Research Methods

for AQA 'A' Psychology

Cara Flanagan

'All you need to know!'

Published in 2005 by:
Nelson Thornes Ltd
Delta Place
27 Bath Road
CHELTENHAM
GL53 7TH
United Kingdom

05 06 07 08 09 / 10 9 8 7 6 5 4 3 2 1

A catalogue record for this book is available from the British Library

ISBN 0 7487 9432 8

Illustrations by Rupert Besley, IFA Design and Angela Lumley
Page make-up by IFA Design

Printed in Croatia by Zrinski

Acknowledgements

The author and publishers are grateful to the following for permission to reproduce photographs and other copyright material in this book:

AQA examination questions are reproduced by permission of the Assessment and Qualifications Alliance; Clegg, Simple Statistics: A Course Book for Students, 1983, Cambridge University Press p.95; FACS coding table reproduced by permission of Joseph C. Hager, A Human Face. p.68; Runyon, Fundamentals of Behavioural Statistics, McGraw-Hill. Reproduced by permission of The McGraw-Hill Companies p.97; KaSo 12 graphs reproduced by permission of University Psychiatric Services, Laupenstrasse 49, CH-3010 Bern, Switzerland p.67; Table 1, p. 579 from Significance Ranking of the Spearman Rank Correlation Coefficient by J.H. Zhar, pp. 578-90, Vol. 67, No. 339, September 1972. Reprinted with permission from The Journal of the American Statistical Association. Copyright 1972 by the American Statistical Association. All rights reserved p.96.

Photo credits:

Aidan Bell, p.47; Alamy, pp29, 32; Alamy/Bill Brookes, p.33; Alamy/Flashpoint Pictures, p.13; Alamy/Kolvenbach, p.27; Alamy/Oote Boe Inc, p.33; Alamy/Pictor International, p.75; Albert Bandura p.25; © Alexandra Milgram, pp.29, 32; Carol Gilligan, p.46; Corbis/Hulton Getty, p.30; FLPA, p.123; From John Henry and hisMighty Hammer by Rozanne Litzinger. Copyright © 1994 by Troll Communications. Reprinted by permission of Scholastic Inc, p.36; Kobal/Paramount, p.38; Newcast/Camelot, p.10; Nick Kim, p.49; Philip Zimbardo, Psychology Department, Stanford University p.72; Powerstock/Age Fotostock, p.4; Retna pictures / Andrew Kent p.9; Richard Duszczak Cartoon Studio Limited, p.45; Science Photo Library/John Cole, p.39; Science Photo Library/Michael Donne, p.74; Science Photo Library/Will & Deni McIntyre, p.19; The Far Side, Gary Larsen/Creators Syndicate, p.34; William B. Swann, Jr., University of Texas, Department of Psychology, p.13; www.york.ac.uk/depts/maths/histstat/people/ p.97.

Royalty free:

Corbis Royalty free p.84 (both); Corel 155 (NT) p.1; Corel 178 (NT) p.26; Corel 250 (NT) pp.12, 49; Corel 283 (NT) p.1; Corel 291 (NT) p.1; Corel 656 (NT) pp.27; Image 100 MRC pp.42, 62; Image 100 SD (NT) p78; Image 100 EE (NT) pp.35, 64; Photodisc 2 (NT) pp.68 (both); Photodisc 6 (NT) p.28; Photodisc 10 (NT) p.50; Photodisc 41 (NT) p.10; Photodisc 43 (NT) p.66; Photodisc 44 (NT) pp.28 (both); Photodisc 45 (NT) pp. 22, 99; Photodisc 50 (NT) pp.4, 52, 52; Photodisc 67 (NT) p.54; Photodisc 73 (NT) pp.1,12; Rubberball WW (NT) p.6; Tom LeGoff/Digital Vision HU (NT) p.14.

Every effort has been made to contact copyright holders, and we apologise if any have been overlooked. Should copyright have been unwittingly infringed in this book, the owners should contact the publishers, who will make corrections at reprint.

Contents

p1 **Introduction**

p2 **Experiments**   Chapter 1

p22 **More about experiments:** field experiments and natural experiments   Chapter 2

p42 **Self-report measures:** questionnaires, interviews and studies using correlational analysis   Chapter 3

p62 **Observations and a few other things**   Chapter 4

p79 **Coursework**   Chapter 5

p99 **Review exercises**   Chapter 6

Appendices
Appendix I: AQA (A) AS specification
Appendix II: How exam questions are marked and where candidates go wrong
Appendix III: Ideas for research activities related to the AQA (A) AS specification
Appendix IV: Websites

p134 **Glossary**

p140 **References**

How to use this book

This book is intended to form the basis of a short course in research methods for the AQA 'A' AS research methods exam. It contains many activities, loads of questions and exam questions, with student answers and examiner's comments. A chapter on coursework has been included even though it is part of the A2 specification because some teachers decide to do this at the end of the AS course.

Experience has found that the length of time needed to cover each of the four main chapters is between 4 and 10 hours, depending on how many of the activities you do. Many questions/activities can be set as homework. You may do the course all at once (which may be too much) or spread it out over weeks or even months. Some teachers have done the first two chapters in class and then encouraged students to complete the rest of the book in their own time.

This book does not cover everything there is to know about research methods in psychology but intends to do enough for the AQA 'A' AS specification. If you wish to read more, we recommend Hugh Coolican's books listed in the reference section (Coolican, 1996, Collican, 2004b).

This book aims to provide a thorough understanding of the required concepts. Some users have commented that there is too much depth in some areas, but this has been necessary in order to ensure that students *do* understand what often appear to be deceptively simple concepts. Students and teachers who have used this book report that the activities made them think a lot, that they felt they really came to understand research methods, and that they found the book interesting and humourous!

So sit back and enjoy yourself.

EXTRAS

There is an AQA student workbook to go with this book. Students can use this to record details of all the terms in the book and then use this booklet for revision. You can download this booklet from the Nelson Thornes website (www.nelsonthornes.com/researchmethods).

Also available is a set of answers to all the **Qs** questions.

In addition, you can obtain from the website a Word file containing templates for certain activities as well as other resources such as graphs, tables, etc., wherever you see this icon 🖳 .

Acknowledgements

First and foremost, a huge thanks to Hugh Coolican for answering all my picky questions with picky answers, and always being ready to help.

Thanks also to so many different people who have contributed ideas, jokes, comments ... Adrian Frost, Sara Berman, Julia Russell, Beth Black and those unsung others from whom I have stolen ideas and forgotten the source.

The first draft benefited from the critical comments of my daughter Philippa, who kept me company over the hot summer during which I wrote the bulk of this book. Thanks too to the rest of the family: Rob and Jack, and Rosie (who asked the question that starts the book, see the page opposite).

And finally, thanks to the team at Nelson Thornes, who have provided the enthusiastic back-up I have come to expect: Rick Jackman, Nigel Harriss and Tracy Hall, who are such a delight to work with.

Special thanks to the guinea pigs

This book has benefited enormously from the feedback given by the teachers and students of Bristol City College (Tony Willner, Maria Kamba and Lana Crosbie), Claires Court School (Sara Berman) and St Mary Redcliffe & Temple School (Grace Pittman and Rob Endley). They kindly had a go at using the first draft of this book and gave me invaluable feedback.

Introduction

The other day, my younger daughter Rosie said to me, 'So what is it psychologists do?', and I answered that they try to explain why people do certain things.

Her next question was, 'How do they do that?'

The answer is that they do research studies to test their beliefs about why people do the things they do.

My younger daughter Rosie.

One way to conduct research is to ask people why they do what they do, or ask them what they think and feel. This method of conducting research is called an **interview**.

We will look at how to conduct interviews in Chapter 3.

Or they could write a **questionnaire** containing a variety of questions.

This research method is also looked at in Chapter 3.

Another way to conduct research is to watch what people do. This method of conducting research is called an **observation** or observational study.

We will look at observational studies in Chapter 4.

If we want to know what causes people to do certain things, we have to conduct an **experiment**.

There are different kinds of experiment, which are the topic of Chapters 1 and 2.

All of these are **research methods** – a way of finding things out in a systematic manner.

Once we have decided on a **method**, we need to **design** the particulars.

Research design is like designing a room – it is the plan of what you are going to do.

Try to bear this in mind – there are research methods and research designs (experimental design, the design of observations, the design of questionnaires, etc.).

Qs   **1**

1. Think about how you might conduct your own research.

   The topic is television advertisements. The question is 'What adverts are most effective?'. Suggest **two or more** ways in which you might investigate this research question.

2. What would be the aim of this research?

*Every study has a **research aim** – what it is that the researcher wants to find out, which may include one or more research questions.*

These are all bathrooms – but each one has a different **design**.

Symbols used in this book

Qs   **1**

On most spreads, there are questions for you to answer.
Suggested answers can be found at www.nelsonthornes.com/reseachmethods.

Activity **1**   **A simple experiment:**

Activities are indicated with this symbol and sometimes accompanied by this icon which indicates that the materials can be found on the website if you wish to print extra copies.

The box on the right identifies the terms (key terms and other terms) that you should record notes on in your AQA student workbook, which can be found on the Nelson Thornes website. When you have finished this book, you will have a set of revision notes that you have made.

Key terms to record
(these are terms that you must know):
    Aims
    Research design
    Research method

Other terms to record:
(these are terms that are not part of the specification so exam questions will not use these terms, although you will need them when answering questions)

Contents

pages 4–5

What is an experiment?

Activity 1: A simple experiment: Does noise affect memory?

Another experiment: Drunken goldfish

And another experiment: Is performance affected by expectation?

Activity 2: Reading in colour – the Stroop effect

 Qs **2**

pages 6–7

Reading in colour – the Stroop effect. A debriefing

Explanation of the Stroop effect

Stroop's findings

Pilot studies

Hypotheses

Directional and non-directional hypotheses

One- and two-tailed

Why have directions?

The null hypothesis

 **Q**s **3,4,5**

pages 10–11

Selection of participants
Randomness
Activity 3: How random is random?
Operationalisation

 **Q**s **8,9**

pages 8–9

Repeated measures and independent groups design
Repeated measures design: disadvantages and advantages
Counterbalancing
Independent groups design: disadvantages and advantages
Matched participants design: disadvantages and advantages

 Qs **6,7**

Experiments

pages 12–13

Experimental control

Extraneous variables

Confederates

Ethics

Debriefing

 **Qs** 10,11

pages 14–15

DIY: Design It Yourself

Activity 4: Memory and organisation

Activity 5: Emotion

Descriptice statistics: How to represent your data

Measures of central tendency

Measures of dispersion

Graphical representation  **Qs** 12,13

pages 16–17

More on graphs

Aims, procedures, findings and conclusions

Multiple choice questions

Qs 14

pages 18–21

Exam-style questions 1 and 2

Model answers for exam-style questions 1 and 2

Answers to multiple choice questions

What is an experiment?

An experiment is a way of conducting research where:

One **variable** is made to change (by the experimenter)

(This is called the **independent variable** or **IV**)

The effects of the IV on another variable are observed or measured

(This variable is called the **dependent variable** or **DV**).

A variable is just a thing – something that can change. For example, noise is a variable. It can be soft or loud.

You actually know all about experiments – you conduct them without thinking. For example, when you start a new class with a new teacher, you see how he or she responds to your behaviour – you might make a joke or hand your homework in on time (both IVs) to see whether the teacher responds well (the DV). You are experimenting with cause and effect.

Activity 1

A simple experiment: Does noise affect memory?

The variable we are going to change (the **IV**) is noise.

The variable we are going to measure (the **DV**) is performance on a memory task.

You will need a radio and two lists of 20 words each. You can use the right-hand wordlist on page 14. There are 40 words in the list.

Divide your class in half: Group N (noise) and Group S (silent).

Group N should have the radio playing very loudly when they are shown the list of words. They have 1 minute to try to remember them and then 1 minute to write them down.

Group S should do the same task, in silence, with the second list of words.

Which group remembered most words?

And another experiment: Is performance affected by expectation?

If you want people to perform better, does it help to lie to them about the quality of materials they are using? Do people perform better if they think the materials they are using are better?

A study by Weick *et al*. (1973) tested this by telling two jazz bands (Band A and Band B) that the piece of music they were rehearsing was either (1) by a composer whose work was well respected or (2) by a composer whose work had been negatively reviewed. Weick *et al*. found that people performed better if they thought they were playing a well-respected work. Participants also remembered the piece better and liked it better.

However, this finding might be because Band A was actually a better band than Band B. To overcome this problem, the experiment was designed so that both bands played both musical pieces: Piece 1 and Piece 2.

Band A were told that Piece 1 was by the superior composer and Piece 2 was by the inferior composer.

Band B were told that Piece 1 was by the inferior composer and Piece 2 was by the superior composer.

Many things that are called experiments are actually investigations. An experiment must have an IV and a DV.

And another experiment: Drunken goldfish

Many early psychology experiments focused on learning in animals. The learning involved simple mazes where the animal was rewarded if it turned in the desired direction at the end of a maze shaped like a Y.

In one experiment, goldfish were trained in a maze and afterwards placed in a water solution high in alcohol. Some of them keeled over.

When the goldfish were retested a week later, those goldfish who had not been exposed to alcohol could remember the maze task perfectly, but those who blacked out in the alcohol solution had no memory for the task. This demonstrates the severe effects of alcohol on learning (Ryback, 1969).

Psychology has been plagued by many foolish experiments – of which this is one. Don't try it at home.

Qs 2

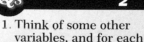

1. Think of some other variables, and for each say how they can vary.
2. Does noise affect your memory?
   a. What was the IV?
   b. What was the DV?
   c. What was the aim of this experiment?
3. Drunken goldfish
   a. What was the IV?
   b. What was the DV?
4. Is performance affected by expectation?
   a. What was the IV?
   b. What was the DV?
   c. What was the aim of this experiment?

KEY TERMS

Dependent variable
Experiment
Independent variable

Activity 2 — Reading in colour – the Stroop effect

Students should work in pairs. One person (the participant) reads the word lists while the other person (the experimenter) times how long it takes to read each list (all mobile phones have timers so this should be easy to arrange!).

There is an alternative, specification-related laboratory experiment on levels of processing on page 130, plus an experiment on the Mere Exposure effect is described on www.nelsonthornes.com/researchmethods.

Instructions:

1 Participants should read the practice list first so both participant and experimenter can practise what they have to do:

- Cover up lists 1–4.

- Participants should state the colour of the word, not what the word says. For example, for the word 'BLUE' they should say 'red', for the word 'BROWN' they should say 'brown'.

- Participants should take great care to say the colour correctly and not race against the clock. Mistakes should be corrected.

- The experimenter should check that the words are read correctly. In order to do this, a non-colour version is printed below.

- The experimenter says 'start' to signal to the participant to begin reading the first list.

- The participant says 'stop' at the end of the list, so the experimenter can record how long it took to read the list.

2 Participants should now read the remaining lists. Each time, they should cover up the other lists and follow the same instructions as above.

Practice	List 1	List 2	List 3	List 4
green	blue	blue	green	red
blue	red	green	purple	blue
brown	brown	purple	blue	green
red	purple	red	green	red
blue	blue	brown	blue	brown
brown	green	red	brown	blue
green	brown	blue	purple	green
blue	red	green	red	purple
brown	blue	brown	blue	brown
purple	purple	purple	green	red
blue	red	brown	blue	purple
green	green	purple	red	blue
purple	brown	red	brown	purple
green	green	blue	purple	brown
purple	brown	red	green	purple
red	purple	green	brown	blue
blue	red	blue	purple	green
purple	blue	brown	red	brown
red	brown	purple	brown	blue
green	green	green	red	brown
purple	blue	purple	blue	red
blue	purple	red	purple	green
red	red	green	brown	red
green	green	blue	green	brown
red	brown	red	purple	green
brown	green	brown	blue	purple
blue	purple	blue	red	red
green	red	green	brown	blue
brown	blue	brown	green	purple
blue	purple	purple	red	green
stop	stop	stop	stop	stop

Practice	List 1	List 2	List 3	List 4
brown	red	blue	green	brown
green	blue	green	purple	red
red	green	purple	blue	brown
purple	brown	red	green	purple
red	purple	brown	blue	green
brown	blue	red	brown	purple
green	red	blue	purple	brown
blue	brown	green	red	brown
red	green	brown	blue	red
blue	red	purple	green	purple
purple	purple	brown	blue	green
red	red	purple	red	brown
purple	blue	red	brown	green
green	brown	blue	purple	red
purple	purple	red	green	blue
red	red	green	brown	purple
green	green	blue	purple	red
red	purple	brown	red	green
purple	blue	purple	brown	red
green	purple	green	red	blue
purple	brown	purple	blue	green
blue	green	red	purple	brown
green	brown	green	brown	blue
brown	red	blue	green	purple
blue	green	red	purple	blue
purple	purple	brown	blue	red
blue	brown	blue	red	green
green	blue	green	brown	purple
brown	purple	brown	green	blue
purple	blue	purple	red	brown
stop	**stop**	**stop**	**stop**	**stop**

When you have finished, turn the page for the next step ...

EXPERIMENTS

A debriefing

You no doubt realized that in lists 1 and 4, the colour words were written in conflicting colours, which made these lists take longer to read than lists 2 and 3. This is called *The Stroop effect* after a study first conducted by J. Ridley Stroop in 1935. You can read his original article at http://psychclassics.yorku.ca/Stroop/.

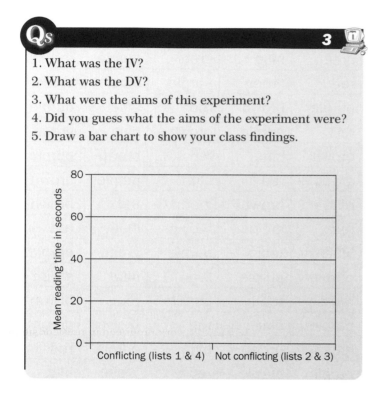

Qs 3

1. What was the IV?
2. What was the DV?
3. What were the aims of this experiment?
4. Did you guess what the aims of the experiment were?
5. Draw a bar chart to show your class findings.

People who take part in an experiment are called **participants**. *Psychologists used to use the term 'subjects'.*

Explanation of the Stroop effect

The interference between the different information (what the words say and the colour of the words) that your brain receives causes a problem. One way to explain this is in terms of automatic processing – we read words automatically so when trying to name the colours, we cannot help but read the words, and this causes interference.

A way to test this is to see if children who are only just learning to read have as much difficulty with the task. They can read the words, but reading is not yet an automatic activity and therefore they are not as affected by the conflict. Try this out on some small children who know their colours but cannot yet read! We would imagine that the children would not get confused by this puzzle because the words would not be read automatically. Research studies support this expectation.

The Stroop effect is not just an interesting phenomenon, it is also useful. It is used to identify people with brain-damage because they find the task more difficult than non-brain damaged people.

Stroop's findings

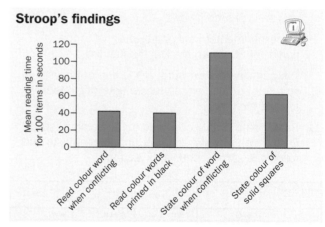

Pilot studies

If you tried one or more of the experiments, you were probably aware that there were flaws. Did you realize beforehand that there would be flaws? Or did some of the flaws become apparent after conducting the experiment? If you did not try these experiments, can you think what flaws there might be?

It is always a good idea to conduct a **pilot study** before the experiment proper. A pilot study is a small-scale trial of a research design run before doing the real thing. It is done in order to find out whether certain things do not work. For example, participants may not understand the instructions or they may guess what the experiment is about, or they may get very bored because there are too many tasks or too many questions.

KEY TERMS

Pilot study

Qs 4

Consider that the experiments you have conducted were pilot studies.

Suggest one thing you might change about each of the experiments so they worked better.

Hypotheses

A **hypothesis** states what you believe to be true. It is a precise and testable statement of the relationship between two variables.

The hypothesis for Stroop's experiment is:

'*People take longer to state the colour of a word when it is written in a conflicting colour than when the word and the colour it is written in are the same.*'

OR '*It takes longer to read a list of conflicting words than non-conflicting words.*'

The hypothesis is sometimes called the **experimental hypothesis** (H^1) or the **alternative hypothesis** (alternative to the null hypothesis H_0).

A hypothesis is not the same as the research aims.

When writing your own hypothesis it is essential that you say how the variables were measured or manipulated. This is called operationalisation -see page 11.

Qs   5

1. Write a hypothesis for the experiment on noise and performance on a memory task.

2. State whether your hypothesis is directional or non-directional and explain why you choose this kind of hypothesis.

3. What were the aims of this experiment?

4. For each of the following, decide whether it is a directional or a non-directional hypothesis:

   a. Boys score differently on aggressiveness tests from girls.

   b. Students who have a computer at home do better in exams than those who do not.

   c. People remember the words that appear early in a list better than the words that appear later.

   d. People given a list of emotionally charged words recall less than participants given a list of emotionally neutral words.

   e. Hamsters are better pets than budgies.

   f. Words presented in a written form are recalled differently from those presented in a pictorial form.

5. Now write your own. For each of the following experiments, write a directional and a non-directional hypothesis, and a null hypothesis:

   a. A study to find out whether girls watch more television than boys.

   b. A study to see whether teachers give more attractive students higher marks on essays than students who are less attractive.

   c. A study to investigate whether lack of sleep affects schoolwork.

Directional and non-directional hypotheses

A **directional hypothesis** states the kind of difference or relationship between two conditions or two groups of participants.

A **non-directional hypothesis** simply predicts that there will be a difference or relationship between two conditions or two groups of participants.

Directional	People take *longer* to state the colour of a word when it is written in a conflicting colour than when the word and the colour it is written in are the same.
Non-directional	Performance speeds are *different* when people state the colour of a word when it is written in a conflicting colour than when the word and the colour it is written in are the same.
Directional	People who do homework *without* the TV on produce *better* results than those who do homework with the TV on.
Non-directional	There is a *difference* between work produced in noisy or silent conditions.

One-tailed and two-tailed

Some people say 'one-tailed' instead of 'directional' and 'two-tailed' instead of 'non-directional'. When you look at a one-tailed cat you know which way it is going!

The null hypothesis (H_0)

In some circumstances (that you don't need to bother about), there is a need to state a null hypothesis – this is a statement of *no difference* or *no relationship* between the variables.

For example:

- There is no difference between work produced in noisy or silent conditions.

- There is no relationship between age and intelligence.

NOTE: *A hypothesis should concern populations and not samples. These concepts are explained on page 10.*

Why have directions?

Justifying the use of directional and non-directional hypotheses

Why do psychologists sometimes use a directional hypothesis instead of a non-directional one?

Psychologists use a directional hypothesis when past research (theory or study) suggests that the findings will go in a particular direction.

Psychologists use a non-directional hypothesis when past research is unclear or contradictory.

KEY TERMS
Directional hypothesis
Experimental/alternative hypothesis
Hypothesis
Non-directional hypothesis

OTHER TERMS
Null hypothesis

Repeated measures and independent groups design

The experiment on noise and memory is an example of an **independent groups design.**

Each participant was tested in only one condition (noise or no noise.

There were two separate (independent) groups of participants.

We could redesign this as a **repeated measures design**.

Each participant would be tested in both conditions. They would be tested in the noise condition and retested in the no noise condition.

Repeated measures
Same participants in each condition (noise or no noise).

Independent groups
Two (or more) groups of participants, one for each condition.

*These are called **experimental designs**.*

The experiment on the Stroop effect was an example of a **repeated measures design**.

Each participant was tested on both conditions (i.e. variations of the IV) – words that were either conflicting or not conflicting.

Learning about research methods is a bit like learning a foreign language. When you learn a foreign language, you have to learn a new set of words and more especially what they mean. One of the best ways to do this is to speak the language – the same is true for research methods. Don't hold back, start using the words.

Qs 6

Noise and memory

1. Write a suitable hypothesis for the new version of the experiment that uses a repeated measures design.

2. Explain why you think that the repeated measures design would not be as good as the independent groups design.

Stroop effect

3. How could you do this study as an independent groups design?

4. What might be the disadvantage of using an independent groups design for this experiment?

Alcohol and goldfish

5. Was this an independent groups design or a repeated measures design?

Is performance affected by expectation?

6. Was this an independent groups design or a repeated measures design?

7. What do you think was the advantage of choosing this design?

For each of the following experiments, state whether it is a repeated measures or an independent groups design.

To do this, ask yourself, 'Would the findings be analysed by comparing the scores from the same person or by comparing the scores of two (or more) groups of people?' (Write your answer down.)

8. Boys and girls are compared on their IQ test scores.

9. Hamsters are tested to see if one genetic strain is better at finding food in a maze than another group.

10. Reaction time is tested before and after a reaction time training activity to see if test scores improve after training.

11. Participants are tested on a memory task in the morning and in the afternoon.

12. Three groups of participants are each asked to remember different word lists (one with nouns, one with verbs and one with adjectives) to see which is easier to recall.

13. Participants are asked to give ratings for attractive and unattractive photographs.

Try this one

In Stroop's original study, the participants had two word lists: one of colour words in a conflicting colour, the other was of colour words printed in black. There were two groups of participants:

• Group 1 read conflicting colour and then black words.

• Group 2 read black and then conflicting colour words.

This was done to control for practice and fatigue (called **order effects**, as you will see on the next page).

Is this now an independent groups design, or is it still a repeated measures?

It is still repeated measures because the analysis still involves comparing the same individual's performance on two conditions (conflicting colour and black words).

KEY TERMS
Experimental design
Independent groups design
Repeated measures design

Repeated measures

Disadvantages

1. One of the memory tests may be more difficult than the other and this is why the participants do better in one condition (the noise condition) than the other (no noise condition).
2. When the participants do the second memory test, they may guess the purpose of the experiment, which may affect their behaviour. For example, some participants may purposely do worse on the second test because they want it to seem as if they work better in noisy conditions.
3. The order of the conditions may affect performance (an **order effect**). Participants may do better on the second test because of a **practice effect** OR participants may do worse on the second test because of being bored with doing the same test again (**boredom** or **fatigue effect**).

Advantages

You can work out the advantages by looking at the disadvantages of independent groups design.

Dealing with the problems created by repeated measures design

Dealing with point 1.

You can make sure the tests are equivalent. Create a list of 40 words and **randomly allocate** these to two lists so both lists are equivalent.

Dealing with point 2.

You can lie to the participants about the purpose of the test to try to prevent them guessing what it is about. This is called a **single blind** design (the participant is blind to the aim of the study).

Dealing with point 3.

You can use **counterbalancing** (see right).

Independent groups

Disadvantages

- No control of **participant variables** (i.e. the different abilities of each participant). For example, participants in Group 1 might be more able than those in Group 2.
- You need twice as many participants.

Advantages

You can work out the advantages by looking at the disadvantages of repeated measures design.

Dealing with the problems created by independent groups design

1. Randomly allocate participants to conditions to ensure that the groups are equivalent (see 'randomness' on page 10).

2. Match participants in each group on key variables (see below).

Matched participants design

This is a third kind of experimental design. It involves the use of independent groups, but each participant in Group A is paired with one in Group B. This is done by pairing participants on key variables (e.g. IQ, memory ability, gender – any characteristic that might affect the findings) and then placing one member of each pair into each group.

Disadvantages

- Very time-consuming to match the participants.
- May not control all the participant variables.

Advantages

- Controls some participant variables.
- Participants won't guess study's aims.

Counterbalancing

Counterbalancing ensures that each condition is tested first or second in equal amounts, as we did for the Stroop effect (see page 5). If participants read a conflicting list first and then a non-conflicting list, we might expect them to read the second list more quickly because they had had more practice.

There are two ways to counterbalance order effects:

Way 1. Counterbalancing

Group 1: the participants do the conflicting list first and then the non-conflicting words.

Group 2: participants do the non-conflicting list first and then the conflicting list.

This is still a repeated measures design even though there are two groups of participants because a comparison will be made for each participant on their performance on the two conditions (conflict and no conflict).

Way 2. ABBA

Condition A: conflicting lists.

Condition B: non-conflicting list.

Each participant takes part in every trial.

Trial 1: Conflicting list A

Trial 2: Non-conflicting list (B)

Trial 3: Non-conflicting list (B)

Trial 4: Conflicting list A

Counterbalancing literally means achieving balance by having an equal weight at both ends.

Qs 7

1. Which of the two forms of counterbalancing (1 or 2) did we use in the experiment on the Stroop effect on page 5?
2. What participant variables might have affected the findings of the Stroop effect study?
3. To what extent were these participant variables controlled?
4. Look back to the experiment 'Is performance affected by expectation?' on page 4. Counterbalancing has been used here, although not for order effects. Explain in what way this design is counterbalanced.
5. *A psychologist conducted a study to see whether visual imagery helps memory. To do this, there were two lists to be recalled – one had words only, the other had images instead of words.*
   a. Describe how you could conduct this study using (a) a repeated measures design, (b) an independent groups design and (c) a matched pairs design.
   b. Which design would be best? Explain your answer.
   c. For which kind of design would counterbalancing be necessary?
   d. Explain how you would design the counterbalancing.

Advantages ☺ *and disadvantages* ☹ *of*
Independent groups design
Matched participants design
Repeated measures design

OTHER TERMS
Boredom effect
Counterbalance
Fatigue effect
Order effect
Participant variables
Practice effect
Random allocation
Single blind design

Selection of participants

When conducting any research study you need to find some participants!

Participants are drawn from **'the target population'**: the group of people that the researcher is interested in.

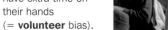

This is a selection or **sample** of the target population.

Opportunity sample

How? Ask people walking by you in the street, i.e. select those who are available.

☺ The easiest method because you just use the first participants you can find.

☹ Inevitably biased because the sample is drawn from a small part of the target population. For example, if you do an experiment using people in the street, the sample is selected from people walking around the centre of a town – not those who work, or those living in rural areas.

Volunteer sample

How? Advertise in a newspaper or on a noticeboard.

☺ Access to a variety of participants.

☹ The sample is biased because the participants are likely to be more highly motivated and/or have extra time on their hands (= **volunteer** bias).

Researchers make generalisations about the target population from the sample as long as the sample is *representative of the target population* (i.e. represents the target population).

*All sampling methods aim to produce a **representative** sample but are inevitably **biased**.*

A sampling method is about how participants are identified NOT about who eventually takes part. For example, in an opportunity or random sample, some potential participants may refuse to take part. The remaining participants are 'volunteers'.

This is not true for all opportunity/random samples as in a field experiment described in chapter 2, where participants cannot refuse.

Random sample

How? Put the names of the target population into a hat and draw out the required number.

☺ Unbiased: all members of the target population have an equal chance of selection.

☹ You usually end up with a biased sample (e.g. more boys than girls) because the sample is usually too small (see Activity 3).

Many students mistake a **systematic sample** for a random sample – selecting every 10th person is not random, it is a systematic method of selection. However, if you select a number using a random method and start with this person and then you select every10th person, this would be a random sample.

If you want equal numbers of girls and boys (or 10 and 11th years, etc.), one way to do this is to put all the boys' names in hat and draw out 5, and do same for the girls' names. This is called a **stratified sample**.

Randomness

The most obvious way to obtain a random selection is to draw numbers or names *'out of a hat'*. It is sometimes called the 'lottery method'.

Random selection is used to obtain a **random sample** of participants (as described above) or for the **random allocation** of participants to conditions when using an independent measures design (as described on the previous page). For random allocation, for example, you put all the participants' names into a hat and draw out half of the names for group 1 and place the remaining names in group 2.

Activity 3 — How random is random?

Take 40 pieces of paper and write 20 boys' names and 20 girls' names.

Put them in a hat and draw out 10 slips of paper. If the selection is unbiased, you should ideally get five boys and five girls.

Put the slips of paper back and draw 10 out again. Repeat this a total of four times and then try it with a larger sample. Each time, record how many boys' and girls' names were drawn. You can record your results in the table below.

	Sample size 10				Sample size 20				Total
Trial no:	1	2	3	4	1	2	3	4	
Boys									
Girls									

The point is that, in principle, random selection results in an unbiased and representative sample, but only if the sample is large enough.

Is this what you found? What happens if you put 40 boys' names and 40 girls' names in the hat?

KEY TERMS

Advantages ☺ and disadvantages ☹, and how to do:

Opportunity sample
Random sample
Volunteer sample
Selection of participants

OTHER TERMS

Random allocation
Stratified sample
Systematic sample
Target population
Volunteer bias
Research prediction

Random
means that each member of the population has an equal chance of being selected.

Operationalisation

Qs   **8**

1. Look back to page 7, Question 5. You were asked to write a hypothesis for three studies. Now write an aim and a research prediction for each of these three studies.

2. *A psychologist conducted a study to look at whether watching certain films made children more helpful (one film was about being helpful, the other was neutral). He advertised for participants in the local newspaper. A large number of children volunteered, and a sample of 30 was selected for the actual experiment.*

   a. What is the IV in this experiment?

   b. What is the DV?

   c. How could you operationalise the DV?

   d. State a suitable hypothesis and/or research prediction for this study.

   e. Is your prediction directional or non-directional?

   f. Explain your choice of direction.

   g. What kind of experimental design would you use in this study?

   h. Describe **one** disadvantage of this experimental design.

   i. How could you deal with this problem?

   j. Describe the target population.

   k. What kind of sample was obtained?

   l. Suggest how the experimenter might select the sub-sample from all those who applied.

3. *A psychology experiment aims to investigate how preschool children differ from those already at school in terms of their ability to remember symbols that look like letters.*

   a. If the experimenter wanted to obtain a random sample of each of the two age groups, how might this have been done?

   b. Explain the purpose of using a random sample.

   c. What is the IV in the experiment?

   d. What is the DV?

   e. The children were shown 20 different symbols. Why was it better to use 20 symbols rather than just two?

   f. Why might it be better to use two rather than 20 symbols?

4. *Mary Smith organises a project to enable her psychology class to have a go at using a matched pairs design. The class is divided into two groups; one will receive word list A (nouns) and the other word list B (verbs). They will be tested on recall.*

   a. Suggest **two** participant variables that could be used to match the classmates.

   b. Explain why each of the variables you chose would be important to control in this study.

   c. What are the two conditions in the experiment?

   d. If Mary decided to use an independent measures design, suggest **two** ways in which participants could have been allocated to the conditions.

   e. The teacher used words that were all of two syllables and of similar length. Give **one** reason why.

   f. The teacher decided to repeat the study using all the pupils in the school. She selected every fifth pupil on the register. Why is this not a random sample?

A 'good' hypothesis should be written in a testable form, i.e. in a way that makes it clear how you are going to design an experiment to test the hypothesis.

Think back to the Stroop effect. Stroop's research aim was to investigate the effects of interference on performance speeds. To turn this aim into an experiment, he needed to state his belief:

Hypothesis *People take longer to perform a task when word and colour conflict with each other than when they do not.*

The concept of 'interference' has been **operationalised** in order to produce a testable hypothesis ('interference' = 'word and colour conflict'). 'Operationalisation' means specifying a set of operations or behaviours that can be measured or manipulated. For example:

Hypothesis *People work better in quiet rather than noisy conditions.*

What precisely do we mean by 'work better' and 'quiet' and 'noisy'? We need to define the operations:

> 'work better' = obtain a higher score on a memory test
> 'quiet' = no sound
> 'noisy' = radio playing.

Operationalised hypothesis *People obtain a higher score on a memory test when tested in quiet (no sounds) rather than noisy (radio playing) conditions.*

Hypothesis *People are happier if they work.*

> 'happier' = higher score on happiness questionnaire
> 'work' = have a full-time job (over 40 hours per week).

Operationalised hypothesis *People obtain a higher score on a happiness questionnaire if they work full time (over 40 hours per week) than if they work part time (less than 20 hours per week).*

Don't make the mistake of confusing the terms hypothesis and research prediction. There is an important difference. A hypothesis is a general claim about the world. In order to test a hypothesis, we need a prediction about how the participants in a study will behave.

The **hypothesis** is about **populations** (people). It states our expectation about the world. It can be operationalised.

The **research prediction** is about **samples** (participants). It predicts what we expect to find in a study. It is stated in the future tense and must be operationalised.

Qs   **9**

1. Do older people sleep more or less than younger people?

   a. Identify the IV and DV in this experiment.

   b. How could you operationalise the IV and DV?

   c. Write a fully operationalised directional hypothesis.

   d. Write a fully operationalised non-directional hypothesis.

2. *People rate food as looking more attractive when they are hungry.* Answer questions a–d above.

3. *A teacher wishes to find out whether one maths test is harder than another maths test.* Answer questions a–d above.

Experimental control

There are DVs and IVs, and then there are extraneous variables . . .

Order effects are an **extraneous variable**.

For example, in the noise and memory experiment (*repeated measures design*), noise (IV) should affect recall (DV).

1. Participants do the memory test with noise.

2. Participants do the memory test without noise.

They do better on the second test.

Is this because they do better when tested without noise? (Noise/no noise is the IV.)

Or because they have *practised* doing the test? (Practice/no practice has become an alternative and unintentional IV.)

Practice/no practice is an extraneous variable.

> The experiment 'controls' the IV in an experiment – making it change to see what happens. The experimenter also has to control other variables (**extraneous variables**) to make sure they do not change – otherwise this may spoil the experiment.

*An **extraneous variable** is a variable other than the IV that may affect the DV and should thus be controlled. The term is used interchangeably with the term **uncontrolled variables**.*

*A **confounding variable** is a variable other than the IV that has affected the DV and has thus confounded the findings of the study.*

another extraneous variable . . .

Noise and memory experiment (*independent groups design*)

Group 1 do the noisy test in the morning.

Group 2 do the test without noise in the afternoon.

Group 2 do better on the test.

Is this because people do better when tested without noise? (Noise/no noise is the IV.)

Or because people do better on memory tests when tested in the afternoon?

Time of day has become a substitute IV – it is an extraneous variable.

Qs   10

1. In the repeated measures study described above, how could you control the extraneous variable?

2. In the independent groups study described on the right, how could you control the extraneous variable?

still more extraneous variables . . .

Consider the Stroop effect study. Imagine that each participant is tested individually. In this situation, there may be both **situational** and **participant extraneous variables**.

- Some participants are tested in a noisy classroom, whereas others are tested in a quiet one-to-one situation.

- One participant is wearing tinted glasses.

- Some participants are uncertain so the experimenter offers to help them fill in the answer sheet.

- In later test sessions the sun is setting and making the test room glow orange.

All of these variations may affect participant performance and may affect the DV.

*Standardised procedures include **standardised instructions** – the instructions given to participants about what to do*

and a final extraneous variable . . .

Finally, we can consider **investigator effects.** The behaviour of an investigator/experimenter may affect the participants and thus affect the DV.

For example, the way in which the investigator asks a question may *lead* the participant to give the answer the investigator 'wants'.

Or the way in which the investigator responds may encourage certain kinds of response. For example, the investigator may smile as if to say 'Yes, that's the right answer'.

How to deal with this extraneous variable

Experimenters use **standardised procedures** to ensure that all participants receive the same instructions and to prevent the experimenter affecting participants' behaviour, for example by using leading questions.

Standardised procedures are like a recipe – if different procedures are used, the different outcomes may be due to the procedures and not the IV.

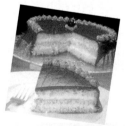

How to deal with investigator effects

Investigators use **standardised instructions** to prevent using leading questions.

Or you can use a **double blind** design – neither the participant nor the person conducting the experiment (who has not designed it) knows the aims of the experiment; therefore, the experimenter cannot affect the participants' performance.

The way in which an investigator asks a question (the words used, the tone of voice, the facial expression) may affect the responses that are given.

KEY TERMS

Control
Extraneous variable
Investigator effects

OTHER TERMS

Confederate
Confounding variable
Debriefing
Double blind
Situational variable
Standardised instructions
Standardised procedures

Confederates

The IV in an experiment is sometimes a person.

For example, you might want to find out if people respond differently to orders from someone wearing a suit or dressed in causal clothes. In this experiment, the IV would be the clothing worn by a 'friend' of the experimenter. The experimenter would arrange for a person to give orders either dressed in a suit or dressed casually. This person is called a **confederate**.

Confederates are not always an IV; they may simply help to guide the experiment.

Confederates are individuals in an experiment who are not real participants and have been instructed how to behave by the experimenter.

The woman on the left in the photograph (a confederate) talks 'blirtatiously' (loudly and effusively) to see what this effect this has on the person who is studying.

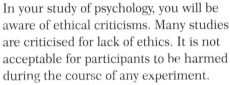

This experiment may damage your health

Briefing for an experiment

This experiment is concerned with reading coloured print. Some people find it harder to identify certain colours. You will be shown five word lists and asked to identify the colours of the written words.

Ethics

In your study of psychology, you will be aware of ethical criticisms. Many studies are criticised for lack of ethics. It is not acceptable for participants to be harmed during the course of any experiment.

What, however, constitutes 'harm'? Is it harmful for a person to experience mild discomfort or mild stress?

Is it acceptable to lie to participants about what an experiment is about? Such deception may be necessary so that participants' behaviour is not affected by knowing the aim of the experiment.

One way to deal with deception is to **debrief** participants afterwards. At the start of an experiment, participants are briefed about what the task will involve. At the end, they are debriefed.

This debriefing has two functions:

1. *Ethical*: It is an opportunity to reassure the participant about their performance. If any deception took place, participants are told the true aims of the study and offered the opportunity to discuss any concerns they may have. They may be offered the opportunity to withhold their data from the study.

2. *Practical*: The debrief allows the researcher to thank individuals for participating. The experimenter may ask for further information about the research topic. For example, he or she may ask why the participant found one condition more difficult, or may ask whether the participant believed the set-up.

Debriefing

Thank you for taking part in the experiment. The true purpose of the study was to find out if it takes longer to identify the word colour when the word and colour are conflicting. This is called the Stroop effect.

1. Would you like to know the overall findings from the study?   YES/NO

2. Did you feel distressed by any aspect of the study?   YES/NO

3. What did you think the purpose of the study was?

4. Did you think that some of the lists were harder to read than others?   YES/NO
   If yes, which lists?

5. Do you think this might have affected your performance?   YES/NO
   If yes, in what way?

Qs   11

1. Who was the confederate in Milgram's study?

2. Why do you need to 'brief' participants?

3. Why is it necessary to debrief participants?

4. Why would it be necessary to deceive participants in the study described on the left?

5. Imagine you were given the briefing and debriefing on shown here. What answers would you give to Questions 3 and 4?

DIY Design it yourself

Two possible activities are suggested on this page. They enable you to try to design and conduct your own experiment. Questions 12 will guide you in designing and conducting your experiment.

Activity 4 — Memory and organisation

A favourite experiment for students is one that concerns organisation and memory. If words are presented to a participant in categories (as shown on the near right), they are more easily memorised than if they are presented in a random order (list on the far right).

Organised list	Random list
Dogs	Pear
Labrador	Beagle
Beagle	Clarinet
Boxer	Hail
Spaniel	Rain
Fruit	Drinks
Apple	Rose
Pear	Squash
Plum	Hand
Orange	Boxer
Weather	Iron
Snow	Coke
Rain	Gold
Sleet	Harp
Hail	Piano
Flowers	Metal
Daffodil	Apple
Rose	Body
Pansy	Fruit
Tulip	Instruments
Instruments	Daffodil
Harp	Plum
Piano	Nose
Flute	Weather
Clarinet	Copper
Drinks	Labrador
Water	Water
Milk	Flowers
Squash	Brass
Coke	Foot
Body	Tulips
Nose	Pansy
Foot	Dogs
Toe	Sleet
Hand	Milk
Metal	Orange
Brass	Toe
Gold	Snow
Copper	Flute
Iron	Spaniel

Qs 12

Design decisions to make – answer these questions for either Activity 4 or Activity 5 (whether or not you are actually doing the activities).

1. What is the IV and what is the DV?
2. How should the IV be operationalised?
3. How will the DV be operationalised (i.e. how will you measure it?)?
4. Should you use repeated measures or independent groups? Write down the relative advantages/disadvantages of each.
5. Write a suitable aim and hypothesis for your study and a research prediction.
6. How many participants will you need?
7. How will you select these participants? (For ethical reasons, you should only use participants over the age of 16.)
8. Are there any extraneous (situational or participant) variables that need to be controlled?
9. How will you control these?
10. Are there any investigator effects to control?
11. How can you control these?
12. Write your standardised procedure, including a briefing and a debriefing.

    NOW conduct a pilot study and make any alterations to the design that are necessary.

13. After you have conducted the study, record the findings for each participant in a table.
    If you do not have time to conduct this experiment yourself, invent an appropriate set of data.
14. What do you conclude from your findings?
15. Identify **one** problem you discovered when conducting this study.

*A **conclusion** is the statement(s) you make about human behaviour (populations) on the basis of your research study with a small set of participants (a sample). Conclusions should be written in the present tense and be about 'people' rather than 'participants'.*

Activity 5 — Emotion

One theory of emotion proposes that we experience general levels of physiological arousal and label these as love, attraction, fear, stress, etc. according to the cues that are available.

For example, if you are physiologically aroused (e.g. from watching a scary movie) and at the same time are in the presence of an attractive man or woman, you might feel the arousal is because that person is attractive to you.

One experiment that tested this arranged for participants to run on the spot for one minute (creating physiological arousal) and then rate a set of photographs for attractiveness. Those people who did not run on the spot gave lower ratings than those who did (White et al., 1981).

Does this photograph look more attractive to someone who has been running on the spot for a minute?

KEY TERMS

Bar chart
Histogram
Measures of central tendency
Measures of dispersion
Mean
Median
Mode
Range
Standard deviation

NOIR (see page 95 for an explanation)
Nominal data
Ordinal data
Interval data
Ratio data
Conclusions

You might describe your findings using the methods outlined on page 15.

Descriptive statistics: How to represent your data

There are three ways to **describe** *the data that you found from your research.*

Measures of central tendency

Measures of central tendency inform us about central (or middle) values of a set of data. There are three different 'averages' – ways of calculating a typical value for a set of data.

The **mean** is calculated by adding up all the numbers and dividing by the number of numbers.

☺ It makes use of the *values* of all the data.

☹ It can be misrepresentative of the numbers if there is an extreme value.

☹ It can only be used with **interval** or **ratio** data (see page 95).

The **median** is the *middle* value in an *ordered* list.

☺ It is not affected by extreme scores.

☺ It can be used with **ordinal data**.

☹ It is not as 'sensitive' as the mean because not all values are reflected in the median.

The **mode** is the value that is *most* common.

☺ It is useful when the data are in categories (such as number of people who like pink), i.e. **nominal data**.

☹ It is not a useful way of describing data when there are several modes.

Measures of dispersion

A set of data can also be described in terms of how dispersed, or spread out, the numbers are.

The easiest way to do this is to use the **range**. Consider the data sets below:

3, 5, 8, 8, 9, 10, 12, 12, 13, 15

　　mean = 9.5　　range = 12 (3 to 15)

1, 5, 8, 8, 9, 10, 12, 12, 13, 17

　　mean = 9.5　　range = 16 (1 to 17)

The two sets of numbers have the same mean but a different range, so the range is helpful as a further method of describing the data. If we just used the mean, the data would appear to be the same.

The **range** is the difference between the highest and lowest numbers.

There is a more precise method of expressing dispersion, called the **standard deviation**. This is a measure of the spread of the data around the mean.

The standard deviation for the two sets of numbers above is 3.69 and 4.45 respectively. This can be worked out using a mathematical calculator.

Graphical representation

A picture is worth a thousand words! Graphs provide a means of 'eyeballing' your data and seeing the findings at a glance.

Bar chart: The height of the bar represents frequency. Unlike a histogram, you can exclude empty categories. There is no true zero, and data on the horizontal axis are not continuous. Suitable for words and numbers.

Histogram: Essentially a bar chart except that the area within the bars must be proportional to the frequencies represented and the horizontal axis must be continuous. *There should be no gaps between bars.*

	Advantages	Disadvantages
Range	Provides you with direct information Easy to calculate	Affected by extreme values Does not take into account the number of observations in the data set
Standard deviation	More precise measure of dispersion because all values are taken into account	May hide some of the characteristics of the data set (e.g. extreme values)

Qs *13*

1. For each of the data sets below, calculate the (a) mean, and (b) median and (c) mode, (d) state which of these would be most suitable to use and why.

	Data set
1.	2, 3, 5, 6, 6, 8, 9, 12, 15, 21, 22
2.	2, 3, 8, 10, 11, 13, 13, 14, 14, 29
3.	2, 2, 4, 5, 5, 5, 7, 7, 8, 8, 8, 10
4.	cat, cat, dog, budgie, snake, gerbil

2. Why is it better to know about the mean and range of a data set rather than just the mean?

3. Explain why it might be better to know the standard deviation of a data set rather than the range.

4. Standard deviation tells us on average how close each of the numbers is to the mean – it tells us how a set of numbers are distributed around the mean. Look at the following data sets. Which one do you think would have the *smaller* standard deviation?

Data set A: 2 2 3 4 5　9 11 14 18 20 21 22 25

Data set B: 2 5 8 9 9　10 11 12 14 15 16 20 25

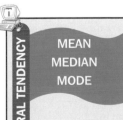

CENTRAL TENDENCY

MEAN
MEDIAN
MODE

Special tip

Many candidates find it hard to remember the link between 'measures of central tendency' and 'mean, median, mode'.

One way to help you remember links is to produce memorable pictures. The flag above is an attempt to illustrate the idea of a central tendency and link this to the three appropriate terms. Try to develop your own memorable picture for this and other concepts – the more outrageous, the better!

More on graphs

A graph should be simple. It should clearly show the findings from a study.

There should be a short title.

The *x* axis must be labelled (the *x* axis goes across the page; it is usually the IV).

The *y* axis must be labelled (the *y* axis goes up vertically; it is usually the DV or 'frequency').

Always use squared paper if you are hand-drawing graphs.

Aims, procedures, findings and conclusions

When psychologists conduct research, they write a report of their study that contains the following information: **aims** (the intended area of study), **procedures** (a description of the **standardised procedures** so that the study can be repeated), **findings** (the data or results produced by the study) and **conclusions** (an interpretation of the findings).

This is an example of a finding:

Participants obtained a higher score when tested in the no noise condition.

This is an example of a conclusion:

The findings suggest that people work better on memory tasks when there is little noise.

The distinction is subtle but important. One is a fact about the *participants*, the other is a generalisation made about what *people* do. Like the distinction between a hypothesis and a research prediction, findings are about *samples*, conclusions are about *populations*.

Qs 14

1. Why is Graph A meaningless?
2. Write a title that would be suitable for all three graphs.
3. Describe the *y* axis of all three graphs.
4. A class of psychology students studies the Stroop effect and produces the following data showing the time taken (in seconds) to read each kind of word list:

Student	1	2	3	4	5	6	7	8	9	10	11	12
Colour conflict	29	25	20	26	22	31	28	28	26	28	21	29
No conflict	20	16	14	20	18	21	20	17	20	19	15	16

(a) Calculate the mean, median, mode and range for each data set.
(b) What measure of central tendency would be most suitable to use to describe this data?
(c) The standard deviations were as follows: colour conflict (3.48) and no conflict (2.34). What does this tell you about the data sets?
(d) Draw both a bar chart and a histogram to represent the data from this study.

Each of the graphs below presents the data collected in an experiment on organisation and memory.

Only one of these graphs is useful; two of them are a 'waste of time' – which one is the useful one?

Graph A
Participant number 1 in the organised word group is placed next to participant number 1 in the random word group. Students like to draw 'participant charts' BUT THEY ARE TOTALLY MEANINGLESS.

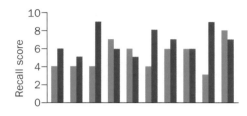

■ Organised word list ■ Random word list

Graph B
The findings from each participant are shown in this graph. They are grouped together so that you can see all the scores from participants in the organised word group and all the scores from the participants in the random word group.

This is *slightly better* than Graph A because we can just about tell that the random word list led to better recall – but a glance at the means (as in Graph C) shows this effortlessly.

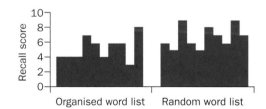

Graph C
This graph shows the mean scores for each group. The findings are clear, which is the point of using a graph.

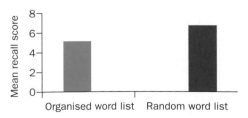

Note: *the horizontal axis of a graph is called the x axis, and the vertical axis is called the y axis.*

Procedures
Findings
Conclusions

Multiple choice questions

1. The independent variable in a study is
   a. The one that is excluded.
   b. The one that is manipulated by the experimenter.
   c. The one that is observed or measured.
   d. Not of interest to the experimenter.

2. A pilot study is
   a. The first study conducted by a research team.
   b. A preliminary investigation.
   c. A small-scale trial run of a research design.
   d. A research project on efficient flying of aeroplanes.

3. Which of the following hypotheses is a non-directional hypothesis?
   a. Participants in the no noise condition do better on the memory test than those in the noise condition.
   b. Participants who drink alcohol have a slower reaction time than those who have no alcohol.
   c. Participants like words that are familiar more than those that are not familiar.
   d. Participants who expect to perform better perform differently from those given lower expectations.

4. One reason for using a directional hypothesis is because
   a. Past research suggests that participants will do better on one condition than another.
   b. Past research is uncertain about how participants will perform.
   c. There is no past research.
   d. The researcher wants to make a strong statement.

5. An extraneous variable is a variable that
   a. Has been controlled by the experimenter.
   b. Confounds the findings of the study.
   c. May influence the dependent variable.
   d. The experimenter wants to find out more about.

6. A student plans to investigate the effects of practice on IQ test performance. Some participants are given two practice tests prior to the IQ test, whereas others do no test beforehand. The dependent variable in this study is
   a. The participants.
   b. The effects of practice.
   c. The IQ test performance before the study.
   d. The IQ test performance at the end of the study.

7. The study described in question 6 is
   a. A repeated measures design.
   b. An independent groups design.
   c. A matched pairs design.
   d. A careful design.

8. In an independent groups design
   a. There are two or more separate groups of participants.
   b. The analysis involves comparing measures from two or more separate groups of people.
   c. The analysis involves comparing two measures from the same person.
   d. Both a and b.

9. One advantage of doing a matched pairs design is
   a. You need fewer participants than for repeated measures.
   b. You can control some participant variables.
   c. Order effects are not a problem.
   d. Both b and c.

10. The letters 'ABBA' refer to a research design
    a. Created by a Swedish rock band.
    b. To control participant variables.
    c. To counterbalance for order effects.
    d. To control extraneous variables.

11. All sampling methods are
    a. Representative of the target population.
    b. Biased.
    c. Random.
    d. Difficult to conduct.

12. Selecting participants who just happen to be available is called
    a. Opportunity sampling.
    b. Volunteer sampling.
    c. Random sampling.
    d. Quota sampling.

13. Which of the following could not be an extraneous variable in a study
    a. An investigator effect.
    b. A confederate.
    c. An order effect.
    d. A lack of standardised procedures.

14. One way to improve the design of a study is to:
    a. Conduct a pilot study beforehand to see if some things do not work.
    b. Have lots of variables.
    c. Use a repeated measures design.
    d. Use a confederate.

15. Which of the following is a disadvantage of using a repeated measures design?
    a. It does not control participant variables.
    b. You have to use more participants than for an independent groups design.
    c. There are more likely to be investigator effects than for an independent groups design.
    d. There may be order effects.

16. In an experiment, half the participants do Condition A first followed by Condition B, whereas the other participants do the conditions in the reverse order. This procedure is called
    a. Countercontrol.
    b. Countercalling.
    c. Counterbalancing.
    d. Counteracting.

17. An individual who is instructed about how to behave by the researcher, often acting as the IV, is called
    a. An extraneous variable.
    b. A dependent variable.
    c. The investigator.
    d. A confederate.

18. Which of the following is a random sample?
    a. Names drawn from a hat.
    b. Asking people if they would like to take part.
    c. Using every 10th name on a register.
    d. Taking whoever happens to be there.

19. Which of the following is a measure of central tendency?
    a. Range.
    b. Bar chart.
    c. Mode.
    d. Interval.

20. Debriefing involves
    a. Telling a participant the true aims of a study.
    b. Giving participants a chance to discuss any psychological harm they may have experienced.
    c. Asking participants for feedback about the experiment.
    d. All of the above.

Answers are on page 20

Exam-style question 1

One area of psychological research concerns prejudice – people make biased judgements of another person's abilities based on ethnic group, age, gender, etc.

Many studies have looked at the effects of gender. For example, in one experiment participants were asked to mark students' essays. Those essays supposedly written by boys were given higher marks, on average, than girls' essays.

A group of psychology students decided to repeat this research to see if students today were still prejudiced about gender. The researchers selected four essays (Essay 1, Essay 2, Essay 3, Essay 4). All the essays had been given a C grade by their teacher.

The participants were divided into two groups. For Group 1, Essays 1 and 2 were given girls' names and Essays 3 and 4 were given boys' names. For Group 2, this was reversed.

Participants were asked to give a mark out of 10 to the essays, where 10 was excellent. The mean scores for boys and girls essays are shown in the graph below.

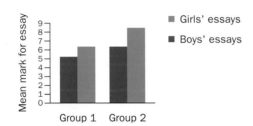

(a) (i) Write a suitable hypothesis for this study.   (2 marks)

   (ii) Identify whether your hypothesis is directional or non-directional and explain why you chose such a hypothesis.
                                                (1 mark + 2 marks)

(b) The student researchers decided to conduct a pilot study.
   (i) Why would it be a good idea to conduct a pilot study?
                                                        (2 marks)

   (ii) Explain how the student researchers would conduct a pilot study.   (2 marks)

(c) Identify **one** method of selecting participants for this study and describe **one** advantage and **one** disadvantage of using this method.   (1 mark + 2 marks + 2 marks)

(d) (i) Explain the term 'investigator effect'.   (2 marks)

   (ii) Suggest **one** investigator effect that may have been a problem in this study.   (2 marks)

   (iii) Explain how you could have dealt with this effect.   (2 marks)

(e) Explain why the experiment was designed so that half the participants had girls' names for Essays 1 and 2 and the other half had girls' names for Essays 3 and 4.   (3 marks)

(f) (i) What measure of central tendency was used to describe the findings?   (1 mark)

   (ii) Explain why this measure was used to give the average for this data.   (2 marks)

(g) Describe **one** finding and **one** conclusion that can be taken from the bar chart.   (2 marks + 2 marks)

Examiner's tips for answering this question

The number of marks available for each part of the question indicates the amount of detail required. When there are 2 marks available, you should ensure that you give more than a brief answer – you need to provide further details, such as saying more than 'a small-scale study' for a pilot study or saying more than 'it is easy' as an advantage of opportunity sampling.

(a) Remember that the hypothesis should be about populations and not samples. And it should be in the present and not the future – it is not a research prediction.

(b) Take care specifically to answer the two questions 'why' (in i) and 'how' (in ii).

(c) and (d) If you are asked to provide 'one' of anything, only your first answer will be marked. Positive marking is not used when 'one' is specified in the question (positive marking is when marks are awarded for the best answer).

(d) (i) This is one of the 'key terms' of the specification so you need to make sure that you can provide a suitable definition if required.

(d) (iii) When you are asked how to deal with something, make sure that you focus on what you would do, rather than (for example) writing about why you would do it.

(f) Remember that your answer must be either mean, median or mode.

(g) Students find it difficult to distinguish between findings and conclusions. Conclusions are about people (rather than participants) and are stated in the present tense (rather than the past tense). They are statements made about the target population on the basis of what was found with the selected participants.

Exam-style question 2

A classic experiment in psychology looked at the effect of experimenter expectations on the performance of participants – the participants in this study were rats who were being tested on their ability to learn the route through a maze (Rosenthal and Fode, 1963). In order to see if the experimenter's expectations would affect the rats' performance, psychology students were asked to train rats to learn their way around a maze. They were told that there were two groups of rats: one group were 'fast learners' having been bred for this characteristic, whereas the other group were 'slow learners'.

In fact, there were no differences between the rats. They were all from the same litter and had been randomly assigned to the students. Despite this, the findings of the study showed that the supposedly brighter rats actually did better. When the students were asked about their rats afterwards, those with 'fast learning' rats described them as smarter, more attractive and more likeable.

The only explanation can be that the students' expectations affected the rats' performance.

(a) What was the aim of this research? (2 marks)

(b) (i) Identify the independent and dependent variables in this study. (2 marks)

    (ii) Explain how the independent variable was operationalised. (2 marks)

(c) (i) Explain the meaning of the phrase 'rats were randomly assigned to students'. (2 marks)

    (ii) Why was it important to 'randomly assign' the rats to the students? (2 marks)

(d) When the investigators produced the findings, they described the data using the mean and standard deviation.

    (i) What does the mean tell us about data? (1 mark)

    (ii) What does the standard deviation tell us about data? (2 marks)

    (iii) Describe **one** advantage of using the mean. (2 marks)

(e) (i) The 'real' participants in the study were the students. Identify **one** suitable method of selecting these participants. (1 mark)

    (ii) Explain how the investigators could have carried out this method of selection. (2 marks)

(f) (i) Identify **one** ethical issue that might arise in this study. (1 mark)

    (ii) Explain how the investigators might have dealt with this issue. (2 marks)

(g) (i) What experimental design was used in this study? (1 mark)

    (ii) Describe **one** advantage and **one** disadvantage of using this experimental design. (2 marks + 2 marks)

    (iii) Identify an alternative experimental design that could have been used in this study. (1 mark)

    (iv) Explain how you could conduct a study with the same aims using this alternative design. (3 marks)

Examiner's tips for answering this question

(a) Don't be afraid to simply lift words from the stimulus material when answering the question.

(b) (ii) This is an example of how your knowledge is tested in research methods questions. You are rarely asked to define a term (although there are sometimes questions like that). Most often, you are required to *use* this knowledge. If you repeat the definition to yourself, you should be able to create an answer.

(c) This is another case of having to use your knowledge to work out the answer. If you understand the term 'random' and know how random allocations are done, you should be able to answer this question.

(e) (i) You might be tempted to list all the methods you know – but only the first will be taken as your answer and will be taken as the basis for (ii). So if you said 'opportunity or random' for part (i) and then in (ii) described how to collect a random sample and then how to do an opportunity sample, this would get zero because the examiner must presume that the first answers each time are linked.

(g) This question is about experimental design. This is one of the questions that students always find difficult. When asked to name the experimental design, they do not appear to remember that the answer is one of the following: repeated measures, independent groups, matched pairs. To help you remember, think of:

Expe**RIM**ental design

R = repeated measures

I = independent groups

M = matched pairs

(g) (ii) There is no reference in this question to the study so you do not need to set your answer in the context of the study. You can just write the answer you have learned.

(g) (iv) This last part is worth 3 marks so take care to provide sufficient details for the marks available. You can include any details related to design, such as how you would deal with order effects.

Model answer for question 1

(a) (i) Write a suitable hypothesis for this study. (2 marks)

Essays that appear to be written by boys get higher marks than essays written by girls.

(ii) Identify whether your hypothesis is directional or non-directional and explain why you chose such a hypothesis. (1 mark + 2 marks)

The hypothesis is directional. I chose this because past research suggests that boys will do better.

(b) The student researchers decided to conduct a pilot study.

(i) Why would it be a good idea to conduct a pilot study? (2 marks)

A pilot study would enable you to check aspects of your research design so that you could put it right before doing the full-scale study.

(ii) Explain how the student researchers would conduct a pilot study. (2 marks)

They would get a small group of people and then try out their design, including the standardised instructions and other standardised procedures.

(c) Identify **one** method of selecting participants for this study and describe **one** advantage and **one** disadvantage of using this method. (1 mark + 2 marks + 2 marks)

One method would be to use an opportunity sample.

One advantage is that it is easy because you just use the first participants you can find.

One disadvantage is that the sample is biased because it is drawn from a small part of the target population.

(d) (i) Explain the term 'investigator effect'. (2 marks)

An investigator effect is anything the investigator does that has an effect on the participant's performance other than what was intended.

(ii) Suggest **one** investigator effect that might have been a problem in this study. (2 marks)

A possible investigator effect would be that some of the psychology students would encourage the participants to give better marks to the boys' essays.

(iii) Explain how you could have dealt with this effect. (2 marks)

You could make sure that the psychology students do not talk to the participants so they don't have an opportunity to communicate their expectations.

(e) Explain why the experiment was designed so that half the participants had girls' names for Essays 1 and 2 and the other half had girls' names for Essays 3 and 4. (3 marks)

This design would counterbalance any order effects. For example, if everyone had the same essays with girls' names, it might be that those essays were slightly worse and this would act as an extraneous variable.

(f) (i) What measure of central tendency was used to describe the findings? (1 mark)

The mean.

(ii) Explain why this measure was used to give the average for this data. (2 marks)

The mean takes all the values of the scores into account, and it can be used with these numerical data.

(g) Describe one finding and one conclusion that can be taken from the bar chart. (2 marks + 2 marks)

The participants in both groups gave lower ratings to the girls, which suggests that people do have gender biases against women.

Examiner's comments

(a) (i) 1 mark would be given if the answer were 'Essays that appear to be written by boys get higher marks' because it is incomplete.

(a) (ii) If your answer to the first part of this question is wrong, you will get no marks for the second part. You would get no marks for saying 'because I said that boys would do better than girls' as this explains the direction but does not justify it. You would get 1 mark for saying 'I chose this because past research suggests it'.'

(b) (i) You might get 1 mark for explaining what a pilot study is. The full 2 marks is for specifically answering the question 'Why?'

(b) (ii) In this part, the focus is on 'how'. It would be tempting to explain why, but this would not be creditworthy here.

(c) You would get only 1 mark for an advantage that said 'it is easy'. Easier than what? Why is it easy? For the disadvantage, you again need to provide detail. An answer that said 'because the sample is biased' would only get 1 mark because the same is true for all sampling methods.

(d) (i) This is a belt-and-braces definition; something briefer could still get full marks as long as it is clear that it is something that the investigator does (usually unconsciously) that affects the participant's behaviour.

(d) (ii) There are various possible answers to this question. One of the major problems is that candidates write about how participants might respond. This is not an investigator effect – the focus must be on what the investigator is doing.

(d) (iii) You would get no marks for (iii) if you got no marks for (ii).

(e) This is the only question worth 3 marks so you have to be sure to squeeze out some extra material for those extra marks. Just saying 'counterbalance' would only receive 1 mark. You need to explain this concept and make sure you place it in the context of this study (in other words, if you just describe the principle of counterbalancing, you will not get full marks).

(f) This is just about OK but does rely rather heavily on defining the term rather than explaining why it was used.

(g) The two answers have been given in one sentence and are sufficiently accurate and detailed for the full marks. You do not always have to write lots in order to get full marks.

*A model answer is an answer that would get full marks. However, it is not the only possible answer that would get full marks, it is simply one possible answer.

	1b	2c	3d	4a	5c	6d	7a	8d	9d	10c
	11b	12a	13b	14a	15d	16c	17d	18a	19c	20d

Model answer for question 2

(a) What was the aim of this research? (2 marks)
The aim of the study was to find out if the experimenters' expectations influence the participants' behaviour.

(b) (i) Identify the independent and dependent variables in this study. (2 marks)
The IV is expectation and the DV is how well the rats learned the maze.

(ii) Explain how the independent variable was operationalised. (2 marks)
The expectations were created by telling students that their rats were maze-bright or dull.

(c) (i) Explain the meaning of the phrase 'rats were randomly assigned to students'. (2 marks)
This means that the rats were placed with each student using a random method such as giving each student a number and picking them out one at a time and assigning them to the rats in order.

(ii) Why was it important to 'randomly assign' the rats to students? (2 marks)
This would prevent any bias because otherwise the best students might select certain rats.

(d) When the investigators produced the findings, they described the data using the mean and standard deviation.
(i) What does the mean tell us about data? (1 mark)
It tells us what the average value of the scores is.

(ii) What does the standard deviation tell us about data? (2 marks)
It tells us the average distance of each score from the mean.

(iii) Describe **one** advantage of using the mean. (2 marks)
The mean takes the value of all scores into account.

(e) (i) The 'real' participants in the study were the students. Identify **one** suitable method of selecting these participants. (1 mark)
You could use an opportunity sample.

(ii) Explain how the investigators could have carried out this method of selection. (2 marks)
They could just use all of the students in one psychology class and ask all of them if they would be willing to participate.

(f) (i) Identify **one** ethical issue that might arise in this study. (1 mark)
Deception.

(ii) Explain how the investigators might have dealt with this issue. (2 marks)
Debrief the participants after the study and tell them the true aims of the study and see if they are feeling distressed in any way.

(g) (i) What experimental design was used in this study? (1 mark)
Independent groups.

(ii) Describe **one** advantage and **one** disadvantage of using this experimental design. (2 marks + 2 marks)
One advantage: you avoid order effects such as the boredom effect, which are a problem if you used repeated measures.

One disadvantage: you can't control participant variables, which may act as an extraneous variable.

(iii) Identify an alternative experimental design that could have been used in this study. (1 mark)
Matched pairs.

(iv Explain how you could conduct a study with the same aims using this alternative design. (3 marks)
I would decide on certain key participant variables such as willingness to please and assess the potential participants. Then I would pair them on these variables and randomly allocate them to one of the two groups. I would get the participants in the first place by using volunteer sampling.

Examiner's comments

(a) If you wrote 'To study experimenter's expectations', this would receive only 1 mark as it lacks important details.

(b) (i) In this question a brief answer is acceptable for a total of 2 marks.

(b) (ii) A 1-mark answer might simply refer to rats being maze-dull or maze-bright. A definition of operationalisation would receive no marks.

(c) (i) This is again a question that requires you to use your knowledge rather than just explaining the meaning of 'random'. An equally acceptable answer would say that it means that each rat had an equal chance of being allocated to either group.

(c) (ii) Not an easy question, but make sure that you saying more than 'prevent bias'. Provide a bit more detail.

(d) (i) This is only worth 1 mark so simply knowing that the mean is an average or a measure of central tendency is fine.

(d) (ii) This is a more difficult concept so there are more marks. You would possibly get 2 marks for saying 'spread of scores around the mean'.

(d) (iii) This is sufficiently detailed although brief for the full 2 marks. The key word is 'values'.

(e) (i) Any sampling method would be equally creditworthy, but maybe it is best to consider part (ii) to decide which one to use.

(e) (ii) A short answer, but it is hard to know what else could be said.

(f) (i) Debriefing would not get any marks as the issue.

(f) (ii) For 2 marks, you would need to say more than 'I would debrief them.' You need to explain what this would involve.

(g) (i) Remember **RIM**.

(g) (ii) If you did not get (i) right, you automatically get zero marks for (ii).

(g) (iii) This is a good choice because there are a range of design issues for matched pairs design. You would get zero if you said 'independent groups' because that was the answer to (i).

(g) (iv) Just writing about matching participants would not be enough for the full 3 marks.

Contents

pages 24–25

Field experiments

Activity 6: A field experiment

Lab versus field experiments

Lab experiments are artificial or 'contrived'

Field experiments are not all good

 **Qs** 15,16

pages 26–27

Validity: internal validity

Participant effects

Investigator effects

Paying homage to formal terms

Experimenter bias

The bottom line

 **Qs** 17

pages 28–29

Validity: external validity

Explaining ecological validity

A study can have mundane realism but lack ecological validity

Milgram (1963): Obedience to unjust authority

Hofling *et al*. (1966): Obedience in the real world

Rank and Jacobsen (1975): More nurses

The bottom line

Qs 18,19

pages 30–31

Qs 20,21

Natural experiments

Activity 7: A natural experiment

Generalisability of natural experiments

Difference studies

Comparing lab, field and natural experiments

CHAPTER

2

More about experiments

field experiments and natural experiments

pages 38–41

Exam-style questions 3 and 4

Model answers for exam-style questions 3 and 4

Answers to multiple choice questions

Experimental and control groups

Thinking back to Milgram and Hofling

John Henry effect

Activity 9: What is validity all about?

Multiple choice questions

 24

pages 36–37

How to deal with ethical issues

Ethical guidelines

Debriefing

Presumptive consent

Ethical committees

Activity 8: Ethical committee

How to deal with particular ethical issues

Qs 23

pages 34–35

Ethical issues

Deception

Protection from physical and psychological harm

Informed consent

Confidentiality

Privacy

Confidentiality and privacy – what's the difference?

The right to withdraw

More on Milgram

 22

pages 32–33

Field experiments

In Chapter 1, we considered experiments. All experiments have an independent variable and a dependent variable.

There are different kinds of experiment:

Laboratory experiment
An experiment conducted in a *special environment* where variables can be *carefully controlled*. Participants are aware that they are taking part in an experiment, although they may not know the true aims of the study.

Field experiment
An experiment conducted in a more *natural environment*, i.e. 'in the field'. As with the laboratory experiment, the independent variable is still *deliberately manipulated* by the researcher. Participants are *often not aware* that they are participating in an experiment.

Field study
Any study that is conducted in a natural environment. Note that not all studies conducted in a laboratory are experiments. There are controlled observations that are conducted in a laboratory (which we will look at in Chapter 4).

*An experiment permits us to study **cause and effect.** It differs from non-experimental methods in that it involves the manipulation of one variable (the independent variable – IV), while trying to keep all other variables constant. If the IV is the only thing that is changed, then it must be responsible for any change in the dependent variable (DV).*

Qs 15

1. What are the research aims of the experiment on the left?

2. How do you know it is an experiment?

3. How do you know it is a field experiment?

4. Write a suitable hypothesis for this experiment.

5. Why should the same person dress in the two different outfits (instead of using two confederates)?

6. What is a 'confederate'?

7. What method did you use to select your participants?

8. Give **one** advantage and **one** disadvantage of using this method of selecting participants.

9. What was the experimental design that you used?

10. Can you think of **one** ethical issue raised in this study (i.e. something that may harm participants)?

11. Name a suitable measure of central tendency to use with your data and explain why.

12. Present your data in a table like the one below.

	Smartly dressed	Casually dressed
Passer-by said 'yes'		
Passer-by said 'no'		

13. Draw a graph to illustrate your findings.

14. What do you conclude?

Activity 6 — A field experiment

(There is an alternative, specification-related field experiment on *Conformity* on page 131)

A number of studies have investigated the effects of appearance on behaviour, for example:

Bickman (1974) left a dime in a telephone box. If the experimenter was dressed in a suit, he got the dime back 77% of the time; if he was wearing unkempt work clothes, there was a 38% return rate.

Bickman also found that New York pedestrians were more likely to obey someone dressed as a guard than someone in a milkman's uniform or casually dressed. The confederates issued orders to passers-by to 'Pick up this bag for me', 'This fellow is overparked at the meter but doesn't have any change; give him a dime', or 'Don't you know you have to stand on the other side of the pole?'.

In these field experiments, the IV is appearance and the DV is helping behaviour.

Students may work in pairs. One member of the pair is the observer and the other is the confederate who wears one of two outfits:

1. Smartly dressed.
2. Casual.

The task is to ask people if they would be prepared to stop and answer some questions for a school project.

If the passer-by says 'no', then thank them.

If the passer-by says 'yes' then explain that this was an experiment for your school work and all you wished to know was whether they were prepared to help or not.

The observer should record :

1. How many passers-by said yes or no for each condition (smart or casual).
2. Any other comments made by passers-by.

Lab versus field experiments

It may help you to understand the difference between lab and field experiments by looking at the examples on this page.

A Helping behaviour was investigated in a study on the New York subway. A confederate collapsed on a subway train and investigators noted whether help was offered. The confederate was either holding a black cane or carrying a paper bag with a bottle of alcohol and smelled of alcohol (thus appearing drunk). Piliavin *et al.* (1969) found that when the victim carried a cane, 95% of bystanders helped within 10 seconds; if he appeared drunk, help came in only 50% of the trials.

B Participants were asked to wait in a room before the experiment began. There was a radio playing either good or bad news, and a stranger was present. When participants were asked to rate the stranger, the degree of liking was related to the kind of news they had been listening to, showing that people are attracted to others who are associated with positive experiences (Veitch and Griffitt, 1976).

C The participants were children aged 3–5 years old. Each child was taken on their own to a special room where there were lots of toys including, in one corner, a 5-foot inflatable Bobo doll and a mallet. The experimenter invited the 'model' to join them and then left the room for about 10 minutes. Half of the children watched the model playing aggressively with a life-sized Bobo doll while the others watched the model play non-aggressively with the doll. Later they were given an opportunity to play with toys, including the Bobo doll, and were observed through a one-way mirror. The children who saw the aggressive behaviour were more likely to behave aggressively (Bandura *et al.*, 1961; see right).

D One group of school pupils were given information about how their peers had performed on a maths task. They were either told that their peers had done well or that they had done poorly on the test. The children were later given a maths test in class. Those who expected to do well did better than those led to expect they would do poorly (Schunk, 1983).

E The Hawthorne Electric factory in Chicago asked researchers to study what factors led to increased worker productivity. The study found that increased lighting led to increased productivity – but then also found that decreased lighting led to increased activity (Roethlisberger and Dickson, 1939).

The conclusion was that the participants knew they were being studied and this interest in their work was what explained their increased output, masking the real IV. This has been called the **Hawthorne effect**.

F Participants were tested in their teaching room, given nonsense trigrams (e.g. SXT) and then asked to count backwards until told to stop. The participants were then asked to recall the trigram. The counting interval was used to prevent the trigram being rehearsed. When the counting interval was 3 seconds, participants could recall most trigrams; when it was 18 seconds, they could not recall many trigrams (Peterson and Peterson, 1959).increased output, masking the real IV. This has been called the **Hawthorne effect**.

Lab experiments are artificial or 'contrived'

- Participants know they are being studied, and this is likely to affect their behaviour.

- The setting is often not like real life. This is described as being low in **mundane realism**. People behave more like they 'normally' do when a study is high in mundane realism.

- The IV or DV may be operationalised in such a way that it does not represent real-life experiences, e.g. using trigrams to test how memory works.

For all these reasons, participants in a laboratory experiment are less likely to behave as they would in real life.

The same problems may also arise in field experiments; so that field experiments are not necessarily more like real life then laboratory experiments.

Mundane realism refers to how an experiment mirrors the real-word. 'Mundane' means 'of the world', commonplace, ordinary.

Qs   16

For each of the examples on the left (A–F), answer the following questions:

1. Identify the IV and DV.

2. Was the task required of participants artificial contrived?

3. Was the study conducted in a natural setting?

4. Was the setting high or low in mundane realism?

5. Did the participants know they were being studied?

6. Were the participants brought into a special (contrived) situation, or did the experimenter go to them?

7. What relevant variables might not have been controlled?

8. Do you think this was a lab or a field experiment?

Field experiments are not all good

Field experiments may be more natural but it is more difficult to control extraneous variables in the 'field'.

There is also a major ethical issue – if participants do not know they are being studied, is it right to manipulate and record their behaviour?

KEY TERMS

Field experiment
Lab experiment

OTHER TERMS

Field study
Laboratory
Mundane realism

Validity: internal validity

Losing sight of the wood for the trees

Does it matter whether an experiment is classified as a field experiment or a lab experiment? No. What matters is an understanding of the bigger picture (the wood instead of the trees).

The bigger picture:

- *Participant awareness.* Awareness factors are threats to **internal validity**.

- *Experimental control.* Lack of experimental control is a threat to **internal validity**.

- *Artificiality* (*low mundane realism*) is a threat to **external validity** (which we will look at on pages 28 and 29).

*The term **'validity'** refers to how true or legitimate something is.*

Internal validity is the degree to which an observed effect is due to the experimental manipulation rather than other factors such as extraneous variables.

If internal validity is low, the results have little value.

Internal validity in an experiment is concerned with the following questions:

- Did the IV produce the change in the DV?

- Or was the change in the DV caused by something else?

High internal validity means that the differences that were found between groups on the DV in an experiment were directly related to what the researcher did to the IV and not due to some other unintended variable (confounding variable). Internal validity is also an issue in questionnaire or observational studies, see chapter 4.

Participant effects

Why don't we want participants to be aware that they are participating in a study? Knowing that you are being studied (increased attention) may act as an alternative IV (a **confounding variable**), as it did in the Hawthorne study. This is known as the **Hawthorne effect** (see page 25).

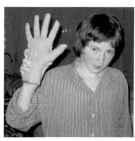

Participants want to offer a helping hand. If they know they are in an experiment, they usually want to please the experimenter and be helpful; otherwise, why are they there? This sometimes results in them being over-cooperative – and behaving artificially.

The opposite effect is also possible when a participant deliberately behaves in such a way as to spoil an experiment. This is sometimes called the '**screw you effect**.'

Social desirability bias is a form of participant reactivity. Participants wish to present themselves in the best possible way and therefore may not behave according to personal preference but behave in the most socially acceptable way for the purposes of a research study.

Demand characteristics create participant effects

We always seek cues about how to behave, particularly in a new environment such as being in an experiment and particularly if a person knows they are in an experiment. Participants actively look for clues as to how they should behave. The result is that they do not behave as they usually would.

Thus, demand characteristics may act as a substitute IV (confounding variable) because they explain the change in the DV.

Participant effects occur because of cues in an experimental situation that may bias a participant's behaviour, e.g. because they know they are being studied or because of demand characteristics.

Demand characteristics are cues in an experimental situation that may unconsciously affect a participant's behaviour.

Dealing with participant effects

Single blind design
The participant does not know the true aims of the experiment or does not know that they are involved in an experiment.

Or the person conducting the experiment (who has not designed it) does not know the aims of the experiment and therefore cannot produce cues about what he or she expects.

Double blind design
Both the participant and the person conducting the experiment (who has not designed it) are 'blind' to the aims.

Experimental realism
If you make the experimental task sufficiently engaging, participants pay attention to the task and not to the fact that they are being observed.

Paying homage to formal terms*

As we have already said, learning about research methods is a bit like learning a foreign language. You have to learn to use a whole new vocabulary, and you have to learn the meaning of this vocabulary. The problem with the vocabulary is that the meaning of the terms is not always black and white. You have to learn to look for the 'general drift' and not be fazed when you find that there are slightly different meanings as your understanding increases.

*An excellent phrase 'invented' by Hugh Coolican (2004a) to explain this problem.

Qs   17

1. *In a study, participants' memory was tested in the morning and in the afternoon to see if there was any difference in their ability to recall numbers.*

    a. Give an example of **one** possible investigator effect in this study.

    b. Describe how you might deal with this investigator effect.

    c. Give an example of how the participant's understanding of the study might affect the findings of this experiment.

    d. Describe how you might deal with this problem of participant reactivity.

    e. Give an example of a possible demand characteristic in this study.

    f. Describe how you might deal with this problem.

2. *A study looked at whether first impressions matter. Participants were given a list of adjectives describing Mr. Smith. One group had positive adjectives first, followed by negative adjectives. The other group had the adjectives in reverse order. They were all then asked to describe Mr Smith.*

    a. Give an example of a possible demand characteristic in this study.

    b. Describe how you might deal with this problem.

Investigator effects

Investigator effects, like participant effects, may reduce the internal validity of an experiment.

Direct effects

An investigator may directly affect a participants' behaviour. This was described in chapter 1. An investigator might design a study AND conduct it, however, in many experiments the person who designs the experiment is not the same as the minion who actually deals with the participants. To distinguish these roles we talk of investigators and **experimenters**.

It is the person who interacts directly with participants who will be the source of direct investigator effects.

Indirect effects

An investigator may indirectly affect a participant in a number of ways, such as:

- *Investigator experimental design effect:* The investigator may operationalise the measurement of variables in such a way that the desired result is more likely or may limit the duration of the study for the same reason.

- *Investigator loose procedure effect:* The investigator may not clearly specify the standardised instructions and/or procedures which leaves room for the results to be influenced by the experimenter.

Some people take a narrower view and define investigator effects only as the direct effects of an investigator/experimenter on the behaviour of participants rather than the effects of the investigator on the overall design of the experiment.

Investigator effects: *investigator affects participant directly or indirectly (through the design of the study).*

Experimenter effects: *those effects due to direct interaction with the participant.*

Participant reactivity: *participant responds to unconscious cues from the investigator.*

The bottom line ...
Investigator effects are any cues (other than the IV) from an investigator/ experimenter that encourage certain behaviours in the participant, leading to a fulfilment of the investigator's expectations. Such cues act as a confounding variable.

KEY TERMS

Demand characteristics
Internal validity
Investigator effects
Participant effects
Validity

OTHER TERMS

Experimental realism
Experimenter
Experimenter bias
Hawthorne effect
Investigator
Participant reactivity
Social desirability bias

Experimenter bias

This is the term used to describe the effects of an experimenter's expectations on a participant's behaviour, a form of investigator effect. A classic demonstration of this was in the experiment by Rosenthal and Fode described on page 19, which showed that even rats are affected by an experimenter's expectations.

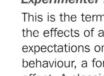

Validity: external validity

Internal validity is about what caused changes in the DV. (Was it the IV or was it something else? If it were something else, the conclusions about cause and effect are not valid).

External validity is related to generalising – can the findings from an experiment be generalised (applied) beyond a particular experiment?

Can we generalise to:

- Different places or settings (**ecological validity**)
- Different people or populations (**population validity**)
- Different times (e.g. 1950s or 1990s) (**historical validity**)

External validity (the ability to generalise) will be stronger the more you **replicate** your study and produce the same findings.

Experimental validity concerns the validity of experiments, both internal and external.

Internal validity concerns what goes on inside the experiment.

It is about control.

External validity concerns what goes on outside the experiment.

It is about representatitiveness and generalising.

A study that is low in internal validity is also low in external validity.

Ecological validity is one form of external validity. It is the extent to which the results of an experiment can be generalised from the set of environmental conditions created by the researcher to other environmental conditions – chiefly to 'real life'.

Explaining ecological validity

Many people mistakenly think that ecological validity means 'the degree to which the behaviours observed and recorded in a study reflect the behaviours that actually occur in natural settings'.

This is not wrong – but it is not right.

1. Part of ecological validity concerns whether the experiment mirrors the real world. This is mundane realism or '**representativeness**'.

2. Another part of ecological validity concerns '**generalisability**' – the extent to which findings from one study (conducted in a unique setting) can be generalised to other settings (including the 'real world').

Invariably, studies in psychology involve a trade-off between control and generalisability. Greater control exists in the laboratory. However, it is debatable to what extent findings from the laboratory can be generalised to other environments, especially the less controllable environments in which everyday life is lived.

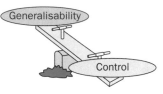

Validity is like a see-saw with control on one side and generalisability on the other.

Different ecologies

KEY TERMS
Ecological validity
External validity

OTHER TERMS
Experimental validity
Generalisability
Historical validity
Population validity
Replication
Representativeness

In field research, there is too little control to allow for definite conclusions, whereas in laboratory research, there is too much control to allow for interesting conclusions.

 Qs   **18**

On this spread and the previous one, a number of terms have been used that relate to validity. Use the terms below to fill in the blanks. Some terms may be used more than once.

Internal, external, ecological, population

1. *In a repeated measures study participants are able to guess the aim of the study.* This would be a threat to _____ validity because participants' answers (the measure of the DV) may reflect their guesses rather than the IV.

2. *A study on stress used an opportunity sample of people living in a city.* This study would lack population validity and might also lack _____ validity.

3. *Participants in a lab experiment know they are being studied.* This could affect the _____ validity of the study.

4. *A study was replicated. and the same findings were produced.* This suggests that the study has high _____ validity.

5. Being able to apply the findings of a study to other settings is called _____ validity, which is a kind of _____ validity.

6. A field experiment is conducted in a more natural setting, which may increase its _____ validity but decrease its _____ validity.

A study can have mundane realism but lack ecological validity

Consider the following three studies (which you will probably read about during your AS year, if you have not done so already).

Milgram (1963) Obedience to unjust authority

Forty male participants were told that the study was investigating how punishment affects learning. There were two confederates: an experimenter, and a 'learner'. The participant drew lots with the confederate and always ended up as the 'teacher'. He was told that he must administer increasingly strong electric shocks to the participant each time he got a question wrong. The machine was tested on the participant to show him that it worked.

The 'learner' is attached to an electric shock machine by experimenters.

The learner, sitting in another room, gave mainly wrong answers and received his (fake) shocks in silence until they reached 300 volts (a very strong shock). At this point, he pounded on the wall and then gave no response to the next question.

Milgram found that 65% of the participants were fully obedient, i.e. continued to obey up to the maximum voltage of 450 volts.

Milgram repeated this study in many different situations:

- The location was moved to a run-down office (48% obedience).
- The teacher was in the same room as the learner (40% obedience).
- The teacher held the learner's hand on the shock plate (30% obedience).

These replications show that the initial conclusion was correct: situational factors affect obedience to unjust authority.

Hofling et al. (1966) Obedience in the real world

Hofling et al. conducted a study in a US hospital. Nurses were telephoned by a 'Dr Smith' who asked that they give 20 mg of a drug called Astroten to a patient. This order contravened hospital regulations in a number of ways:

- Nurses were told not to accept instructions over the phone,
- Nor from an unknown doctor,
- Nor for a dose in excess of the safe amount (the dosage being twice that advised on the bottle),
- Especially for a unknown drug.

Nevertheless, 21 out of 22 (95%) nurses did as requested. When the nurses involved in the study were interviewed afterwards, they said, in their defence, that they had obeyed because that is what doctors expect nurses to do – they behaved as nurses do in real life. Or did they?

Rank and Jacobsen (1977): More nurses

In another study (this time in Australia), nurses were also asked to carry out an irregular order. This time, 16 out of 18 (89%) refused. There were important differences:

- The drug was familiar (Valium).
- The nurses could consult with peers.

The bottom line ...

A study is not high in ecological validity just because it has been carried out in a natural setting. Similarly, it is not low in ecological validity just because it has been conducted in a laboratory.

Ecological validity is established by representativeness and generalisability (some people make the mistake of thinking it is just representativeness).

Representativeness can be established through mundane realism.

Generalisability can be established by confirming the original findings through replication.

You might think that the study of nurses by Hofling *et al.* had high mundane realism and high ecological validity. However, *it had low mundane realism*. Even though it was conducted in a natural setting, the tasks were quite artificial. Rank and Jacobsen's study used *more real-life tasks* – the nurses dealt with a familiar drug and were allowed to consult with each other.

Nevertheless, Hofling *et al.*'s study was conducted in a more natural setting than Milgram's, although this *does not automatically mean that it had higher ecological validity*. You must always explain why a study has high ecological validity. *The replications of Milgram's study* suggest that his findings do apply to other settings, whereas the same is not true for the study by Hofling *et al.* Furthermore, *Milgram's study concerned the obedience of ordinary people to perceived authority*, (e.g. obeying an experimenter), so it wasn't really artificial at all.

Furthermore, the doctor–nurse authority relationship is a special one so it is not reasonable to generalise from this to all other kinds of obedience. It is part of a nurse's job to obey orders from doctors, as the nurses in Hofling *et al.*'s study argued in their defence.

Qs 19

An area of study that has interested psychologists is massed versus distributed practice, i.e. whether learning is better if you practise something repeatedly (massed) or space your periods of practice (distributed). This topic has been studied in different settings.

- *Study 1: Participants were required to recall nonsense syllables on 12 occasions spread over 3 days or 12 days (Jost, 1897). Recall was higher over 12 days. This finding has been supported by subsequent research.*

- *Study 2: Post office workers had to learn to type postcodes either using massed or distributed practice (Baddeley and Longman, 1978). Distributed practice was again found to be superior.*

Present arguments for why each of these studies could be viewed as having high and low ecological validity.

Natural experiments

There is a third kind of experiment, called a natural experiment. In a **natural experiment**, the IV has not been deliberately manipulated by the experimenter so the situaton is described as 'natural'.

The reason for doing such experiments is that there are some IVs that cannot be manipulated directly for practical or ethical reasons.

Strictly speaking, an experiment involves the deliberate manipulation of an IV by an experimenter so natural experiments are not 'true experiments' because no one has *deliberately* changed the IV to observe the effect on the DV.

An example of a natural experiment

A study was conducted in St Helena to see whether the introduction of TV would produce an increase in anti-social behaviour (Charlton *et al.*, 2000). The residents of this tiny island (47 square miles) received TV for the first time in 1995.

The vast majority of the measures used to assess pro- and anti-social behaviour showed no differences after the introduction of TV. This finding is in contrast with an earlier study by Williams (1985) of a Canadian town where TV was introduced for the first time. In this study, anti-social behaviour was found to increase.The difference may be explained in terms of social norms. In St Helena, there was a community with a strong sense of identity and no reason to be aggressive, whereas this was not true of the Canadian town.

ctivity 7   A natural experiment

You can conduct similar research to Schellenberg's making use of existing data and thus conduct a natural experiment.

Music lessons can boost IQ (Schellenberg, 2004)

The participants (aged 6 years old) had their IQs tested before the study began. They were allocated to one of four groups: two groups had 36 weeks of extra-curricular music tuition: one had singing-based tuition, the other studied keyboard. A third group had extra drama lessons on top of normal school, and the last, (control) group simply attended school as usual. The children completed IQ and other tests at the end of the school year. Schellenberg found that the music groups IQ performance increased significantly more than that of the drama and control groups.

IV: Divide your class into those who have received extra music lessons and those who have not. You must operationalise this IV – i.e. decide what constitutes 'having music lessons'. Would 1 week of lessons count?

DV: For each member of your class, calculate a GCSE score.

PARTICIPANT	**GCSE SCORES** Grade A*=9, A=8, B=7, C=6, D=5, E=4, F=3, G=2, U=1, X=0																				*Total score* Add white columns	*Final score* Total score ÷ number of scores	*Music lessons* (Y/N)
	Grade	Score	Grade	Score	Grade	Score	Grade	Score	Grade	Score	Grade	Score	Grade	Score	Grade	Score	Grade	Score	Grade	Score			
1																							
2																							

Analysis

Combine the data collected by your classmates. Calculate a mean score for all pupils with music lessons and without music lessons and draw a graph to illustrate this data.

What can you conclude?

Another natural experiment: Deprivation dwarfism

Physical underdevelopment occurs when children do not have sufficient food. But it also occurs when children are deprived of emotional care – a condition called 'deprivation dwarfism'.

One study demonstrating this was conducted by Widdowson (1951). He recorded the case of a group of apparently malnourished orphanage children. Despite being given dietary supplements, they remained underdeveloped. However, when a new supervisor arrived who gave them better emotional care, they began to improve. It is possible that the hormones produced by stress affect growth.

Qs   20

1. Answer the following questions for both of the studies above (the St Helena and orphanage studies):
   a. Identify the IV and DV.
   b. How was the IV manipulated?
   c. Identify at least **one** threat to internal validity. (Hint: think of extraneous variables.)
   d. Identify at least **one** potential threat to external validity.
   e. What were the aims of this study?
   f. Write a suitable hypothesis for this experiment.
   g. Identify the target population.
   h. What was the experimental design?
2. The study by Schellenberg (on the left) was not a natural experiment. What kind of experiment was it?

Generalisability of natural experiments

Drawing valid conclusions from natural experiments is problematic because:

- Participants are not **randomly allocated** to conditions, which means that there may be biases in the different groups of participants. For example, in the study on music and IQ, there are likely to have been other factors that differentiated between the music lesson and non-music lesson groups. This would act as a **confounding variable**.

- The sample studied may have unique characteristics. For example, in the St Helena study, the people were part of a pro-social community, which means that the findings cannot be generalised to other cultures and social groups.

Comparing lab, field and natural experiments

Nature and Use	Advantages ☺	Disadvantages ☹
Laboratory experiment To investigate causal relationships under controlled conditions	Well controlled, confounding variables are minimised, thus higher **internal validity** Can be easily replicated, demonstrating **external validity**	Artificial, a contrived situation in which participants may not behave naturally **Investigator effects** and **participant effects**, may reduce **internal validity**.
Field experiment To investigate causal relationships in more natural surroundings	Less artificial, usually higher **mundane realism** and **ecological validity** Avoids **participant reactivity** (because participants are not aware of study), may increase **internal validity**	Less control of **extraneous variables**, reduces **internal validity** More time-consuming and thus more expensive
Natural experiment To investigate causal relationships in situations where the IV cannot be directly manipulated	Allows research where the IV cannot be manipulated for ethical or practical reasons, e.g. studies of deprivation Enables psychologists to study 'real' problems such as the effects of disaster on health (increased **mundane realism** and **ecological validity**)	Cannot demonstrate causal relationships because the IV is not directly manipulated Inevitably many **confounding variables** (e.g. allocation of participants to groups), threat to **internal validity** Can only be used where conditions vary naturally Participants may be aware of being studied.

KEY TERMS

Natural experiment

Advantages ☺ and disadvantages ☹ of
Field, laboratory and natural experiments

OTHER TERMS

Difference studies

Difference studies

A naturalistic study is only a natural experiment if there is an IV and a DV.

Some people consider that studies of gender differences, for example comparing whether boys or girls have higher IQs, are natural experiments. They would say that gender is the IV and IQ score is the DV.

But no one has manipulated gender. It is a naturally occuring variable, not a naturally *manipulated* one.

Gender studies are **difference studies**. They are not experiments. We cannot draw a causal conclusion. We cannot say that gender causes an individual to have a higher IQ. We can only conclude that gender is related to IQ.

An IV must be manipulated by someone in order for us to claim that a cause and effect have been identified.

Qs 21

1. Fill in the right-hand column in the table below with the words lab, field, natural. There may be more than one answer in a box. For example, you could place 'lab' in both high and low internal validity. Explain your answers.

| High internal validity |
| Low internal validity |
| High external validity |
| Low external validity |

2. Four studies are described below. Identify each study as a lab, field or natural experiment and explain your decision:

   a. *Two primary schools use different reading schemes. A psychological study compares the reading scores at the end of the year to see which scheme was more effective.*

   b. *Children take part in a trial to compare the success of a new maths programme. The children are placed in one of two groups – the new maths programme or the traditional one – and taught in these groups for a term.*

   c. *The value of using computers rather than books is investigated by requiring children to learn word lists, either using a computer or with a book.*

   d. *The effect of advertisements on gender stereotypes is studied by showing children ads with women doing feminine tasks or doing neutral tasks and then asking them about gender stereotypes.*

   e. *A study investigated the anti-social effects of TV by seeing whether people who watch a lot of TV (more than 5 hours a day) are more aggressive than those who do not.*

Ethical issues

In Chapter 1, we considered ethics. There is, however, considerably more to ethics than what was discussed there.

*An **ethical issue** is a conflict between what the researcher wants and the rights of participants. It is a conflict about what is acceptable.*

For example, an experimenter might want to study the effects of tattooing on self-esteem. But you cannot tattoo someone without their permission. And even if you did have their permission, there would have to be a very good reason for doing this study in order to justify the procedures used.

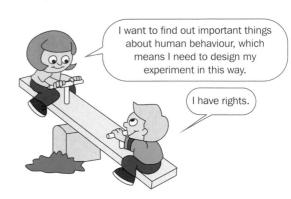

I want to find out important things about human behaviour, which means I need to design my experiment in this way.

I have rights.

Ethical issues are like a see-saw.

Deception

Is it acceptable to deceive a participant about the true aims of a study?

From the researcher's point of view, deception is sometimes necessary because otherwise participants might alter their behaviour to fit the experimenter's expectations.

From the participant's point of view, deception is unethical – you should not deceive anyone without good cause. Perhaps more importantly, deception prevents participants being able to give informed consent. They may agree to participate without really knowing what they have let themselves in for, and they might be quite distressed by the experience.

Deception also leads people to see psychologists as untrustworthy. It means that a participant may not want to take part in psychological research in the future.

Informed consent

From the researcher's point of view, informed consent means you have to reveal the true aims of the study – or at least you have to tell participants what is actually going to happen, and then participants are likely to guess the aims.

From the participant's point of view, you should be told what you will be required to do in the study so that you can make an informed decision about whether you wish to participate. This is a basic human right (established during the Nuremburg war trials – Nazi doctors had conducted various experiments on prisoners without their consent).

Protection from physical and psychological harm

From the researcher's point of view, some of the more important questions in psychology involve a degree of distress to participants.

From the participant's point of view, nothing should happen to you during an experiment that will make you less happy, lower your self-esteem or feel embarrassed about your behaviour – i.e. have negative feelings.

Research participants should be protected from undue risk during an investigation. There are many ways in which you can cause harm to participants, some physical (e.g. getting them to smoke, drink alcohol or drink coffee excessively), some psychological (e.g. making them feel inadequate, embarrassing them, etc.).

Normally, the risk of harm must be no greater than in ordinary life.

Participants should be in the same state after an experiment as they were before *unless they have given their informed consent otherwise.*

This is a photograph of one of Milgram's studies of obedience. The confederate (on the right) is screaming because he is supposedly receiving an electric shock as the participant presses the confederate's hand on the shock plate.

Do you think that the participant would be unduly distressed by the experience of thinking that he was causing such harm to another? If so, is this 'acceptable' psychological harm?

Confidentiality

From the researcher's point of view, it may be difficult to protect confidentiality because the researcher wishes to publish the findings. A researcher may guarantee *anonymity* (withholding your name), but even then it may be obvious who has been involved in a study. For example, knowing that a study was conducted in St Helena permits some people to be able to identify participants.

From the participant's point of view, the Data Protection Act makes confidentiality a legal right. It is acceptable for personal data to be recorded if the data are not made available in a form that identifies the participants (i.e. confidentiality through anonymity).

Confidentiality and privacy – what's the difference?

The words confidentiality and privacy are sometimes used interchangeably, but there is a distinction between the two.

Confidentiality *concerns the communication of personal information from one person to another, and the trust that this information will then be protected.*

Privacy *refers to a zone of inaccessibility of mind or body, and the trust that this will not be 'invaded'.*

In other words, we have a right of privacy. If this is invaded, confidentiality should be respected.

The right to withdraw

From the researcher's point of view, it may not be possible to offer participants this right, e.g. when conducting a field experiment and participants are not aware they are being studied.

From the participant's point of view, if you have been deceived about the aims of the study you still ought to have the option to quit if you find that you do not like what is going on. This compensates for the fact that you did not give informed consent. Even with informed consent, you may not fully understand what is involved.

Privacy

From the researcher's point of view, it may be difficult to avoid invasion of privacy in a field experiment.

From the participant's point of view, people do not expect to be observed by others in certain situations. We have a right to privacy.

In one study, psychologists investigated invasion of personal space by conducting a field experiment in a urinal. There were three conditions: a confederate stood either immediately next to a participant or one urinal away, or was absent. The experimenter recorded micturation times (how long they took to pee) as an indication of how comfortable the participant felt (Middlemist et al., 1976).
Is it unacceptable to observe people in such a place?

Qs   22

1. Do you think that participants in Milgram's study would have been unduly distressed by taking part?
2. If they were distressed, do you think that this is acceptable?
3. Do you think it is unacceptable to observe people in a public urinal?
4. In Milgram's experiment, do think it was acceptable to deceive his participants?
5. Did Milgram obtain informed consent from his participants? Explain your answer.
6. Did Milgram give participants the right to withdraw from his experiment? Explain your answer.

More on Milgram

The participants in Milgram's study were told that it concerned the effect of punishment on learning. They were asked for their consent to take part and told they would be paid $4.50 for taking part. Furthermore, they were told that they could withdraw from the experiment at any time and would still be paid for having taken part.

During the experiment, if a participant asked to stop, the experimenter had been instructed deliver a set of 'prods' such as saying, 'It is absolutely essential that you continue' or 'You have no other choice; you must go on.'

Does this count as informed consent?

Does this count as the right to withdraw?

KEY TERMS
Ethics
Ethical issues
OTHER TERMS
Confidentiality
Deception
Informed consent
Privacy
Protection from psychological harm
Right to withdraw

How to deal with ethical issues

There are many ways to deal with ethical issues. We will consider a few of them and, for each one, offer some evaluation.

Ethical guidelines

Psychologists are a group of professionals (like solicitors, doctors, etc.). They have a professional organisation consisting of fellow professionals that monitors their behaviour – in the UK, it is the Bristish Psychological Society (BPS); in the US, it is the American Psychological Association (APA). These associations draw up a set of guidelines or principles, or a code of conduct, that tells psychologists what behaviours are not acceptable and tells them how to deal with ethical dilemmas.

BUT

The existence of guidelines means that each individual researcher can say 'I have followed the guidelines and therefore my study is ethically acceptable'. A researcher is, in a way, absolved of responsibility for thinking or making any decisions. Guidelines close off discussions about what is right and wrong.

Ethical guidelines are concrete, quasi-legal documents that help to guide conduct within psychology by establishing principles for standard practice and competence.

Issues versus guidelines

This is another case of 'homage to formal terms'. Issues are not the same as guidelines even though informed consent is both an issue and a guideline. An issue is a conflict; a guideline is a means of resolving this conflict.

*Note that **debriefing** is a not an issue.*

Debriefing

A way to compensate for deception is to inform participants of the true nature of the study, after the research has taken place. In general, the aim of debriefing is to restore the participant to the state he or she was in at the start of the experiment. (A debriefing may also be used to collect useful extra information from participants).

BUT

You cannot put the clock back. If a participant was distressed by taking part in the experiment, this is difficult to undo. Participants may say they did not mind and enjoyed the experience even if this was not the case.

THE FAR SIDE® BY GARY LARSON

Sorry, your highness, but you're really not the dictator of Ithuvania, a small European republic. In fact, there is no Ithuvania. The hordes of admirers, the military parades, this office -- We faked it all as an experiment in human psychology. In fact, your highness, your real name is Edward Belcher, you're from Long Island, New York, and it's Time to go home, Eddie.

© 1993 FarWorks, Inc. All Rights Reserved/Dist. by Creators Syndicate

The Far Side® by Gary Larson © 1993 FarWorks, Inc. All Rights Reserved. Used with permission.

Presumptive consent

There are situations in which it is not possible to obtain informed consent (such as field experiments or where informed consent would invalidate the study). An alternative to gaining informed consent from participants is to gain informed consent from others. This can be done, for example, by asking a group of people whether they feel that the study is acceptable. We then *presume* that the participants themselves would have felt the same had they been given the opportunity to say so.

Ethical committees

All institutions where research takes place have an ethical committee, and the committee must approve any study before it begins. They look at all possible ethical issues and at how they have been dealt with, weighing up the value of the research against the possible costs in ethical terms. In some cases, the balance is seen to be reasonable; in other cases, it is decided that the costs are simply too great or the research is simply not of sufficient value.

The BPS guidelines contain the following comments:

On deception:
Intentional deception of the participants over the purpose and general nature of the investigation should be avoided whenever possible. Participants should never be deliberately misled without extremely strong scientific or medical justification. Even then there should be strict controls and the disinterested approval of independent advisors.

On informed consent:
Wherever possible, the investigator should inform all participants of the objectives of the investigation. The investigator should inform the participants of all aspects of the research or intervention that might reasonably be expected to influence their willingness to participate. The investigator should, normally, explain all other aspects of the research or intervention about which the participants enquire. Failure to make full disclosure prior to obtaining informed consent requires additional safeguards to protect the welfare and dignity of the participants.

On children:
Research with children or with participants who have impairments that limit understanding and/or communication such that they are unable to give their consent requires special safe-guarding procedures.

On protection from harm:
Investigators have a primary responsibility to protect participants from physical and mental harm during the investigation. Normally the risk of harm must be no greater than in ordinary life i.e. participants should not be exposed to risks greater than or additional to those encountered in their normal life styles.

If harm, unusual discomfort, or other negative consequences for the individual's future life might occur, the investigator must obtain the disinterested approval of independent advisors, inform the participants, and obtain real, informed consent from each of them.

Activity 8 **Ethical committee**

Divide your class into groups. Each group should devise a study that raises one of the ethical issues listed in the table below – but not a wild idea! Something that might be just acceptable. Look through your psychology textbook for ideas.

Write a research proposal that identifies the ethical issues and how you intend to deal with them. You should also be clear about the aim of the research and why it is important.

Then present your proposal to an ethical committee. This committee should be composed of people who represent the different interests: for example, university psychology department, researchers, participants.

 ## How to deal with particular ethical issues

Ethical issue	How to deal with it	Limitations
Deception	The need for deception should be approved by an ethical committee, weighing up benefits (of the study) against costs (to participants)	Cost–benefit decisions are flawed because both are subjective judgements. And the costs are not always apparent until after the study
	Participants should be fully debriefed after the study and offered the opportunity to withhold their data	Debriefing cannot turn the clock back – a participant may still feel embarrassed or have lowered self-esteem
Informed consent	Participants are asked to formally indicate their agreement to participate, and this should be based on comprehensive information concerning the nature and purpose of the research and their role in it	If a participant knows such information, this may invalidate the purpose of the study
		Even if researchers have sought and obtained informed consent, that does not guarantee that participants really do understand what they have let themselves in for
	An alternative is to gain **presumptive consent**	
	You could also offer the right to withdraw	The problem with presumptive consent is that what people say they would or would not mind is different from actually experiencing it
The right to withdraw	Participants should be informed at the beginning of a study that they have the right to withdraw	Participants may feel they should not withdraw because it will spoil the study
Protection from	Avoid any situation that may cause harm a participant to experience psychological (e.g. negative feelings) or physical damage	In many studies, participation is a requirement of an undergraduate psychology course so students would not feel that they could withdraw
Confidentiality	Researchers should not record the real names of any participants; they should use numbers or false names instead	Researchers are not always able to accurately predict the risks of taking part in a study
Privacy	Do not observe anyone without their informed consent unless it is in a public place	It is sometimes possible to work out who the participants were on the basis of the information that has been provided, e.g. the geographical location of a school
	Participants may be asked to give their retrospective consent or withhold their data	There is no universal agreement about what constitutes a public place
		Not everyone feels this is acceptable, e.g. lovers on a park bench.

 Qs **23**

Study A

In order to study the effects of sleep deprivation, students are asked to limit their sleep to 5 hours for three nights and then sleep normally for the next three nights. Each day, the students' cognitive abilities are assessed using a memory test.

Study B

Participants volunteer to take part in a study. They are told that the study is about public speaking, but the real aim is to see how people respond to encouragement by others. Some participants speak in front of a group of people who smile at them, whereas others talk to a group who appear disinterested.

Study C

Marathon runners are assessed on how much sleep they have the night before and the night after a race to see what the effects of exercise are on sleep.

Study D

A teacher is doing a psychology course and decides to try a little experiment with her class of 8-year-olds. She gives half the class a test in the morning, whereas half of them do the same test in the afternoon to see if time of day affects performance.

For each study, answer the following questions:

1. Identify the IV and DV.
2. How could you operationalise the DV?
3. Identify **one** possible extraneous variable.
4. In what way is this study high or low in external validity?
5. What kind of experiment do you think this is? (Explain your answer.)
6. Identify at least **two** possible ethical issues.
7. Describe how you would deal with each ethical issue.
8. Describe **one** limitation for each of your methods of dealing with the ethical issues.

KEY TERMS
OTHER TERMS

Ethical guidelines

Debriefing
Ethical committee
Presumptive consent

MORE ABOUT EXPERIMENTS

Experimental and control groups

A researcher might want to investigate the effect that rewards have on performance. To do this, children are asked to collect rubbish from a playground and offered a chocolate bar as a reward. They collect several bags of rubbish.

We cannot conclude anything about the effects of the reward because all the children were told that they would receive a reward. We need to have a control group so that we can make a comparison.

We need two groups: an **experimental group** (offered a reward) and a **control group** (offered no reward). This allows us to compare the effects of the reward (IV) on collecting rubbish (the DV).

Or we need to have two conditions: an **experimental condition** (children offered a reward on one occasion) and a **control condition** (offered no reward on another occasion).

Threats to internal validity

If there is an experimental group and a control group, it is possible that the experimental group will perform differently for reasons other than the IV (experimental treatment).

Consider a study on the effectiveness of a new teaching programme. One class are taught using the new programme (experimental group) and compared with another class taught using the 'old' programme (control group).

- The experimental group might improve simply because the teaching programme is new.
- The classes may have had different teachers.
- Or the control group might try extra hard to show that the old way is just as good or better than the new approach. This is called the **John Henry effect**.

John Henry is an American legend. He worked on building the railroads, drilling holes by hitting thick steel spikes into rocks. There was no one who could match him, although many tried.

Then one day someone tried to sell a steam-powered drill to the railroad company, claiming that it could out-drill any man. They set up a contest between John Henry and that drill. The foreman ran the newfangled steam-drill. John Henry pulled out two 20 pound hammers, one in each hand. They drilled and drilled, dust rising everywhere. The men were howling and cheering. At the end of 35 minutes, John Henry had drilled two 7-foot holes – a total of 14 feet, whereas the steam drill had only drilled one 9-foot hole.

Thinking back to Milgram and Hofling

After Milgram's research, another study found real-life support for the findings. Dicks (1972) interviewed former German soldiers and found that they displayed the same psychological mechanisms of obedience shown by participants in laboratory-based obedience research. However, one event of the Second World War found the opposite (Mandel, 1998). In an encounter between German troops and civilians, the commander, Major Trapp, had orders to kill all the Jews in a small town – but Trapp told his men that if they did not wish to obey orders, he would assign them to other duties. Nevertheless, most of the men did obey – despite the fact that, according to Milgram, the task involved many of the factors that should lead to reduced obedience (face-to-face contact, some disobedient peers, absence of pressure from an authority figure).

This challenges our original conclusion because now it appears that Milgram's findings have not been replicated in other settings.

The moral of the story: Don't assume that any study has **ecological validity** – search for confirming evidence. All research conducted in the real world is not automatically ecologically valid, and all laboratory studies are not automatically ecologically *invalid*. Every study has some ecological validity – some are just more ecologically valid than others.

> Control group/condition
> Experimental group/condition
> John Henry effect

 **Qs** **24**

A playgroup wishes to investigate whether children play differently if an adult is present or not.

1. Describe how you might design a study to investigate this using an independent groups design.

2. Which is the experimental group and which is the control group?

3. Identify **one or more** ethical issues and suggest how you would deal with these.

4. To what extent would the findings of your study have representativeness?

5. To what extent would the findings of your study have generalisability?

6. How could you conduct a study with the same aims using a repeated measures design?

7. Identify the experimental and control conditions in this new study.

8. Describe **one** advantage and **one** disadvantage of using a repeated measures design in this study.

 Activity 9 **What is validity all about?**

Using what you have learned in this chapter, create something to represent the various aspects of validity. It could be a PowerPoint presentation, a mobile, a poster for your classroom, a leaflet, a cartoon strip, a poem, a rap song – anything that is entertaining AND forces you to process the material (as processing leads to deeper understanding and long-term memories).

Multiple choice questions

1. Which of the following is *not* a characteristic of a field experiment?
   a. It is conducted in a natural environment.
   b. The IV is directly manipulated by the experimenter.
   c. Extraneous variables can be well controlled.
   d. Participants are often not aware that they are being studied.

2. Which of the following is *not* a characteristic of a lab experiment?
   a. It is conducted in a natural environment.
   b. The IV is directly manipulated by the experimenter.
   c. Extraneous variables can be well controlled.
   d. Participants are often aware that they are being studied.

3. Mundane realism refers to
   a. Using video film to capture participants' behaviour.
   b. An experiment being boring and therefore not holding the participant's interest.
   c. The extent to which an experiment mirrors the real world.
   d. A Spanish football team.

4. Variables in an experiment are operationalised, which means they are
   a. Understandable to participants.
   b. Used in a medical experiment.
   c. Described in a way that can be easily measured or manipulated.
   d. Turned into numbers.

5. Lab experiments are sometimes artificial because
   a. Participants know they are being studied and this may affect their behaviour.
   b. The setting may lack mundane realism.
   c. The IV may be operationalised in such a way that it does not represent real-life experiences.
   d. All of the above.

6. Internal validity is concerned with
   a. The generalisability of research findings.
   b. The consistency of measurement.
   c. Whether an observed effect can be attributed to the IV.
   d. Whether the findings are what the experimenter expected.

7. External validity refers to
   a. The generalisability of research findings.
   b. Whether the findings are what the experimenter expected.
   c. Whether an observed effect can be attributed to the IV.
   d. All of the above.

8. Which of the following is *not* a kind of external validity?
   a. Ecological validity.
   b. Mundane validity.
   c. Population validity.
   d. Historical validity.

9. Demand characteristics are
   a. Features of an experiment that cannot be controlled.
   b. Threats to external validity.
   c. Problem behaviours.
   d. Cues in an experimental situation that unconsciously affect a participant's behaviour.

10. Which of the following would *not* be a threat to internal validity?
    a. Experimenter bias.
    b. Participant reactivity.
    c. Social desirability bias.
    d. Single-blind design.

11. The person who designs an experiment is called the
    a. Investigator.
    b. Experimenter.
    c. Participant.
    d. Designer.

12. An investigator effect is any effect the investigator has on
    a. An investigation.
    b. Participants' behaviour.
    c. Extraneous variables.
    d. All of the above.

13. Ecological validity concerns
    a. Representativeness.
    b. Generalisability.
    c. Representativeness and reliability.
    d. Representativeness and generalisability.

14. Which of the following is the best definition of ecological validity?
    a. Ecological validity is the degree to which behaviour in the laboratory reflects real life.
    b. Ecological validity is the extent to which

findings can be generalised from the lab to the real world.
    c. Ecological validity is the extent to which findings can be generalised from the experimental setting to other settings.
    d. Ecological validity is the degree to which findings can be generalised from one group of people to the target population.

15. If the participants in a study are only men, we might think the study had low
    a. Population validity.
    b. Ecological validity.
    c. External validity.
    d. Both a and c.

16. In a natural experiment
    a. The IV is controlled by an experimenter.
    b. The IV varies naturally.
    c. The DV is controlled by an experimenter.
    d. The DV varies naturally.

17. Natural experiments are not 'true' experiments because
    a. Participants are not randomly allocated to conditions.
    b. The sample studied may have unique characteristics.
    c. The IV is not directly manipulated by the experimenter.
    d. All of the above.

18. Studies that compare the behaviour of males and females (gender studies) are:
    a. Difference studies.
    b. Field experiments.
    c. Natural experiments.
    d. Both a and c.

19. Debriefing is
    a. An ethical issue.
    b. An ethical guideline.
    c. An ethical issue and an ethical guideline.
    d. A folder for research notes.

20. If informed consent is not possible, a possible alternative is to
    a. Give participants the right to withdraw.
    b. Debrief participants.
    c. Obtain presumptive consent.
    d. All of the above.

Answers are on page 41

Exam-style question 3

A very recent study (Schutheiss *et al*, 2004) looked at whether one can explain people's responses to films in terms of hormones. Hormones are chemical substances produced in the body in response to certain situations. Different hormones have different effects. Female hormones are related to relaxation, whereas male hormones are related to aggression. Men and women have both male and female hormones (strange but true).

The research question was whether hormones could explain why people feel more lovey-dovey after watching a romantic film and more aggressive after watching an exciting film.

In this study, there were three groups of participants. One group viewed a romantic scene from *The Bridges of Madison County*, the second group watched an exciting scene from *The Godfather, part II*, and the third group watched a documentary on the Amazon rainforest. The films were shown in a cinema.

Each participant had their hormone levels tested before and immediately after viewing the 45-minute film clip.

The study found that both men and women experienced raised levels of female hormones when watching the romantic film. In the group watching the exciting scene, the men had raised levels of male hormones, whereas these hormones were lowered in the women. The third group, watching the Amazon rainforest, showed no significant change in hormone levels.

(a) (i) What was the experimental design in this study?   (1 mark)

    (ii) Describe **one** advantage of using this design.   (2 marks)

(b) (i) Identify a suitable sampling method for this study.   (1 mark)

    (ii) Explain how you would carry this out.   (2 marks)

(c) (i) Explain why this study could be considered to be a field experiment.   (2 marks)

    (ii) Describe **one** advantage and **one** disadvantage of doing a field experiment.   (2 marks + 2 marks)

(d) (i) Explain what is meant by demand characteristics.   (2 marks)

    (ii) Describe a way in which demand characteristics might have been a problem in this study.   (2 marks)

(e) Identify **one** ethical issue and say how you would deal with it.   (3 marks)

(f) Explain why the third group watched a documentary on the Amazon rainforest.   (2 marks)

(g) (i) Explain what is meant by external validity.   (1 mark)

    (ii) Describe **one** reason why this study might lack external validity.   (2 marks)

(h) Describe **one or more** conclusion(s) that could be drawn from this study.   (3 marks)

(i) (i) Identify a suitable graph that could be used to show the findings from this study.   (1 mark)

    (ii) What labels would you put on the *x* and *y* axes (horizontal and vertical axes) of this graph?   (2 marks)

Examiner's tips for answering this question

(a) Remember the **RIM** tip from last chapter – candidates always find it difficult to work out what answers are possible – but remember that if you learn the three alternatives and guess, you have a 33% chance of getting it right!

(b) The question does say 'suitable' so you should bear this in mind – how is the researcher likely to obtain his sample?

(c) It is arguable whether this study is a field experiment, but you are only asked to say why it might be considered to be one. Don't write a novel! There are only 2 marks available. But equally, don't write only a few words.

(c) (ii) In questions like this, there is no requirement to set your answer in the context of the study – but you can do this as a way of providing the extra detail required. Don't forget to make comparisons (e.g. 'Field experiments *are better than* lab experiments in terms of ...' rather than just saying that they are better).

(d) (i) This is one of the rare occasions on which you are simply asked to define one of the key terms; more often, you are required to *apply* your knowledge of the terms to answer questions.

(d) (ii) Here, you have to apply your knowledge to this study.

(e) Sometimes there are two parts to the question, as here. Take care to answer both parts clearly and provide sufficient details about how you would deal with the ethical issue – e.g. don't just say, 'I would debrief them.'

(f) Here is another example of having to *apply* your knowledge.

(g) (ii) Remember that if you are asked to provide 'one' of anything, only your first answer will be marked.

(h) You have the option, if you wish, of describing more than one conclusion in order to provide 3 marks' worth of material. Don't be afraid to state the obvious, but remember that conclusions are not the same as findings. You can state the findings and then (for the creditworthy bit) say, 'This suggests that ...'.

(i) (i) This is another question where you have a limited choice of answers: the answer must be a bar chart or histogram – but don't write both of them (remember there is no positive marking).

(i) (ii) It might help to sketch the graph.

Exam-style question 4

A local hospital decides to have mixed wards rather than separate wards for men and women. Before introducing this new scheme to all wards, the hospital management decide to compare the effects of mixed versus separate wards on patient well-being. They offer participants the choice of whether they are in mixed or single-sexed wards.

The hospital employs a psychologist to conduct a study into the effects of mixed versus single-sex wards on the health and happiness of the patients. Health outcomes were determined by looking at whether patients recover more quickly in one type of ward than another, and also at whether they have better signs of health (e.g. lower blood pressure).

(a) (i) Write a suitable non-directional hypothesis for this study.
(2 marks)

   (ii) Explain why you would use a non-directional hypothesis instead of a directional hypothesis.   (2 marks)

(b) (i) Identify the independent variable and the dependent variable in this study.   (2 marks)

   (ii) Suggest **two** ways in which you could operationalise the dependent variable.   (2 marks + 2 marks)

(c) (i) Explain why this study could be considered to be a natural experiment.   (2 marks)

   (ii) Describe **one** advantage and **one** disadvantage of conducting a natural experiment.   (2 marks + 2 marks)

(d) (i) How could the relationship between the researcher and the participants have affected the validity of this study?   (2 marks)

   (ii) How could you deal with the problem identified in (i)?
(2 marks)

(e) (i) Identify the experimental design used in this study.   (1 marks)

   (ii) Describe **one** disadvantage of this design in the context of this study.   (2 marks)

   (iii) Explain **one** way of dealing with this disadvantage.   (2 marks)

(f) Explain why a pilot study might have been useful in this   (2 marks)
experiment.

(g) Describe **one** possible extraneous variable in this study and explain how you would deal with it.   (3 marks)

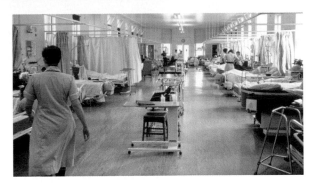

Examiner's tips for answering this question

(a) If you produce a directional hypothesis, you will score zero marks for both parts of this question.

(b) (ii) This is testing your understanding of 'operationalisation'. How would you make the DV into something you could test or measure in some way? There are hints in the stimulus material.

(c) The same advice applies here as stated earlier – there is no need to write a long answer when only 2 marks' worth is required. Just identify one or two features of a natural experiment that are present in this study.

(c) (ii), (e) (ii), (c) (iii) and (g) These questions all have one thing in common – they require only 'one' thing. If you provide more than one, only your first answer will be marked even if a subsequent answer is more detailed. Check your answers and cross out anything that is not relevant or that you do not want marked – this advice does not apply to other parts of the exam.

(c) (ii) So often, candidates just say, 'It is more like real life' or 'It is more difficult.' Such statements need some further explanation.

(d) Some questions are a bit 'wordy' because of the way in which the specification is written (see Appendix I). This question is easier than it looks – you can write about participant reactivity or investigator effects. But again, just write what would be appropriate for 3 marks.

(e) (iii) Don't just identify a way to deal with the problem: *explain* how you would do this.

(f) Make sure you answer the question. Don't explain what a pilot study is or how you would do it – the question is about 'why'.

(g) Take care to answer both parts clearly and provide sufficient detail for 3 marks. Don't just give a 'knee-jerk' answer saying 'noise'. Think of a *likely* extraneous variable – noise would not really be an extraneous variable in this study, unless you could explain why.

Model answer for question 3

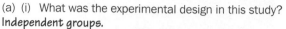

(a) (i) What was the experimental design in this study? (1 mark)
Independent groups.

   (ii) Describe **one** advantage of using this design. (2 marks)
One advantage is that you won't suffer from order effects such as guessing what the study was about if each participant had to watch all three films. You'd also have to wait until the effects of each film wore off, so each participant would have to come back again.

(b) (i) Identify a suitable sampling method for this study. (1 mark)
Volunteer sampling.

   (ii) Explain how you would carry this out. (2 marks)
You would advertise in certain places, like a newspaper, asking for people who would be willing to take part in a psychology experiment.

(c) (i) Explain why this study could be considered to be a field experiment. (2 marks)
The study involves the use of real-life materials (a film) and takes place in a natural environment.

   (ii) Describe **one** advantage and **one** disadvantage of doing a field experiment. (2 marks + 2 marks)
One advantage is that participants behave more like they usually would, and this means that you can generalise to real life better.

One disadvantage is that it is more difficult to control extraneous variables such as noise.

(d) (i) Explain what is meant by demand characteristics. (2 marks)
They are features of an experiment that lead participants to unconsciously respond in predictable ways.

   (ii) Describe a way which demand characteristics might have been a problem in this study. (2 marks)
It might be that other aspects of the romantic film led people to be relaxed, like the music that is used in such films.

(e) Identify **one** ethical issue and say how you would deal with it. (3 marks)
One issue would be psychological harm if a participant didn't want to watch The Godfather. You could deal with it by asking participants for their informed consent before the experiment began, which would involve telling them everything they would be required to do.

(f) Explain why the third group watched a documentary on the Amazon rainforest. (2 marks)
This was a control condition to ensure that the effects were due to the different kinds of film.

(g) (i) Explain what is meant by external validity. (2 marks)
External validity is the extent to which you are able to generalise the findings of a study to other people, other settings and other times.

   (ii) Describe **one** reason why this study might lack external validity. (2 marks)
The sample of participants might be unrepresentative of the wider population, and thus the study would lack population validity.

(h) Describe **one or more** conclusion(s) that could be drawn from this study. (3 marks)
The findings suggest that hormones lead to the responses we recognise when watching certain sorts of film. This is true for romantic films, but it seems that only men are affected by exciting films, which could explain why women find such films boring.

(i) (i) Identify a suitable graph that could be used to show the findings from this study. (1 mark)
Bar chart.

   (ii) What labels would you put on the x and y axes (horizontal and vertical axes) of this graph? (2 marks)
The x axis would be labelled 'Romantic film, exciting film and Amazon rain forest'.
The y axis would be labelled with increase in levels of hormones.

Examiner's comments

(a) (i) Perhaps a bit of a tricky question because each participant was tested twice and therefore it might appear to be a repeated measures design – but the final analysis was a comparison between the three groups.

(a) (ii) Here is an example of a candidate giving two answers when only one is required. Fortunately, both answers are worth 2 marks. Just saying 'order effects' would be worth 1 mark.

(b) (i) Random sampling might not be very suitable; volunteer or opportunity sampling would be the most likely.

(b) (ii) For 2 marks, your answer does not need to be very detailed, but just saying 'I would advertise' would be worth 1 mark.

(c) (i) Two answers have been given, but they are both creditworthy as there is no requirement for only one answer. A 1-mark answer might merely mention that field experiments are those in a natural environment.

(c) (ii) It might appear that two answers have been given for the advantage, but 'and' has been used to link two related points so it is all creditworthy.

(d) (i) This is probably a definition you know or do not know. An answer that said 'unconscious cues' might receive 1 mark.

(d) (ii) This is a difficult question that requires you to think on your feet. You would get a mark for saying anything that suggests you have tried to apply the concept appropriately, i.e. found something in the study that would elicit certain behaviour from the participants – aside from the IV – but you cannot just repeat the definition of demand characteristics again.

(e) Simply saying 'informed consent' would only gain 1 mark.

(f) The term used is 'explain', which means that just saying a 'control condition' would not count as a sufficient answer because it does not really explain why.

(g) (i) An excellent definition and more detail than would be required.

(g) (ii) It is acceptable to describe any of the types of external validity – population, ecological or even historical.

(h) It is useful to start your answer in this way to ensure that you are giving a conclusion and not a finding. The second sentence starts with a finding but does end with a second conclusion.

(i) (i) It would not be a histogram because the X axis is not continuous.

   (ii) Only brief answers are required.

Model answer for question 4

(a) (i) Write a suitable non-directional hypothesis for this study.   (2 marks)
Patients on mixed wards have different health outcomes from those on single-sex wards.

(ii) Explain why you would use a non-directional hypothesis instead of a directional hypothesis.   (2 marks)
It may be that there is no previous research on this topic so it is difficult to predict a direction.

(b) (i) Identify the independent variable and the dependent variable in this study.   (2 marks)
The IV is type of ward and the DV is the effect on health and happiness.

(ii) Suggest **two** ways in which you could operationalise the dependent variable.   (2 marks + 2 marks)
One way is to compare recovery rates. Another way is to measure blood pressure.

(c) (i) Explain why this study could be considered to be a natural experiment.   (2 marks)
There was an IV and DV, and the IV was not directly manipulated by the experimenter.

(ii) Describe **one** advantage and **one** disadvantage of conducting a natural experiment.   (2 marks + 2 marks)
Advantage: can investigate things where it would be difficult to manipulate the IV directly; for example assigning patients to mixed or single-sex wards might be objectionable.

Disadvantage: can't claim to show a causal relationship because the IV is not directly manipulated.

(d) (i) How could the relationship between the researcher and participants have affected the validity of this study?   (2 marks)
If the participants knew about the study, then they might improve in the single-sex wards because they wanted to show that they were just as good.

(ii) How could you deal with the problem identified in (i)?   (2 marks)
You could deceive the participants about the true aims of the study. You could tell them that the study was about a new kind of hospital bed.

(e) (i) Identify the experimental design used in this study.   (1 marks)
Independent groups.

(ii) Describe **one** disadvantage of this design in the context of this study.   (2 marks)
One disadvantage is that there is no control for participant variables – it could be that the patients in one group were healthier at the outset, which is why they got better faster.

(iii) Explain **one** way of dealing with this disadvantage.   (2 marks)
You could use a matched participants design and exclude all participants who were not matched.

(f) Explain why a pilot study might have been useful in this experiment.   (2 marks)
You might find that the measures of heath and happiness didn't provide useful data or data that didn't find differences between the two groups.

(g) Describe **one** possible extraneous variable in this study and explain how you would deal with it.   (3 marks)
One possible extraneous variable would be that people who opt for the mixed-sex wards have a more outgoing personality, which would affect the DV. You could deal with this by matching participants on such traits.

Examiner's comments

(a) (i) You would only get 1 mark for writing 'Patients on mixed wards have different health outcomes'. You need to include the 2nd condition OR operationalise the DV, which could be expressed in lots of ways, for example 'raised blood pressure' or 'quicker recovery'.

(a) (ii) This is a brief answer, but it would be difficult to think of anything else to say. An example of a 1-mark answer is 'There is no previous research.'

(b) (i) There is no need for any more detail.

(b) (ii) There are two examples of operationalisation in the stimulus material, which have been used in this answer. You could provide your own, such as time spent out of bed or a score from a questionnaire to assess happiness.

(c) (i) This answer explains both why it is an experiment and why it is a natural experiment.

(c) (ii) There is no requirement for contextualisation in this question, although you would not be penalised for doing so (as has been done here). In fact, the advantage is sufficiently detailed without this example.

(d) (i) There are lots of possible answers – you could use participant reactivity (as done here) or an investigator effect, such as saying that the researcher's expectations about which ward would be better might lead to changes in the participants' behaviour.

(d) (ii) This answer must be clearly linked to (i) – when you get to part (ii), you may decide to change your answer to part (i) because it does not provide you with a very good answer to part (ii).

(e) (i) RIM.

(e) (ii) An answer that is not contextualised would only get 1 mark, e.g. 'There is no control for participant variables – participants in one group may differ from those in the other group which might explain why they do better.'

(f) There is sufficient detail in this answer, although there is much more one could write. Saying 'It could show you aspects of the design that didn't work' would get 1 mark because there is no reference to this study.

(g) You can get 3 marks by providing extra detail for either part of this question – so you could briefly identify the extraneous variable and give more detail about how you would deal with it, or vice versa.

Answers to MCQs from page 37	1c	2a	3c	4c	5d	6c	7a	8b	9d	10d
	11a	12b	13d	14c	15d	16b	17d	18a	19b	20d

Contents

pages 44–45

Questionnaires

Quantitative and qualitative data

Writing good questions

Designing good questionnaires

Activity 10: Design and use your own questionnaire

 **Qs** 25

pages 46–47

Interviews

Structured and unstructured interviews

Quantitative and qualitative data

Examples of structured and unstructured interviews

Activity 11: Try your own interview

A comparison of questionnaires and interviews

Ethical issues for questionnaires and interviews

 **Qs** 26,27

pages 50–51

Reliability

Assessing reliability

Activity 13: Split-half method and test-retest method

Assessing validity of questionnaires and interviews

Improving reliability

Improving validity

Activity 14: Validity and reliability of a questionnaire

 **Qs** 30

pages 48–49

Correlational analysis

Scattergraphs

Activity 12: Playing with correlation: the Excel method

Significance

Investigations using a correlational analysis

 **Qs** 28,29

Self-report measures

questionnaires, interviews and studies using correlational analysis

pages 52–53

DIY: A study using a correlational analysis

ESP: A 'sheep–goat effect'

Activity 15: Investigating the sheep–goat effect

A final word on correlation

Multiple choice questions

 **Q**s **31**

pages 54–57

Exam-style questions 5 and 6

Model answers to exam-style questions 5 and 6

Answers to multiple choice questions

pages 58–61

Crossword

Belief in the Paranormal Scale

Crossword answers

Questionnaires

A **questionnaire** (or questionnaire survey) is a set of questions.

It is designed to collect information about a topic or even more than one topic.

The two great strengths of questionnaires are:

1. You can collect the same information from a large number of people relatively easily (once you have designed the questionnaire, which is not so easy).

2. You can access what people think – experiments rely on 'guessing' what people think on the basis of how they behave. With a questionnaire, you ask people – whether they give you valid answers is another matter.

Writing good questions

When writing questions, there are three guiding principles:

- *Clarity*. Questions need to be written so that the reader (respondent) understands what is being asked. One way to do this is to **operationalise** certain terms. There should be no ambiguity.

- *Bias*. Any bias in a question might lead the respondent to be more likely to give a particular answer (as in a **leading question**). The greatest problem is probably **social desirability bias**. Respondents prefer to select answers that portray them in a positive light rather than reflect the truth.

- *Analysis*. Questions need to be written so that the answers provided are easy to analyse. If you ask 'What kind of job do you do?' or 'What makes you feel stressed at work?', you may get 50 different answers from 50 people. These are called **open questions**. Alternatively, one can ask **closed questions**, where a limited range of answers are provided, such as listing 10 job categories or 10 sources of stress. Such closed questions are easier to analyse.

Examples of open questions

What factors contribute to making work stressful?

When do you feel most stressed?

Advantages of open questions

- Allows the researcher to collect detailed, qualitative data.

- Allow respondents to express themselves.

- Mean that unexpected information can be collected.

Advantages of closed questions

- Tend to produce quantitative data.

- Easier to analyse the data.

- Easier for respondents to fill in.

BUT the respondents' answers may not be represented so that they are forced to be untruthful.

Quantitative and qualitative data

Questionnaires may collect:

- **Quantitative data**: numerical information for example, about your age, how many hours you work in a week, how highly you rate different TV programmes.

- **Qualitative data**: information that cannot be counted for example, about how you think or feel.

Quantitative data are data that represent how much, how long or how many, etc. there are of something; i.e. behaviour is measured in numbers or quantities.

Qualitative data are a more complex account of what people think or feel. Qualitative data cannot be counted but they can be summarised. They may be converted to quantitative data and then counted.

Qualitative data typically come from asking open questions to which the answers are not limited by a set of choices or a scale, whereas closed questions generate quantitative data directly.

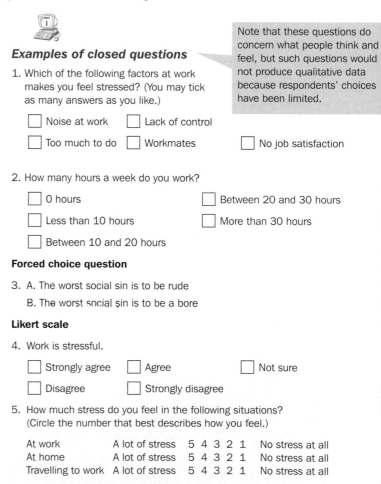

Examples of closed questions

> Note that these questions do concern what people think and feel, but such questions would not produce qualitative data because respondents' choices have been limited.

1. Which of the following factors at work makes you feel stressed? (You may tick as many answers as you like.)

   ☐ Noise at work   ☐ Lack of control

   ☐ Too much to do   ☐ Workmates   ☐ No job satisfaction

2. How many hours a week do you work?

   ☐ 0 hours   ☐ Between 20 and 30 hours

   ☐ Less than 10 hours   ☐ More than 30 hours

   ☐ Between 10 and 20 hours

Forced choice question

3. A. The worst social sin is to be rude

   B. The worst social sin is to be a bore

Likert scale

4. Work is stressful.

   ☐ Strongly agree   ☐ Agree   ☐ Not sure

   ☐ Disagree   ☐ Strongly disagree

5. How much stress do you feel in the following situations? (Circle the number that best describes how you feel.)

At work	A lot of stress	5 4 3 2 1	No stress at all
At home	A lot of stress	5 4 3 2 1	No stress at all
Travelling to work	A lot of stress	5 4 3 2 1	No stress at all

Semantic differential technique (Place a tick to show your feelings.)

6. People who are bosses are usually:

Hard	_ _ _ _ _ _ _ Kind	Small	_ _ _ _ _ _ _ Large
Passive	_ _ _ _ _ _ _ Active	Beautiful	_ _ _ _ _ _ _ Ugly

Designing good questionnaires

A good questionnaire should (obviously) contain good questions. Some other things to consider when designing a good questionnaire:

- *Filler questions*: It may help to include some irrelevant questions to mislead the respondent from the main purpose of the survey. This may reduce **demand characteristics**.

- *Sequence for the questions*. It is best to start with easy ones, saving questions that might make someone feel anxious or defensive until the respondent has relaxed.

- *Pilot study*: The questions can be tested on a small group of people. This means that you can refine the questions in response to any difficulties encountered.

Sometimes people don't know what they think.

 25

A psychology student designed a questionnaire about attitudes to eating. Below are some questions from this questionnaire:

1. Do you diet?
   ALWAYS / SOMETIMES / NEVER
   (circle your answer)

2. Do you think that dieting is a bad idea?

3. Explain your answer to (2).

4. For each question:

   a. State whether it is an open or closed question.

   b. State whether the question would produce quantitative or qualitative data.

   c. Give **one** criticism of the question.

   d. Suggest how you could improve the question in order to deal with your criticism.

   e. Suggest **one** strength of the question.

5. *You have been asked to write a questionnaire about people's attitudes about ghosts and other paranormal phenomena.*

   a. Write **one** closed question that would collect quantitative data.

   b. Write **one** open question that would collect qualitative data.

   c. Write an example of a leading question for this questionnaire.

   d. Explain how social desirability bias might affect the validity of the responses to your questionnaire.

   e. Describe **one** advantage of using questionnaires to collect data in this study.

   f. Describe **one** disadvantage of using questionnaires to collect data in this study.

   g. Explain the difference between qualitative and quantitative data.

   h. Why might it be preferable to collect quantitative data?

   i. Why might it be preferable to collect qualitative data?

A questionnaire can be a research method or a research technique.

The aims of a study may be to find out about smoking habits in young people. The researcher would design a questionnaire to collect data about what people do and why. In this case, the questionnaire is the **research method**.

The aims of a study might be to see if children who are exposed to an anti-smoking educational programme have different attitudes towards smoking than children not exposed to such a programme. The researcher would use a questionnaire to collect data about attitudes, but the analysis would involve a comparison between the two groups of children – an experimental study using a questionnaire as a **research technique**.

Activity **10**   **Design and use your own questionnaire**

Select a suitable topic, for example 'Methods of exam revision', 'Why people choose to study psychology' or you could choose a topic related to your studies, such as a questionnaire on day care experiences or on stress.

Steps in questionnaire design

- Write the questions. (Keep the questionnaire short, somewhere between 5 and 10 questions. Include a mixture of open and closed questions.)

- Construct the questionnaire.

- Write standarised instructions.

- Pilot the questionnaire.

- Decide on a sampling technique.

Conduct the questionnaire

- Collect data.

- Analyse the data. (Just select a few questions for analysis. For quantitative data, you can use a bar chart. For qualitative data, you can identify some trends in the answers and summarise these.)

- Write the report.

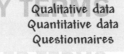

KEY TERMS
Qualitative data
Quantitative data
Questionnaires

OTHER TERMS
Closed questions
Forced choice questions
Leading questions
Likert scale
Open questions
Semantic differential technique

Interviews

A questionnaire can be given in a written form or it can be delivered in real-time (face to face or over the telephone) by an interviewer. There are advantages and disadvantages:

☺ The interviewer can adapt questions according to the interviewee's answers, taking advantage of on-the-spot flexibility. This is sometimes called the **clinical** or **unstructured interview**.

☹ An interviewer may unconsciously lead respondents to provide certain answers by verbal or visual cues.

☹ People may feel less comfortable about revealing personal information.

Quantitative and qualitative data

Questions in an interview, as in a questionnaire, may produce **quantitative** or **qualitative** data. An unstructured interview is more likely to produce qualitative data because the questions that develop are likely to ask respondents to elaborate their answers (e.g. 'Why do you feel that?').

Questions may be quantitative (e.g. 'How often do you feel like that?'), but they are still less predictable than questionnaires.

Advantages and disadvantages

Quantitative data

☺ Easier to analyse because the data are in numbers.

☹ Reduces information about people to over-simplified statistics (statistically significant but humanly insignificant).

Qualitative data

☺ Represents the true complexities of human behaviour and gains access to thoughts and feelings that cannot be assessed using other methods.

☹ More difficult to analyse so that conclusions are difficult to draw.

Activity 11 — Try your own interview

Try out the moral interviews on the right with a partner in class. Take turns being the interviewer and interviewee as you try out both kinds of interview.

Discuss:

- What you found out.
- The differences in the information obtained.
- Which questions worked best and why.
- How truthful the answers were and why.

Qs 26

1. Would you describe Kohlberg's and Gilligan's interviews as structured, unstructured or semi-structured (somewhere in between)? Explain your answer.

2. In the questions on the right, find an example of a closed question, an open question, a question that would produce quantitative data and a question that would produce qualitative data.

Structured and unstructured interviews

An **interview** consists of questions asked to a participant (the interviewee) in real time either face to face or over the telephone.

A **structured interview** has predetermined questions; i.e. a questionnaire that is delivered face to face.

An **unstructured interview** has less structure! New questions are developed as you go along, similar to the way in which your GP might interview you. He or she starts with some predetermined questions, but further questions are developed as a response to your answers. For this reason the unstructured or semi-structured approach is called the **clinical method**.

Examples of structured and unstructured interviews

Lawrence Kohlberg (1978) interviewed boys about their moral views. Interviewers gave the boys an imaginary situation (such as the one below) and then asked a set of questions.

Lawrence Kohlberg

In Europe, a woman was near death from a special type of cancer. There was one drug that the doctors thought might save her. It was a form of radium that a druggist in the same town had recently discovered. The drug was expensive to make but the druggist was charging 10 times what the drug cost him to make. He paid $400 for the radium and charged $4000 for a small dose of it. The sick woman's husband, Heinz, went to everyone he knew to borrow the money, but he could only get together about $2000, which is half of what it cost. He told the druggist that his wife was dying and asked him to sell it cheaper or let him pay later. But the druggist said 'No. I discovered the drug and I'm going to make money from it.' Heinz got desperate and broke into the man's store to steal the drug for his wife.

- Should Heinz steal the drug?
- Why or why not?
- (If the subject originally favours stealing, ask: 'If Heinz doesn't love his wife, should he steal the drug for her?')
- (If the subject originally favours not stealing, ask: 'Does it make a difference whether or not he loves his wife?')
- Why or why not?
- Suppose that the person dying is not his wife but a stranger. Should Heinz steal the drug for the stranger?
- Why or why not?

Carol Gilligan also investigated moral principles (Gilligan and Attanucci, 1988). Participants were asked a set of questions about moral conflict and choice:

Carol Gilligan

- Have you ever been in a situation of moral conflict where you had to make a decision but weren't sure what was the right thing to do?
- Could you describe the situation?
- What were the conflicts for you in that situation?
- What did you do?
- Do you think it was the right thing to do?
- How do you know?

The interviewer asked other questions to encourage the participants to elaborate and clarify their responses, such as saying 'Anything else?'. Special focus was on asking participants to explain the meaning of key terms such as 'responsibility', 'fair' and 'obligation'.

A comparison of questionnaires and interviews

	Advantages ☺	Disadvantages ☹
Questionnaires *Respondents record their own answers*	• Can be easily repeated so that data can be collected from a large number of people relatively cheaply and quickly (once the questionnaire has been designed) • Questionnaires do not require specialist administrators • Respondents may feel more willing to reveal personal/confidential information than in an interview	• Answers may not be truthful, e.g. because of **leading questions** and **social desirability bias** • The sample may be biased because only certain kinds of people fill in questionnaires – literate individuals who are willing to spend time filling them in
Structured interview *Questions predetermined*	• Can be easily repeated • Requires less skill than unstructured interviews • More easy to analyse than unstructured interviews because the answers are more predictable	• The interviewer's expectations may influence the answers the interviewee gives (this is called **interviewer bias**). This may especially be true because people do not always know what they think. They may also want to present themselves in a 'good light' and therefore give 'socially desirable' answers (**social desirability bias**) • In comparison with unstructured interviews, the data collected will be restricted by a predetermined set of questions
Unstructured or semi-structured interviews *Interviewer develops questions in response to respondent's answers*	• Generally more detailed information can be obtained from each respondent than in a structured interview • Can access information that may not be revealed by predetermined questions	• More affected by interviewer bias than structured interviews • Interviews may not be comparable because different interviewers ask different questions (low **inter-interviewer reliability**). **Reliability** may also be affected by the same interviewer behaving differently on different occasions • The answers from unstructured interviews are less easy to analyse because they are unpredictable.

Special tip

Students often write something like 'The advantage of a questionnaire is that you can collect lots of data.' The problem with this is that it is not clear what 'lots of data' means. Compared with what? You can collect lots of data in an experiment or interview.

• You need to provide clear detail. (What is 'lots of data'? Why is there 'lots of data'?)

• You need to offer a comparison. (Compared with what?, eg. compared with an interview).

A good answer would say, 'The advantage of a questionnaire is that you can collect data from more people than you would if using the interview methods, which results in lots more data.'

Qs   **27**

1. Explain the difference between a structured and an unstructured interview.
2. Explain the difference between a questionnaire and an interview.
3. If you wanted to find out about attitudes towards dieting, why would it be preferable to conduct an interview rather than use a questionnaire?
4. Why might it be better to use a questionnaire than conduct an interview?
5. How can 'leading questions' be a problem in interviews or questionnaires?
6. What is the 'social desirability bias'?
7. What kind of data are produced in interviews? Explain your answer.

KEY TERMS
Interview
Advantages ☺ and disadvantages ☹ of
questionnaires and interviews
qualitative and quantitative data

OTHER TERMS
Clinical interview
Inter-interviewer reliability
Interviewer bias
Structured interview
Unstructured interview

Interviewing an elephant for Australian TV.

Ethical issues for questionnaires and interviews

• **Deception** may be necessary.

• Questions may be related to sensitive and personal issues (**psychological harm**). Respondents may feel that they have to present themselves in a good light.

• **Confidentiality** and **privacy** must be respected.

Correlational analysis

A **correlation** is a relationship between two variables. Age and beauty co-vary. As people get older, they become more beautiful. This is a **positive correlation** because the two variables increase together.

You may disagree and think that as people get older they become less attractive. You think that age and beauty are correlated but that it is a **negative correlation**: as one variable increases, the other one decreases.

Or you may simply feel that there is no relationship between age and beauty. This is called a **zero correlation**.

*A **scattergraph** is a graph that shows the correlation between two sets of data (or **co-variables**) by plotting dots to represent each pair of scores.*

*The scatter of the dots indicates the degree of correlation between the co-variables. A statistical test is used to calculate the **correlation coefficient**, a measure of the extent of correlation that exists.*

*Notice that all correlation coefficients are no greater than 1. Some correlation coefficients are written as –0.52, whereas others are +0.52. The plus or minus sign shows whether it is a positive or a negative correlation. The coefficient (number) tells us how closely the co-variables are related. –0.52 is just as closely correlated as +0.52; it's just that –0.52 means that as one variable increases, the other decreases (**negative correlation**), and +0.52 means that both variables increase together (**positive correlation**).*

Scattergraphs

A correlation can be illustrated using a **scattergraph**.

For each individual, we obtain a score for each co-variable – in our case, the co-variables are age and beauty.

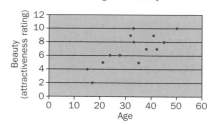

A scattergraph showing the relationship between age and beauty

The top graph illustrates a positive correlation.

The middle graph shows a negative correlation.

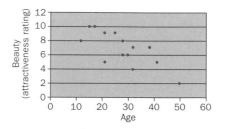

The bottom graph is a zero correlation.

The extent of this correlation is described using a **correlation coefficient** – this is a number between +1 and –1 that is calculated using a statistical test. +1 is a perfect positive correlation, and –1 is a perfect negative correlation.

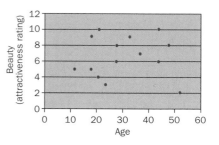

The correlation coefficients for the three graphs are:
(1) 0.76
(2) – 0.76
(3) 0.002

Qs 28

1. Think of two variables that are likely to be positively correlated (such as height and weight).
2. Think of two variables that are likely to be negatively correlated.
3. What does a correlation coefficient tell you about a set of data?
4. Give an example of a positive correlation coefficient and a negative correlation coefficient.
5. Explain what the following correlation coefficients mean:

    +1.00   –1.00   0.00
    –0.60   +0.40   +0.10

Activity 12   Playing with correlation: the Excel method

Using **Excel**, you can enter and alter pairs of numbers to see how this affects a scattergraph and correlation coefficient. Both are produced automatically by Excel if you follow these steps:

1. Open a new document (select <file> <new> <blank workbook>).

2. Select <insert> <chart> <XY (scatter)> and press <next>.

3. Place the cursor at the very top left of the page; click and drag across 2 rows and then down 16 rows. Press <next> <next> <finish>.

4. Now enter pairs of scores in rows 2–16 (these can be invented or you could try entering a real set of numbers to see if they are correlated – such as height and shoe size). Do not enter data in the top row.

5. To calculate the correlation coefficient: Place the cursor in any empty box. Select <insert> <function>. In the top box, type 'correl' and press 'go' and then <OK>.

6. The screen now says 'array1' and 'array2'. Click in 'array1' and then move the cursor to the top of the first column of your numbers; then click and drag to the bottom of the column. Do the same for array2.

7. Try changing some of the numbers and see how this alters your scattergraph and correlation coefficient.

(See the list of websites (page 133) for sites where you can plot correlations.)

Significance

Significance is the extent to which something is particularly unusual.

When we look at a correlation coefficient, we need to know whether it is strong or weak. In order to do this, we use tables of significance, which tell us how big the coefficient needs to be in order for the correlation to be significant (unusual).

The table below gives an approximate idea of the values needed. The more pairs of scores you have, the smaller the coefficient can be.

A coefficient of either −0.45 or +0.45 would be significant if there were 16 pairs of data but not if there were 14 pairs.

The *magnitude* of the number informs us about significance; the *sign* tells us which direction the correlation is in (positive or negative).

Investigations using a correlational analysis

A correlation is not a research method. Therefore we do not talk about a correlational investigation but about an investigation using a correlational analysis.

	Advantages ☺	Disadvantages ☹
Experiments (lab and field)	• Cause can be determined because we observe the effect of an IV on a DV	• May not be possible to manipulate variables because of ethical problems
Investigations using correlational analysis	• Can be used when an experiment would be unethical or impractical • If correlation is significant then further investigation is justified • If correlation is not significant then you can rule out a casual relationship	• People often misinterpret correlations and assume that a cause and effect relationship has been found, but this is not possible • There may be other, unknown (**intervening**) variable(s) that can explain why the co-variables being studied are linked
Both	• The procedures can be repeated which means that the findings are confirmed	• May lack **internal/external validity**.

Qs

29

1. Consider the number +0.36. Identify the magnitude and sign of this number.
2. If this value (+0.36) were obtained after testing 20 people, would it be significant?
3. Sketch a scattergraph to illustrate this correlation.
4. If you conducted a study with 30 participants, would a correlation of +0.30 be significant?
5. Would −0.40 be significant?
6. *A study investigates whether there is a negative correlation between age and liking for spicy foods. Participants are asked to rate their liking for spicy foods on a scale of 1 to 10 where 10 means they liked it a lot.*

   a. What is meant by the term 'negative correlation' in this context?

   b. Why might you expect to find a negative correlation?

   c. Suggest **three** suitable descriptive statistics that could be used in this study.

   d. Describe **one** advantage and **one** disadvantage of this study.

7. *Guiseppe Gelato always liked statistics at school, and now that he has his own ice cream business he keeps various records. To his surprise, he has found an interesting correlation between his ice cream sales and aggressive crimes. He has started to worry that he may be irresponsible in selling ice cream because it appears to cause people to behave more aggressively. The table below shows his data.*

All data rounded to 1000s	Jan	Feb	Mar	Apr	May	Jun	Jul	Aug	Sep	Oct	Nov	Dec
Ice cream sales	10	8	7	21	32	56	130	141	84	32	11	6
Aggressive crimes	21	32	29	35	44	55	111	129	99	36	22	25

   a. Draw a scattergraph to display Guiseppe's data.

   b. What can you conclude from the data and the scattergraph?

   c. What intervening variable might explain the relationship between ice cream and aggression?

   > Remember that conclusions are an *interpretation* of the findings.

   d. Describe how you would design a study to show Guiseppe that ice cream does (or does not) cause aggressive behaviour. (You need to operationalise your variables, decide on a suitable research design and sampling method, etc.)

Significance table

N =	One-tailed test
4	1.000
6	0.829
8	0.643
10	0.564
12	0.503
14	0.464
16	0.429
18	0.401
20	0.380
22	0.361
24	0.344
26	0.331
28	0.317
30	0.306

These values are for Spearman's test of correlation. The full table is given on page 96.

Reliability

Reliability refers to whether something is consistent.

If you use a ruler to measure the height of a chair today and check the measurement tomorrow, you expect the ruler to be reliable (consistent) and provide the same measurement. You would assume that any fluctuation was because the chair had changed.

Any tool used to measure something must be reliable, such as a psychological test assessing personality or an interview about drinking habits.

If the 'tool' is measuring the same thing,it should produce the same result on every occasion. If the result is different, we know that the thing (chair or personality) has changed.

This means that we can feel confident that any difference between objects/people is due to variation in the objects and not the measuring device.

Different archers produce the following patterns of arrows.

Being reliable is being consistent; being valid is being on target (related to what you are aiming to do)

| Reliable, but not valid | Not reliable, not valid | Reliable and valid |

Assessing reliability of questionnaires and interviews

Internal reliability is a measure of the extent to which something is consistent within itself. For example, all the questions on a psychological test should be measuring the same thing.

Internal reliability

e.g. a psychological test (a type of questionnaire)

Split-half method: Two forms of the same test are prepared by dividing the questions on a test in half. For example, Question 1 is placed on Form A, Question 2 is placed on form B, 3 on A, 4 on B, and so on. Or the questions can be divided using a random method.

Therefore, you end up with two forms of the same test. If the items on the test were consistent, each form should yield the same score.

The two scores can be compared by calculating a correlation coefficient.

External reliability is a measure of the extent to which one measure of an object (like a chair) varies from another measure of the same object. Two rulers should give the same measure even if there is a month between measurements.

If the same interview were conducted 1 day and then 1 week later, the outcome should be the same – otherwise the interview is not reliable.

Two interviewers should produce the same outcome. This is called **inter-interviewer reliability**.

External reliability

e.g. a psychological test or in an interview

Test-retest method: Administer the same test twice to see if the same results are obtained. If the test or interview is given at two different times with no 'treatment' in between, it should yield the same results.

For example, give participants a test and then give the same participants the same test a month later to see if they get the same result. The two scores can again be compared by calculating a correlation coefficient.

Or conduct an interview with a set of interviewees and then repeat this a month later using same interviewer and the *same interviewees* to see if the same outcome is produced.

e.g. an experiment

Replication: An experiment is repeated using the same standardised procedures to see if the findings are the same.

Qs 30

In a study on self-esteem, the researcher constructs a scale to measure a person's self-esteem. The scale consists of 30 questions.

1. How could the researcher assess the reliability of the self-esteem scale?
2. Why would it matter if the reliability of the scale were poor?
3. How could the researcher improve the reliability of the scale?
4. How could the researcher assess the validity of the self-esteem scale?
5. Why would it matter if the validity of the scale were poor?
6. How could the researcher improve the validity of the scale?

Activity 13 — Split-half method and test-retest method

Try these methods of assessing reliability yourself. At the end of this chapter (page 60), there is a psychological test – a scale that measures a person's belief in the paranormal.

Split-half method. Construct two smaller versions of this scale to see if it is internally reliable. There are 25 items on this scale so you cannot divide it exactly in half.
Get everyone in your class to do the test and then calculate their score for Form A and Form B. Use the Excel method described on page 48 to calculate the correlation. Is it positive? Is it significant?

Test-retest method. Do the same questionnaire again (after a few days). Compare the second score for each person with their first score. Use the Excel method to calculate the correlation. Is it positive? Is it significant?

Assessing validity of questionnaires and interviews

When conducting questionnaires (including psychological tests and scales) and interviews, we are also concerned with validity.

The **external validity** concerns the extent to which the findings can be generalised (as we studied before on page 28, chapter 2).

But the **internal validity** is now a different matter because there is no IV and DV – therefore, we cannot be concerned with the extent to which the IV solely caused the changes in the DV.

The internal validity of a questionnaire/interview is related to the question of whether the questionnaire or interview or psychological test really measures what you intended to measure.

There are several ways to do this, the most common being:

- **Face validity**. Does the test look like it is measuring what you intended to measure? For example, are the questions obviously related to the topic?

- **Concurrent validity**. This can be established by comparing the current test with a previously established test on the same topic. Participants take both tests and you then compare their scores on the two tests.

Improving reliability

To improve reliability, you first need to assess the reliability of the questionnaire or interview!

Internal reliability: Select the test items that produce the greatest similarity. You can do this by removing certain items and seeing if there is a stronger correlation with the remaining items.

External reliability: This should be improved by greater internal reliability or increased validity.

Improving validity

Validity is also improved first of all by assessing the validity of a questionnaire or interview. If such measures of validity are low:

Internal validity: If one or more measures of internal validity are low, the items on the questionnaire/interview/test need to be revised, e.g. to produce a better match between scores on the new test and an established one.

External validity: Use a different sampling method to improve population validity.

Activity 14 — Validity and reliability of a questionnaire

You can use the quiz on the right or obtain your own questionnaire from a teenage magazine such as *Go Girl* or *Sugar*.

You could try one or all of the following activities:

- Measure the internal reliability of the quiz.
- Measure the external reliability of the quiz.
- Assess the face validity of the quiz.
- Assess the concurrent validity of the quiz by comparing the outcome with an established psychological test that measures the same variable. For example, psychologists may measure sensation seeking using Zuckerman's (1994) Sensation Seeking Scale (You can take the test and get your score at: www.bbc.co.uk/science/humanbody/mind/surveys/sensation/)
- Rewrite the quiz to improve reliability and validity.
- Rewrite the quiz using the knowledge you have gained in this chapter. For example, where tests are presented in 'flowchart'

form (as in the example), these could be rewritten as closed, forced choice questions to investigate the effect of questionnaire design. You might bear in mind the issue of **response set** – in the paranormal scale, some items had reversed scoring. This is to prevent people becoming too accustomed to writing 1 or 5 all the time.

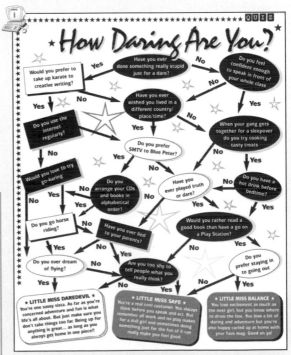

Does this questionnaire look as if it is testing sensation-seeking? If so, it has face validity.

KEY TERMS

Reliability
Internal validity

OTHER TERMS

Concurrent validity
External reliability
Face validity
Inter-interviewer reliability
Internal reliability
Replication
Response set
Split-half method
Test-retest method

DIY A study using a correlational analysis

(There is an alternative, specification-related study using a correlational analysis on Stress and Health on page 132)

ESP. A 'sheep-goat effect'

People who believe in paranormal phenomena are the 'sheep'.

People who do not believe in paranormal phenomena are the 'goats'.

Various studies have looked at the relationship between paranormal beliefs and misjudgements of probability, e.g. that of Brugger *et al.* (1990). People who are sheep (believe in paranormal phenomena) are less good at probabilistic reasoning. Probabilistic reasoning refers to making judgements related to probability. For example, which is more likely:

- I throw 10 dice at the same time and get 10 sixes?

- I throw one dice 10 times in succession and get 10 successive sixes?

In fact, they are both equally likely – if you did not think so, it suggests you are not good at probabilistic reasoning. You probably also think you should never choose the numbers in the lottery that came up last time.

The link between probabilistic reasoning and paranormal belief is that some people like to have an explanation for the things that happen around them. For example, if a door bangs shut on a windless night, such people 'prefer' the explanation that there was a ghost, whereas others prefer to accept that there is no explanation. Those preferring the explanation of causes also do not find it easy to comprehend the idea of chance (probability).

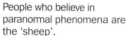 **Activity 15** — **Investigating the sheep–goat effect**

To investigate this, you need:

1. A measure of the degree to which someone believes in paranormal phenomena.

   You can use The Belief in the Paranormal Scale (on page 60) or produce your own questionnaire. A high score on the scale indicates that you believe in paranormal phenomena.

2. A measure of probabilistic reasoning.

   Ask participants to mimic the rolling of a dice by writing or saying a digit between 1 and 6. They should produce a string of 100 numbers.

   The way to score this is printed at the top of page 61. A high score indicates that they are not good at probabilistic reasoning.

 To analyse your data

1. Draw a scattergraph to show the relationship between the co-variables (belief in the paranormal and probabilistic reasoning).

2. Calculate the correlation coefficient.

   What do the graph and correlation coefficient tell you about your findings? Is the correlation strong, moderate or weak?

3. Calculate the mean, median and mode for both sets of data (belief in the paranormal and probabilistic reasoning).

   Which measure of central tendency is the most useful? Why?

   Which measure of central tendency is the least useful? Why?

4. Sort your participants into three groups: sheep, goats and neutral. You need to decide how to define each group; e.g. you might decide that the sheep are all those who scored more than 45.

   Draw a bar chart to show the mean probabilistic reasoning score for each group.

   Compare the scattergraph and the bar chart. Which do you think is more informative?

A final word on correlation

The correlations we have looked at are all **linear** – in a perfect positive correlation (+1) all the values would lie in a *straight* line from the bottom left to the top right.

There is, however, a different kind of correlation – **a curvilinear correlation**. The relationship is not linear – it is curved – but there is still a predictable relationship. For example, stress and performance do not have a linear relationship. Performance on many tasks is depressed when stress is too high or too low; it is best when stress is moderate. The relationship between stress and performance was first identified by Yerkes and Dodson and thus called the Yerkes–Dodson Law. The graph on the right illustrates this relationship.

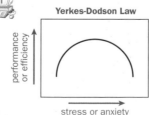

Yerkes-Dodson Law

performance or efficiency

stress or anxiety

Qs — **31**

1. Describe the aims of the sheep–goat study.

2. Would the hypothesis predict a positive or a negative correlation?

3. What conclusions can you draw from your findings?

OTHER TERMS
Curvilinear correlation
Linear correlation

Multiple choice questions

1. **Data related to how people think and feel are called**
   a. Qualitative data.
   b. Quantitative data.
   c. Questionnaire data.
   d. Both a and c.

2. **Data that can be easily counted are called**
   a. Qualitative data.
   b. Quantitative data.
   c. Questionnaire data.
   d. Both a and c.

3. **Closed questions tend to produce**
   a. Qualitative data.
   b. Quantitative data.
   c. Questionnaire data.
   d. Both a and c.

4. **Open questions tend to produce**
   a. Qualitative data.
   b. Quantitative data.
   c. Questionnaire data.
   d. Both a and c.

5. **Respondents often answer questions in a way that makes them look good rather than being truthful. This is called**
   a. A response set.
   b. A leading question.
   c. Social desirability bias.
   d. The Hawthorne effect.

6. **One means of assessing people's attitudes is by using a scale from strongly agree to strongly disagree. This is called**
   a. The semantic differential technique.
   b. A forced choice scale.
   c. A quantitative scale.
   d. The Likert Scale.

7. **Which of the following is *not* an advantage of qualitative data?**
   a. Represent thoughts and feelings that cannot be measured in an experiment.
   b. Easy to analyse the findings.
   c. Represents the true complexity of human behaviour.
   d. Means that unexpected information can be collected.

8. **A clinical interview is a kind of**
   a. Questionnaire.
   b. Structured interview.
   c. Unstructured interview.
   d. Correlation.

9. **One advantage of an interview in comparison with a questionnaire is**
   a. The interviewer can adapt questions as he or she goes along.
   b. People may feel more comfortable about revealing personal information.
   c. Interviews can be delivered by less skilled personnel.
   d. Social desirability bias is less of a problem.

10. **Which of the following is false?**
    a. A questionnaire can collect data from a large number of people in a short space of time.
    b. Questionnaires are less easy to analyse than interviews.
    c. Questionnaires do not require specialist administrators.
    d. Social desirability bias is a problem in a questionnaire.

11. **A leading question is a question that**
    a. Contains the answer in the question.
    b. Is the most important question on a questionnaire.
    c. Suggests what answer is desired.
    d. Tends to confuse respondents.

12. **In a correlation you have**
    a. An IV and a DV.
    b. Co-variables.
    c. Factors.
    d. Both a and b.

13. **A negative correlation is when**
    a. Two variables increase together.
    b. As one variable increases, the other decreases.
    c. There is a weak correlation between two variables.
    d. There is a strong correlation between two variables.

14. **A correlation coefficient of +0.65 indicates.**
    a. No correlation.
    b. A weak positive correlation.
    c. A moderate positive correlation.
    d. A strong positive correlation.

15. **Which of the following could *not* be a correlation coefficient?**
    a. 0
    b. +0.79
    c. +1.28
    d. −0.30

16. **A scattergraph is**
    a. A descriptive statistic.
    b. A graph that illustrates a correlation.
    c. A collection of dots where each dot represents a pair of scores.
    d. All of the above.

17. **Which of the following is *not* an advantage of a study using a correlational analysis?**
    a. Can be used when it is unethical or impractical to manipulate variables.
    b. Useful to help decide whether a more rigorous scientific investigation into the apparent relationship is justified.
    c. If no correlation can be found, you can rule out a causal relationship.
    d. Can demonstrate a causal relationship.

18. **Internal reliability is a measure of the extent to which**
    a. One measure of an object varies from another measure of the same object.
    b. How true or legitimate a measurement is.
    c. You obtain the result you were expecting.
    d. Something is consistent within itself.

19. **One way to assess internal reliability is to**
    a. Replicate the study.
    b. Use the test-retest method.
    c. Use the split-half method.
    d. Ask a friend.

20. **Face validity is an assessment of whether a test**
    a. Looks appealing to participants.
    b. Looks like it is measuring what it intends to measure.
    c. Produces a score similar to the score produced by another test measuring the same thing.
    d. All of the above.

Answers are on page 54

Exam-style question 5

A school decides to conduct a study on the healthy habits of the students in the school, using a questionnaire. They want to collect data about eating habits, exercise and smoking. It is important to know about (a) the students' habits and (b) their attitudes.

The school psychology department was asked to construct a suitable questionnaire. A part of this questionnaire is shown below.

8. Do you smoke?

☐ Never ☐ Occasionally ☐ Frequently ☐ Excessively

9. If you do smoke, or have smoked, at what age did you start?

10. What do you think is the best reason not to smoke?

(a) Outline **one** advantage and **one** disadvantage of using a questionnaire. (2 marks + 2 marks)

(b) Explain **one** reason why a pilot study should have been carried out in the context of this study. (2 marks)

(c) (i) Identify **one** question in the extract above that would providequalitative data. (1 mark)

   (ii) With reference to the question you have identified in part (i), explain why this question would produce qualitative data. (3 marks)

(d) (i) Identify **one** sampling method that could have been used in this study. (1 mark)

   (ii) In the context of this study, explain **one** reason for using the sampling method you have identified in (i). (2 marks)

(e) (i) The questions in the extract above can be criticised. Select **one** question and give **one** criticism of it. (2 marks)

   (ii) Re-write the question you selected so that it overcomes the criticism you identified in (i). (2 marks)

(f) Describe **two** ways of making sure that this study would be carried out in an ethically acceptable way. (3 marks + 3 marks)

(g) (i) Explain what is meant by validity in the context of research. (3 marks)

   (ii) Identify **one** threat to validity in this study. (2 marks)

   (iii) Explain how you would deal with the threat to validity identified in (ii). (2 marks)

Examiner's tips for answering this question

(a) When stating an advantage, be careful to provide sufficient detail and not just say 'a lot of data can be collected' – this could be said to be true for all methods.

Remember, for all the questions with the word 'one' in them, that only your first answer will be marked by the examiner. Do not waste time providing more than one answer.

(b) Many candidates do not read such questions carefully, and they explain either what a pilot study is or how they would do it – the question here asks *why* you would do it, and your answer must be set in the context of this study.

(c) (ii) There are 3 marks for this answer, which means you need to think hard about how you can provide sufficient detail. The question does not restrict you to give 'one' reason why the question would produce qualitative data so you can provide detail by giving a range of answers.

(d) (i) Any sampling method is acceptable but make sure you do give a reason in (ii) for the sampling method you named in (i).

(d) (ii) Watch out for the 'in the context': you must refer to some aspect of the study to get the full marks.

(e) If you select a question and do not provide an appropriate criticism, you get no marks for (i) and no marks for (ii).

(e) (ii) The question says 'rewrite' so don't just give vague details of what you would do; instead, present a new, alternative question – which must overcome the criticism given in (i).

(f) It is rare to be asked for 'two' of anything so this question may stretch your knowledge. Think carefully, otherwise you are throwing away an important 3 marks.

Note that your answer must be contextualised and must focus on what you would do, not on what the issue is. Thus, just writing 'privacy' will get no marks because it is an issue. You need to explain what you would do.

(g) (i) You might want to use the definition of validity provided in this chapter rather than the one provided in Chapter 2. In Chapter 2, we were concerned with the validity of *experiments*, although that answer would also be acceptable.

(g) (ii) The 'threat' may relate to internal or external validity. Note that this question is worth 2 marks so you need to provide sufficient details.

(g) (iii) Clearly, the answer to (iii) must be linked to (ii). Any sensible answer will gain credit, although it must be explained.

Exam-style question 6

Sigmund Freud developed a theory of personality. He proposed that children go through various stages of development, in each stage energy being focused on an area of the body. During the first stage of development, the focus is on the mouth (this stage is called the oral stage). Freud suggested that either too much pleasure or too much frustration at this stage would lead a person to develop an oral personality.

One way to test this is to see if adults with a focus on their mouths also have oral personalities. In one study, mouth focus was assessed by observing the number of mouth movements a participant makes in a 30-minute period.

Oral personality was assessed in an interview, which provided a score for oral personality for each participant. The oral personality scores for 15 participants were:

3, 4, 5, 6, 6, 7, 7, 9, 10, 13, 15, 16, 17, 19, 20

(A highly oral personality would score 20.)

The findings from the study are shown in the graph at the top right of this page. The correlation coefficient is 0.74.

(a) (i) One variable in this study was 'mouth focus'. How was 'mouth focus' operationalised? (2 marks)

  (ii) Identify the second variable in this study. (1 mark)

(b) (i) Identify the kind of graph that has been used to illustrate the findings of this investigation. (1 mark)

  (ii) Write a suitable label for the y axis (vertical axis) of the graph. (1 mark)

(c) (i) What is meant by a correlation coefficient? (2 marks)

  (ii) Using the information from the graph and/or correlation coefficient, describe the relationship between the co-variables. (3 marks)

  (iii) Give **one** advantage of an investigation using a correlational analysis. (2 marks)

(d) A newspaper article reports these findings claiming that 'Mouth focus causes an oral personality'.

  (i) Explain why this is not a valid conclusion. (2 marks)

  (ii) Suggest a more suitable conclusion for this study. (2 marks)

(e) The researcher wished to summarise the findings using a measure of central tendency.

  (i) Identify a suitable measure of central tendency for the scores for oral personality. (1 mark)

  (ii) Explain why this would be a suitable measure of central tendency. (2 marks)

(f) Explain how the researcher could assess the reliability of the interview that was used. (2 marks)

(g) Explain how the researcher could assess the validity of the interview. (2 marks)

(h) The interview produced quantitative data. Give one advantage and one disadvantage of quantitative data compared to qualitative data. (2 marks + 2 marks)

(i) Identify one ethical issue that might arise in this study and explain how you would deal with it. (3 marks)

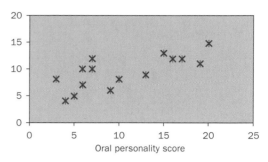

Relationship between mouth focus and oral personality

Oral personality score

Examiner's tips for answering this question

(a) (i) This is an example of the kind of question where you are *not* asked to describe the meaning of a term (in this case, operationalisation) but are required to demonstrate your understanding by applying the definition to this example.

(a) (ii) This study does not have an IV and DV so the variables are actually co-variables – but because the term 'co-variables' is not in the specification, it cannot be included in the question.

(b) These should be easy marks.

(c) (i) It is rare to get a question that simply requires a definition, but there are a few such questions each time, and this is one of them. There is no requirement to contextualise your answer, but you can do this if you think it is a means of providing extra detail.

(c) (ii) Think carefully about how to get 3 marks' worth of detail into your answer.

(c) (iii) There is no requirement to contextualise your answer, but again this may be a helpful way to provide extra detail. Don't forget that you will not get 2 marks and (you might not even get 1 mark) if you provide a statement that could apply to all research methods, such as saying 'It shows you the relationship between two variables.'

(d) (i) This is really just another way of asking about one of the disadvantages of correlational analysis.

(d) (ii) You are being asked to state a conclusion. A helpful way to ensure that you provide a conclusion and not a finding is to start your answer with 'The findings suggest that …'.

(e) (ii) Your answer should be based on the data given in the stimulus material.

(f) and (g) In both of these questions, you must focus on how you would do it and not on what is meant by the terms reliability or validity. You must also avoid writing about *why* you would do it. Finally, you must deal with the interview rather than the measure of mouth focus.

(h) There is no requirement to contextualise this answer.

(i) Remember that debriefing is not an ethical issue but could be mentioned as a way of dealing with an ethical issue.

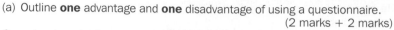

Model answer for question 5

(a) Outline **one** advantage and **one** disadvantage of using a questionnaire.

(2 marks + 2 marks)

One advantage is that you can collect a lot of data from a lot of people quickly and relatively easily.

One disadvantage is that people may want to present themselves in a good light and therefore you don't get truthful (valid) answers.

(b) Explain **one** reason why a pilot study should have been carried out in the context of this study. (2 marks)

You would carry out a pilot study to check the design of the questionnaire, so you could see for example if some of the questions were confusing.

(c) (i) Identify **one** question in the extract above that would provide qualitative data. (1 mark)

Question 10.

(ii) With reference to the question you have identified in part (i), explain why this question would produce qualitative data. (3 marks)

The answer would tell you what people think about smoking and would produce a range of answers that would not be easily quantifiable.

(d) (i) Identify **one** sampling method that could have been used in this study. (1 mark)

An opportunity sample.

(ii) In the context of this study, explain **one** reason for using the sampling method you have identified in (i). (2 marks)

Doing an opportunity sample means that you can obtain your participants easily because they are the first ones, rather than having to contact volunteers. This would mean it was quicker to complete the study.

(e) (i) The questions in the extract above can be criticised. Select one question and give **one** criticism of it. (2 marks)

Question 8. The terms used aren't explained so different people may interpret them differently. One person might think 10 a day was excessive whereas someone else would rate this as moderate.

(ii) Rewrite the question you selected so that it overcomes the criticism you identified in (i). (2 marks)

Instead of using the terms moderate, excessive, etc. I would use numbers, e.g. 0–5 a day, 6–10 a day, 11–20 a day, etc.

(f) Describe **two** ways of making sure that this study would be carried out in an ethically acceptable way. (3 marks + 3 marks)

1. Confidentiality – I would ensure that people did not put their names on the questionnaires and would tell them about their rights of confidentialty as part of the informed consent.

2. Protection from psychological harm – I would make sure that there were no distressing questions, which could be checked during the pilot study.

(g) (i) Explain what is meant by validity in the context of research. (3 marks)

Validity refers to the legitimacy of a study. It concerns both internal validity (the extent to which a study has measured what was intended to be measured) and external validity (the extent to which the findings can be generalised).

(ii) Identify **one** threat to validity in this study. (2 marks)

The questionnaire may not collect the 'right' sort of data, e.g. people may not be truthful about their smoking habits and may lie to make themselves look better.

(iii) Explain how you would deal with the threat to validity identified in (ii). (2 marks)

I would try to reduce dishonest answers by assuring them about confidentiality and that it was important to be honest so the healthy habits of school students could be properly assessed.

Examiner's comments

(a) Saying that an advantage is that questionnaires are 'quick and easy' would receive no marks because it needs more explanation. You could argue that some experiments are also quick and easy.

The disadvantage given here may appear to be two answers (and then only the first would be credited) but the 'and' links two related points. There is no need to use the term 'social desirability bias' because there is enough for two marks as it stands – but it would make the answer clearer.

(b) There is not a great deal of contextualisation here, but enough (the mention of a questionnaire and questions). If the candidate had added, *'I would do this by giving the questionnaire to a small sample'*, this would receive no marks because it is answering the question 'how' instead of 'why'.

(c) (i) The other questions are all quantitative so would not be acceptable answers (and you would get zero for (ii)).

(ii) There is just enough here for 3 marks. An answer that omitted the last six words would only get 2 marks, and an answer that only mentioned *'what people think'* would get 1 mark.

(d) The first sentence is excellent. Notice how the explanation is made more detailed by making a comparison with another method. BUT there is no contextualisation in the first sentence (as required in the question) so the candidate has added another sentence.

(e) (i) The criticism is clearly explained. Just saying *'the words aren't clear'* would not have been detailed enough for 2 marks.

You might criticse the open-ended nature of Question 10 and provide some tick box answers.

(e) (ii) The choice of numbers (0–5, 6–10, 11–20) is a bit erratic but again sufficiently detailed for 2 marks. You do have to actually show what you would do.

(f) Ample detail for both answers, focused on what you would do about the ethical issue.

(g) (i) Detail has been gained by offering definitions of three aspects of validity.

(g) (ii) The first part of this sentence alone would possibly attract 1 mark, but it is fairly woolly. The 'e.g.' provides us with the important information.

(g) (iii) An alternative solution might have been to lie about the aims of the study. Since the word 'one' is not in the answer, you could include a range of ways that would all be creditworthy.

Model answer for question 6

(a) (i) One variable in this study was 'mouth focus'. How was 'mouth focus' operationalised? (2 marks)

By counting the number of mouth movements in a 30 minute period.

    (ii) Identify the second variable in this study. (1 mark)

Oral personality.

(b) (i) Identify the kind of graph that has been used to illustrate the findings of this investigation. (1 mark)

Scattergraph.

    (ii) Write a suitable label for the *y* axis (vertical axis) of the graph. (1 mark)

Number of mouth movements.

(c) (i) What is meant by a correlation coefficient? (2 marks)

It is a measure of the extent to which two variables are related, lying between +1 and −1.

    (ii) Using the information from the graph and/or correlation coefficient, describe the relationship between the co-variables. (3 marks)

They both tell us that there is a reasonably strong positive correlation: as oral personality increases, the mouth focus score increases.

    (iii) Give **one** advantage of an investigation using a correlational analysis. (2 marks)

It allows you to see to what extent two variables are related, e.g. they increase together, or as one increases the other decreases.

(d) A newspaper article reports these findings claiming that 'Being orally satisfied as a child causes an oral personality.'
    (i) Explain why this is not a valid conclusion (2 marks)

You can't claim a causal relationship if you have done a correlational study, so you can't say that early experience causes an oral personality.

    (ii) Suggest a more suitable conclusion for this study. (2 marks)

The findings suggest that people who are focused on their mouth also have an oral personality.

(e) The researcher wished to summarise the findings using a measure of central tendency.
    (i) Identify a suitable measure of central tendency for the scores for oral personality. (1 mark)

The mean.

    (ii) Explain why this would be a suitable measure of central tendency. (2 marks)

It takes the values of all the data into account, which is not true for the median.

(f) Explain how the researcher could assess the reliability of the interview that was used. (2 marks)

The researcher could repeat the interview again a while later using the same participants to see if the same score was produced.

(g) Explain how the researcher could assess the validity of the interview. (2 marks)

Validity could be assessed by seeing if the score obtained on the interview was positively correlated with the score obtained on another measure of oral personality.

(h) The interview produced quantitative data. Give **one** advantage and **one** disadvantage of quantitative data compared with qualitative data. (2 marks + 2 marks)

One advantage is that you can analyse this kind of data more easily because the data are numerical.

One disadvantage is that you force people to over-simplify their behaviour by having to quantify it instead of being able to describe their thoughts.

    (i) Identify **one** ethical issue that might arise in this study and explain how you would deal with it. (3 marks)

One ethical issue is informed consent, which is not mentioned. Participants should be offered the chance to give their informed consent before taking part by being told what the study will involve.

Examiner's comments

(a) (i) Both parts of this answer are required for 2 marks. You would get 1 mark for saying '*counting the number of mouth movements*'.

(c) (i) The key word to include is '*measure*' or some other word that suggests number or quantity. This is what differentiates a correlation coefficient from a correlation. But just saying '*It is a number*' would not be sufficient for 2 marks. It would hardly be worth 1 mark.

(c) (ii) Simply saying a '*positive correlation*' would score only 1 mark. Describing this as a moderate correlation would be wrong; you need to say a '*strong correlation*' and, for the full 3 marks, describe the relationship.

(c) (iii) This is probably more detail than would be required for 2 marks and, despite what was said in the examiner's tips on page 55, you might get 2 marks for saying a '*relationship between two variables*' because it is better than saying a '*link between two things*', which would get 1 mark.

(d) (i) If you just said, '*You can't have cause and effect*', you would only get 1 mark.

(d) (ii) If this answer had been written in terms of participants, it would get zero marks because conclusions are general statements made about the target population, not about the selected participants.

(e) (ii) It might be argued that the mean is unsuitable because the scores for oral personality would be ordinal data – however, it could be argued that this data uses a 'plastic interval scale' (see glossary).

(f) If you said '*repeat the interview*' without saying '*with the same participants*', you would only get 1 mark. Saying '*repeat the study*' would get 0 marks.

(g) You could alternatively describe face validity.

(h) More detail could have been given in these answers by specifying the difference between quantitative and qualitative data, but it is implicit in the answers as they stand.

(i) An alternative way to deal with the issue would be to debrief participants. Other ethical issues, such as confidentiality or privacy, would also be creditworthy.

There is enough detail about how you would deal with the issue. Just saying '*get informed consent*' would not be enough for full marks.

Clues

Across

1. Process of ensuring that variables are in a form that can be easily tested. (18)
5. An investigative method that generally involves a face-to-face interaction with another individual and results in the collection of data. (9)
7. The kind of data that express what people think or feel and cannot be counted. (11)
10. The mode is one measure of central tendency. Name two others. (4,6)
11. The middle value in a set of scores when they are placed in rank order. (6)
13. A statistical measure of the amount of variation in a set of scores around the mean. (8,9)
21. A research design in which neither the participant nor the experimenter is aware of the condition that an individual participant is receiving. (6,5)
22. The extent to which an observed effect can be attributed to the experimental manipulation rather than some other factor. (8,8)
23. The arithmetic average of a group of scores, calculated by dividing the sum of the scores by the number of scores. (4)
24. Data that represent how much, how long or how many, etc. there are of something; i.e. a behaviour is measured in numbers. (12)
25. An experimental technique designed to overcome order effects. (16)
30. The kind of reliability in which something is consistent within itself; e.g. all test items should be measuring the same thing. (8)
31. The most frequently occurring score in a set of data. (4)
32. Kind of sampling in which people are selected who are most easily available at the time of the study. (11)
34. A correlation between two variables such that, as the value of one co-variable increases, the other decreases. (8)
35. In a repeated measures design, a confounding variable arising from the sequence in which conditions are presented, e.g. a practice or fatigue effect. (5,6)
36. In an experiment, the variable that is manipulated by the experimenter (initials). (2)
37. An experiment in which the relationship between an independent and dependent variable is studied within the context in which the behaviour normally occurs, (usually) without the participants knowing they are part of a study. (5)
38. Predicts the kind of difference (e.g. more or less) or relationship (positive or negative) between two groups of participants or between different conditions: _____ hypothesis. (11)
39. A type of frequency distribution in which the number of scores in each category of continuous data are represented by vertical columns. (9)
40. Kind of correlation in which both variables increase together. (8)

Down

2. The extent to which two measures are consistent. (11)
3. A graph used to represent the frequency of data; the categories on the x axis have no fixed order, and there is no true zero. (3,5)
4. Term used to describe instructions or procedures that are the same for all participants to avoid investigator effects and enable replication of the study. (12)
6. A calculation of the extent to which a measure varies from another measure of the same thing. (8,11)
8. A way of conducting research in a systematic manner e.g. experiment or interview. Is this the design or the method? (6)
9. A technique for selecting participants such that every member of the population being tested has an equal chance of being selected. (6)
12. Shows a relationship between two variables. (11)
14. In an experiment, the variable that is measured by the experimenter (initials). (2)
15. A small-scale trial of a study run to test any aspects of the design, with a view to making improvements. (5)
16. A number between −1 and +1 that tells us how closely the co-variables in a correlational analysis are related. (11,11)
17. In an interview or questionnaire, questions that invite the respondents to provide their own answers rather than select one of those provided. (4)
18. A graphical representation of the relationship (i.e. the correlation) between two sets of scores. (12)
19. An experimental design in which participants are randomly allocated to two (or more) groups representing different conditions. (10,6)
20. A type of research design in which the participants are not aware of the research aims or of which condition of the experiment they are receiving. (6,5)
21. Features of an experiment that a participant unconsciously responds to when searching for clues about how to behave. (6,15)
26. A type of experimental design in which each participant takes part in every condition under test. (8,8)
27. A measure of dispersion that measures the difference between the highest and lowest score in a set of data. (5)
28. A type of investigation in which the experimenter cannot manipulate the independent variable directly, but in which it varies naturally. (7)
29. A sampling technique that relies solely on people who offer to participate, usually in response to an advertisement. (9)
33. The overall plan of action to maximise meaningful results and minimise ambiguity using research techniques such as control of variables and selection of participants. Is this the design or the method? (6)

Crossword answers are on page 61

Belief in the Paranormal Scale

This inventory represents an attempt to discover which of the various paranormal events and phenomena you believe to be most likely and which you believe to be least likely. There are no right or wrong answers. Moreover, this is not an attempt to belittle or make fun of your beliefs. Therefore, please indicate your true feelings as well as you can. If you are unsure or ambivalent, indicate this by marking 'undecided' and proceed to the next item. Indicate your answers in the following format:

1 = strongly disagree with this statement
2 = disagree with statement
3 = undecided or don't know
4 = agree with statement
5 = strongly agree with statement

1 2 3 4 5	1.	I believe psychic phenomena are real, and should become part of psychology and be studied scientifically.
1 2 3 4 5	2.	All UFO sightings are either other forms of physical phenomena (such as weather balloons) or simply hallucinations.
1 2 3 4 5	3.	I am convinced the Abominable Snowman of Tibet really exists.
1 2 3 4 5	4.	I firmly believe that ghosts and spirits do exist.
1 2 3 4 5	5.	Black magic really exists and should be dealt with in a serious manner.
1 2 3 4 5	6.	Witches and warlocks do exist.
1 2 3 4 5	7.	Only the uneducated or demented believe in the supernatural.
1 2 3 4 5	8.	Through psychic individuals it is possible to communicate with the dead.
1 2 3 4 5	9.	I believe the Loch Ness monster of Scotland exists.
1 2 3 4 5	10.	I believe that once a person dies his spirit may come back from time to time in the form of ghosts.
1 2 3 4 5	11.	Some individuals are able to levitate (lift objects) through mysterious mental forces.
1 2 3 4 5	12.	I believe that many special persons throughout the world have the ability to predict the future.
1 2 3 4 5	13.	The idea of being able to tell the future through the means of palm reading represents the beliefs of foolish and unreliable persons.
1 2 3 4 5	14.	I am firmly convinced that reincarnation has occurred throughout history.
1 2 3 4 5	15.	I firmly believe that, at least on some occasions, I can read another person's mind via ESP (extrasensory perception).
1 2 3 4 5	16.	ESP is an unusual gift that many persons have and should not be confused with elaborate tricks used by entertainers.
1 2 3 4 5	17.	Ghosts and witches do not exist outside the realm of the imagination.
1 2 3 4 5	18.	Supernatural phenomena should become part of scientific study, equal in importance to physical phenomena.
1 2 3 4 5	18.	Supernatural phenomena should become part of scientific study, equal in importance to physical phenomena.
1 2 3 4 5	19.	All of the reports of "scientific proof" of psychic phenomena are strictly sensationalism with no factual basis.
1 2 3 4 5	20.	Through the use of mysterious formulas and incantations it is possible to cast spells on individuals.
1 2 3 4 5	21.	With proper training anyone could learn to read other people's minds.
1 2 3 4 5	22.	It is advisable to consult your horoscope daily.
1 2 3 4 5	23.	Plants can sense the feelings of people through a form of ESP.
1 2 3 4 5	24.	ESP has been scientifically proven to exist.
1 2 3 4 5	25.	There is a great deal we have yet to understand about the mind of man, so it is likely that many phenomena (such as ESP) will one day be proven to exist.

Scoring for the Belief in the Paranormal Scale (*Jones et al.*, 1977)

Reverse responses for questions 2, 7, 13, 17, 19; i.e. for question 2, if a person responded with 5, then change this to 1; if 4, then change this to 2; 3 stays the same; 2 changes to 4; and 1 changes to 5.

Now add all the responses, giving a maximum score of 125.

In the trial of this scale (with 475 undergraduates) 10% scored less than 50 (low believers) and 10% scored more than 85 (high believers).

Scoring for the probabilistic task

Score this by placing a tick whenever a number is repeated consecutively. The participant's score is the total number of ticks.

Crossword answers

Across

1. OPERATIONALISATION – Process ensuring that variables are in a form that can be easily tested. (18)

5. INTERVIEW – An investigative method that generally involves a face-to-face interaction with another individual and results in the collection of data. (9)

7. QUALITATIVE – The kind of data that express what people think or feel and cannot be counted. (11)

10. MEAN, MEDIAN – The mode is one measure of central tendency. Name two others. (4,6)

11. MEDIAN – The middle value in a set of scores when they are placed in rank order. (6)

13. STANDARD DEVIATION – A statistical measure of the amount of variation in a set of scores around the mean. (8,9)

21. DOUBLE BLIND – A research design in which neither the participant nor the experimenter is aware of the condition that an individual participant is receiving. (6,5)

22. INTERNAL VALIDITY – The extent to which an observed effect can be attributed to the experimental manipulation rather than some other factor. (8,8)

23. MEAN – The arithmetic average of a group of scores, calculated by dividing the sum of the scores by the number of scores. (4)

24. QUANTITATIVE – Data that represent how much, how long or how many, etc. there are of something; i.e. a behaviour is measured in numbers. (12)

25. COUNTERBALANCING – An experimental technique designed to overcome order and practice effects. (16)

30. INTERNAL – The kind of reliability in which something is consistent within itself; e.g. all test items should be measuring the same thing. (8)

31. MODE – The most frequently occurring score in a set of data. (4)

32. OPPORTUNITY – Kind of sampling in which people are selected who are most easily available at the time of the study. (11)

34. NEGATIVE – A correlation between two variables such that, as the value of one co-variable increases, the other decreases. (8)

35. ORDER EFFECT – In a repeated measures design, a confounding variable arising from the sequence in which conditions are presented, e.g. a practice or fatigue effect. (5,6)

36. IV – In an experiment, the variable that is manipulated by the experimenter (initials). (2)

37. FIELD – An experiment in which the relationship between an independent and dependent variable is studied within the context in which the behaviour normally occurs, (usually) without the participants knowing they are part of a study. (5)

38. DIRECTIONAL – Predicts the kind of difference (e.g. more or less) or relationship (positive or negative) between two groups of participants or between different conditions: hypothesis. (11)

39. HISTOGRAM – A type of frequency distribution in which the number of scores in each category of continuous data are represented by vertical columns. (9)

40. POSITIVE – Kind of correlation in which both variables increase together. (8)

Down

2. RELIABILITY – The extent to which two measures are consistent. (11)

3. BAR CHART – A graph used to represent the frequency of data; the categories on the x axis have no fixed order, and there is no true zero. (3,5)

4. STANDARDISED – Term used to describe instructions or procedures that are the same for all participants to avoid investigator effects and enable replication of the study. (12)

6. EXTERNAL RELIABILITY – A calculation of the extent to which a measure varies from another measure of the same thing. (8,11)

8. METHOD – A way of conducting research in a systematic manner e.g. experiment or interview. Is this the design or the method? (6)

9. RANDOM – A technique for selecting participants such that every member of the population being tested has an equal chance of being selected. (6)

12. CORRELATION – Shows a relationship between two variables. (11)

14. DV – In an experiment, the variable that is measured by the experimenter (initials). (2)

15. PILOT – A small-scale trial of a study run to test any aspects of the design, with a view to making improvements. (5)

16. CORRELATION COEFFICIENT – A number between −1 and +1 that tells us how closely the co-variables in a correlational analysis are related. (11,11)

17. OPEN – In an interview or questionnaire, questions that invite the respondents to provide their own answers rather than select one of those provided. (4)

18. SCATTERGRAPH – A graphical representation of the relationship (i.e. the correlation) between two sets of scores. (12)

19. INDEPENDENT GROUPS – An experimental design in which participants are randomly allocated to two (or more) groups representing different conditions. (10,6)

20. SINGLE BLIND – A type of research design in which the participants are not aware of the research aims or of which condition of the experiment they are receiving. (6,5)

21. DEMAND CHARACTERISTICS – Features of an experiment that a participant unconsciously responds to when searching for clues about how to behave. (6,15)

26. REPEATED MEASURES – A type of experimental design in which each participant takes part in every condition under test. (8,8)

27. RANGE – A measure of dispersion that measures the difference between the highest and lowest score in a set of data. (5)

28. NATURAL – A type of investigation in which the experimenter cannot manipulate the independent variable directly, but in which it varies naturally. (7)

29. VOLUNTEER – A sampling technique that relies solely on people who offer to participate, usually in response to an advertisement. (9)

33. DESIGN – The overall plan of action to maximise meaningful results and minimise ambiguity using research techniques such as control of variables and selection of participants. Is this the design or the method? (6)

pages 68–69

Observational studies

Coding systems, checklists and rating scales

The Facial Action Coding System (FACS)

Early Childhood Environmental Rating Scale (ECERS)

Activity 18: DIY Make your own coding system

Evaluating naturalistic observations

Content analysis

Activity 19: DIY Content analysis

Observational studies

Distinctions

Devices for making and recording observations

Analysing observational data

Reliability

Validity

Ethical issues

Training observers

Assessing reliability

pages 66–67

Contents

Naturalistic observation

An example of a naturalistic observation

An example of a controlled observation

An example of an experiment with controlled observational techniques

Activity 16: Making observations

Observation techniques

Observational systems

Sampling procedures

Activity 17: Making systematic observations

pages 64–65

Observations
and a few other things

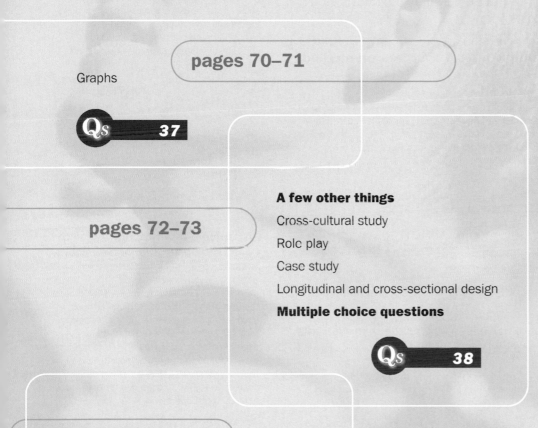

Graphs

pages 70–71

Qs 37

A few other things

Cross-cultural study

Rolc play

Casc study

Longitudinal and cross-sectional design

Multiple choice questions

pages 72–73

Qs 38

pages 74–77

Exam-style questions 7 and 8

Model answers to exam-style questions 7 and 8

Answers to multiple choice questions

Naturalistic observation

Observational research is non-experimental research. There is no independent variable (IV), although a hypothesis concerning an IV may be tested (i.e. you can investigate but not demonstrate causal relationships).

In an observational study, participants are observed engaging in whatever behaviour is being studied. The observations are recorded.

In a **naturalistic observation**, behaviour is studied in a natural situation where *everything* has been left as it *normally* is.

In a **controlled observation**, some variables are controlled by the researcher, reducing the 'naturalness' of the behaviour being studied. Participants are likely to know they are being studied, and the study may be conducted in a laboratory.

Observational methods may also be used in an experiment – in which case observation is a **research technique** instead of a **research method**.

An example of a controlled observation

The same research as described on the right could have been conducted by controlling some of the variables. For example, the researchers might have set up a special playroom in their laboratory with certain types of toys available (male, female and neutral). They could have observed the children through a **one-way mirror** so that the children would be unaware of being observed.

Activity 16 — Making observations

Work with a partner and take it in turns to observe each other. One of you will be Person A, and the other will be Person B.

Person A should have a difficult task to do (e.g. answering one of the exam questions in this book!).

Person B should have a boring task to do (e.g. copying out the exam question).

Each person should spend 5 minutes on the task.

The person doing the observing should note down any aspect of their partner's behaviour.

See questions on this task below.

Qs 32

1. Answer the following questions about the observational study in Activity 16.
   a. Suggest a suitable hypothesis for the study.
   b. If you did the activity, summarise your observations.
   c. What uncontrolled factors might affect your findings?
   d. What can you conclude from your research?
   e. In this study, is 'observation' the method or the technique?
   f. Are the observations controlled or naturalistic?
   g. If you did conduct the observation, can you suggest **one or more** difficulties that you encountered?
2. With reference to the study by Lamb and Roopnarine (an example of a naturalistic observation), give **one** advantage and **one** disadvantage of studying children in this way.
3. With reference to the example of a controlled observation, give **one** advantage and **one** disadvantage of studying children in this way.

An example of a naturalistic observation

Do little boys criticise each other if they behave like girls? Do little boys 'reward' each other for sex-appropriate play? Is the same true for little girls?

One study observed boys and girls aged 3–5 years during their free play periods at nursery school. The researchers classified activities as male, female or neutral, and recorded how playmates responded. Praise and imitation constituted some of the positive responses; criticism and stopping play were some of the negative responses. They found that children generally reinforced peers for sex-appropriate play and were quick to criticise sex-inappropriate play (Lamb and Roopnarine, 1979).

An example of an experiment with controlled observational techniques

In the 'Bobo doll study' described on page 25 (Bandura *et al.*, 1961), the children's aggressiveness was observed at the end of the experiment to see if those exposed to the aggressive model behaved more aggressively. At the end of the experiment, each child was taken to a room that contained some aggressive toys (e.g. a mallet and a dart gun), some non-aggressive toys (e.g. dolls and farm animals) and a 3-foot Bobo doll.

The experimenter stayed with the child while he or she played for 20 minutes, during which time the child was observed through a one-way mirror. The observers recorded what the child was doing every 5 seconds, using the following measures:

- *Imitation of physical aggression*: any specific acts that were imitated.

- *Imitative verbal aggression*: any phrases that were imitated, such as 'POW'.

- *Imitative non-aggressive verbal responses*: such as 'He keeps coming back for more.'

- *Non-imitative physical and verbal aggression*: aggressive acts directed at toys other than Bobo, e.g. saying things not said by the model, or were not demonstrated by the model playing with the gun.

Observation techniques

You might think that making observations is easy, but if you tried Activity 16, you should now realise it is difficult, for two main reasons:

1. It is difficult to work out what to record and what not to record.

2. It is difficult to record everything that is happening even if you do select what to record and what not to record.

Observational research, like all research, aims to be objective and rigorous. For this reason, it is necessary to use observational techniques and conduct systematic observations.

Observational systems

One of the hardest aspects of the observational method is deciding how different behaviours should be categorised. This is because our perception of behaviour is often seamless; when we watch somebody perform a particular action, we see a continuous stream of action rather than a series of separate behavioural components.

In order to conduct systematic observations, one needs to break this stream of behaviour up into different categories. A **coding system** (also called a **behaviour checklist**) is constructed when making preliminary observations. What is needed is **operationalisation** – breaking the behaviour being studied into a set of components. For example, when observing infant behaviour, have a list such as smiling, crying, sleeping, etc., or when observing facial expressions, have a list of different expressions as shown on page 68.

The coding system should:

- Be *objective*: the observer should not have to make inferences about the behaviour and should just have to record explicit actions.

- Cover all *possible component behaviour*s and avoid a 'waste basket' category.

- Each category should be *mutually exclusive*, meaning that you should not have to mark two categories at one time.

In **unstructured observations**, the researcher records all relevant behaviour but has no system. The behaviour to be studied is largely unpredictable.

One problem with this is that the behaviours recorded are often those which are most visible or eye-catching to the observer, but these may not necessarily be the most important or relevant behaviours.

In **systematic** or **structured observations**, the researcher uses various 'systems' to organise observations.

- **Research aims** Decide on an area to study.

- **Observational systems** How to record the behaviour you are interested in.

- **Sampling procedures** Who you are observing and when.

Sampling procedures

Continuous observation Record every instance of the behaviour you see in as much detail as possible. This is useful if the behaviours you are interested in do not occur very often.

In many situations continuous observation would not be possible because there would be too much data to record, therefore there must be a systematic method of sampling observations:

- **Event sampling** Counting the number of times a certain behaviour (event) occurs in a target individual or individuals.

- **Time sampling**. Recording behaviours in a given time frame. For example, noting what a target individual is doing every 30 seconds. You may select one or more categories from a checklist.

Activity 17 — Making systematic observations

The coding system below is adapted from one used by Fick (1993) in a study looking at the effects of having a dog as a pet on the nature and frequency of social interactions in nursing home residents.

You can use this shortened version to make observations of other students in a common room or cafeteria. Shortened coding system:

- *Non-attentive behaviour*: Participant is not engaged in group activity.

- *Attentive listening*: Participant maintains eye contact with other group members.

- *Verbal interaction with another person*: Participant initiates or responds verbally to another person.

- *Non-verbal interaction with another person*: Participant touches, gestures, smiles, nods, etc. to another person.

1. Decide on your research aims; e.g. you could compare social interactions in the morning and afternoon, or differences between boys and girls, or between different environments (such as in class and in the cafeteria).

2. State your hypothesis.

3. Draw up a grid to record your observations.

4. Decide on a sampling procedure.

5. Conduct a pilot study.

In **controlled observations**, *it is the participant's environment that is controlled – not the techniques used to obtain observational data.* **Systematic techniques** *are used in* **naturalistic and controlled observations**.

Observational studies

Distinctions

Method and technique
Remember that all research involves making observations; however, in the case of some research, the overall *method* is observational, where the emphasis is on observing a relatively unconstrained segment of a person's freely chosen behaviour.

Controlled and naturalistic
In both cases, systematic methods are used to record observations. In a controlled observation, the environmental variables are controlled to some extent e.g. the setting may be moved from the person's normal environment, or some of the items in the environment may be deliberately chosen.

Participant and non-participant
In many cases, the observer is merely watching the behaviour of others and acts as a non-participant. In some studies, observers also participate, which may affect their objectivity. A classic example of a participant observation is described on the right.

Disclosed and undisclosed (overt and covert)
One-way mirrors are used to prevent participants being aware that they are being observed. This is called undisclosed (covert) observation. Knowing that your behaviour is being observed is likely to alter your behaviour. Observers often try to be as unobtrusive as possible.

Direct and indirect
In many studies, observations are made of data that has already been collected, e.g. observing advertisements on TV to see what gender bias exists, or observing newspaper advertisements or children's books. This is indirect observation (see 'Content analysis on page 69.)

An undisclosed observation: The eve of destruction
In the 1950s, the social psychologist Leon Festinger read a newspaper report about a religious cult that claimed to be receiving messages from outer space predicting that the end of the world would take place on a certain date in the form of a great flood. The cult members were going to be rescued by a flying saucer so they all gathered with their leader. Festinger was intrigued to know how the cult members would respond when they found that their beliefs were unfounded, especially as many of them had made their beliefs very public. In order to observe this at first hand, Festinger and some co-workers posed as converts to the cause and were present on the eve of destruction. When it was apparent that there would be no flood, the group leader said that their prayer had saved the city. Some cult members did not believe this and left the cult, whereas others took this as proof of the cult 's beliefs (Festinger *et al.*, 1956).

Rescue ship for the religious cult who foretold the end of the world.

Devices for managing and recording observations
The raw data gathered in an observational study can come in visual, audio or written form. To assist the collection of data you might use:

- Binoculars, if you are observing from any distance.
- One-way mirrors, for undisclosed observations.
- A video camera, if you want to replay behavioural sequences or observe people in an unobtrusive manner.
- An audio-cassette recorder, again for replaying sequences so they can be coded later.
- Paper for recording data using a coding system. This can be done 'live' or using video/audio-recording.

Analysing observational data
Unstructured observations produce **qualitative** data.

Structured or systematic observations produce numerical data in categories (**quantitative**) that can be analysed using descriptive statistics.

Qs | **33**

1. Identify what kind of observational study was conducted by Festinger *et al.* (described top right).

2. In each of the following observations, state which sampling procedure would be most appropriate and explain how you would do it:
   a. Recording instances of aggressive behaviour in children playing in a school playground.
   b. Vocalisations (words, sounds) made by young children.
   c. Compliance with controlled pedestrian crossings by pedestrians.
   d. Litter-dropping in a public park.
   e. Behaviour of dog owners when walking their dogs.

3. *A group of students decided to study student behaviour in the school library.*
   a. Suggest **one or more** hypotheses that you might investigate.
   b. List **five** behaviours you might include in a behaviour checklist.
   c. Identify a suitable sampling procedure and explain how you would do it.
   d. How could you observe the students so that they were not aware that they were being observed?
   e. What ethical issues might be raised in this observational study?
   f. For each issue identified in your answer to (e), explain how you could deal with this issue and whether this would be acceptable.
   g. Explain in what way this would be a naturalistic observation.
   h. In this study, is observation a method or a technique?

4. *What distinguishes a successful teacher from an unsuccessful one? A group of students decide to observe various teachers while they are teaching.*
   a. Identify **two** ways in which you could operationalise 'successful teaching behaviour'.
   b. Describe **one** way in which you could minimise the intrusive nature of your observations.
   c. How would you record the data in this observational study?
   d. Suggest **one** advantage and **one** disadvantage of conducting an observational study in this context.
   e. Describe **two** ways of ensuring that this study would be carried out in an ethically acceptable manner.
   f. In this study, is observation a method or a technique?

Reliability

Observations should be consistent, which means that two observers should ideally produce the same record. The extent to which two (or more) observers agree is called inter-rater or **inter-observer reliability**. This is measured by correlating the observations of two or more observers (see 'Assessing reliability' below). A general rule is that if (Total agreements) ÷ (Total observations) > 0.80, the data have inter-observer reliability.

Dealing with low reliability

Observers should be trained in the use a coding system/behaviour checklist. They should practise using it and discuss their observations.

Training observers

The Behavioural Observation unit (BEO) at the University of Bern trains people in the use of observational techniques (BEO, 2004). They have a nursery school at the unit where the children can be observed through a one-way mirror. The data collected have been used for various studies such as comparing twins. The unit has devised a coding system (called KaSo 12):

No social participation
1. Occupied alone participation
2. Hanging around alone
3. Alone – onlooker
4. Alone – unclear
Social participation
5. Parallel behaviour 1
6. Parallel behaviour 2
7. Loosely associated but interactive
8. Role play – identifiable
9. Social participation unclear
Not identifiable
10. Child not in view, generally unclear

Validity

External validity

Observational studies are likely to have high **ecological validity** because they involve more natural behaviours (but remember the discussion in Chapter 2 – naturalness does not always mean greater ecological validity).

Population validity may be a problem if, for example, children are observed only in middle-class homes. The findings may not generalise to all children.

Internal validity

Observations will not be valid (or reliable) if the coding system/behaviour checklist is flawed. For example, some observations may belong in more than one category, or some behaviours may not be codeable.

The validity of observations is also affected by **observer bias** – what someone observes is influenced by their expectations. This reduces the objectivity of observations.

Dealing with low validity

Conducting observations in varied settings with varied participants (improves external validity).

Dealing with low reliability (improves internal validity).

Using more than one observer to reduce observer bias and averaging data across observers (balances out any biases).

Assessing reliability

The graph below show observations made of two children in the nursery class using KaSo 12. Each time, three observers were used (blue, red and green lines). The figures represent the relative duration of a specific behaviour category in per cent.

Child 1: Mean correlation of the 3 profiles: r = 0.86.

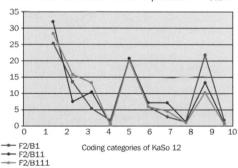

—•— F2/B1
—•— F2/B11
—•— F2/B111
Coding categories of KaSo 12

Child 2: Showing a markedly different distribution of behaviour patterns but an even closer correlation: r = 0.93.

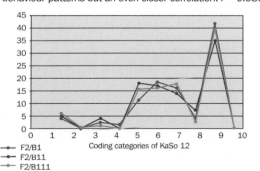

—•— F2/B1
—•— F2/B11
—•— F2/B111
Coding categories of KaSo 12

Ethical issues

In a naturalistic observation, participants may be observed without their **informed consent**.

Some observations may be regarded as an invasion of **privacy**. Participant **confidentiality** should be respected.

The use of one-way mirrors involves **deception**/lack of informed consent.

Dealing with ethical issues

Informed consent: In some cases, it may be possible to obtain informed consent. For example, in the observations of nursery children by the BEO (see below left), parental permission was obtained for all children attending the nursery.

Invasion of privacy: **Ethical guidelines** generally advise that it is acceptable to observe people in public places (places where people expect to be seen by others).

Ethical committees can be used to approve observational designs.

Qs   34

1. On the left are two graphs showing the observations of two children by three observers. Do you think that the graphs indicate an acceptable level of inter-observer reliability?

2. *A psychologist decided to observe the non-verbal behaviours between two people having a conversation. (Non-verbal behaviours are those which do not involve language – such as smiling, touching, etc.)*

   a. Explain why it would be desirable to conduct a pilot study.

   b. If this is to be a naturalistic observation, *where* should the student researchers make their observations?

   c. Each conversation is observed by two students. Identify **one** way in which you could ensure reliability between the different observers and explain how you might put this into practice.

   d. Describe **two** features of the study that might threaten its validity.

   e. Explain how you could deal with these two features that might threaten validity.

   f. Draw a suitable table for recording observations, showing some of the possible categories.

   g. Describe **one** way of ensuring that this study would be carried out in an ethically acceptable manner.

   h. Evaluate your method of dealing with ethics.

KEY TERMS

Improving reliability
Improving validity

OTHER TERMS

Inter-observer reliability
Non-participant observation
Observer bias
Undisclosed observations

Observational studies

Coding systems, categories and rating scales

Using a **coding system** (see right) means that a code is invented to represent each category of behaviour. A **behaviour checklist** is essentially the same thing, although a code may not be given to each behaviour.

A further method is to provide a list of behaviours or characteristics and ask observers to rate each one using a **rating scale** (see below).

Early Child Environment Rating Scale (ECERS) (Harms et al., 1998)

This scale has been used in numerous studies of child development to record observations of a child's early environment. A positive correlation has generally been found between higher scores on ECERS and child development outcomes in areas that are considered to be important for later school success.

The observer rates each of the 43 items on a 7-point scale: 1 (inadequate), 3 (minimal), 5 (good) and 7 (excellent). The 43 items are:

	Space and Furnishings			
1.	Indoor space	22.	Blocks
2.	Furniture for routine care, play and learning	23.	Sand/water
		24.	Dramatic play
3.	Furnishings for relaxation and comfort	25.	Nature/science
4.	Room arrangement for play	26.	Maths/number
5.	Space for privacy	27.	Use of TV, video and/or computers
6.	Child-related display	28.	Promoting acceptance of diversity
7.	Space for gross motor play		**Interaction**
8.	Gross motor equipment	29.	Supervision of gross motor activities
	Personal Care Routines	30.	General supervision of children (other than gross motor)
9.	Greeting/departing	31.	Discipline
10.	Meals/snacks	32.	Staff–child interactions
11.	Nap/rest	33.	Interactions among children
12.	Toileting/diapering		**Programme Structure**
13.	Health practices	34.	Schedule
14.	Safety practices	35.	Free play
	Language-Reasoning	36.	Group time
15.	Books and pictures	37.	Provisions for children with disabilities
16.	Encouraging children to communicate		**Parents and Staff**
17.	Using language to develop reasoning skills	38.	Provisions for parents
		39.	Provisions for personal needs of staff
18.	Informal use of language	40.	Provisions for professional needs of staff
	Activities	41.	Staff interaction and cooperation
19.	Fine motor	42.	Supervision and evaluation of staff
20.	Art	43.	Opportunities for professional growth
21.	Music/movement		

There is an alternative, specification – related observational study on stress behaviour on page 132.

There is an alternative, specification – related observational study on stress behaviour on page 132.

Qs 35

Imagine that you wished to investigate interpersonal deception to see if it was possible to use facial expressions to tell whether or not someone was lying.

1. Describe how you would design a study using observational techniques to investigate this. Record at least six design decisions and describe each one carefully.

2. Would you describe your study as a naturalistic observation, a controlled observation or a natural, field or lab experiment? Explain why.

3. How could same study be done using a different method?

4. What would be the relative advantages of doing this study as a naturalistic observation or as a lab experiment?

Facial Action Coding System (FACS) (Ekman and Friesen, 1978).

Paul Ekman and others have used this coding system to investigate how people display and recognise emotion using non-verbal cues and to study interpersonal deception.

For the full illustrations, see www-2.cs.cmu.edu/afs/cs/project/face/www/facs.htm

Code	Description		
1	Inner brow raiser	26	Jaw Drop
2	*Outer brow raiser	27	Mouth stretch
4	Brow lowerer	28	Lip suck
5	Upper lid raiser	41	Lid droop
6	Cheek raiser	42	Slit
7	Lid tightener	43	Eyes closed
9	Nose wrinkler	44	Squint
10	Upper lip raiser	45	Blink
11	Nasolabial deepener	46	Wink
12	Lip corner puller	51	Head turn left
13	Cheek puffer	52	Head turn right
14	Dimpler	53	Head up
15	Lip corner depressor	54	Head down
16	Lower lip depressor	55	Head tilt left
17	Chin raiser	56	Head tilt right
18	Lip puckerer	57	Head forward
20	Lip stretcher	58	Head back
22	Lip funneler	61	Eyes turn left
23	*Lip tightener	62	Eyes turn right
24	Lip pressor	63	Eyes up
25	Lips part	64	Eyes down

*Outer brow raiser

*Lip tightener

Activity 18 — DIY

Make your own coding system

A number of studies have looked at how males and females are represented in children's books. For example, Crabb and Bielawski (1994) examined American preschool books and found that female characters were more likely to be pictured using household objects, whereas males were more likely to be using production objects (e.g. items related to agriculture, construction, transportation – i.e. work outside the home).

Develop your own coding system to record the way in which males and females are represented in preschool children's books. Start by looking at some children's books and the activities that men and women, boys and girls are engaged in.

Once you have developed a coding system, you may investigate the hypothesis that children's books support gender stereotypes.

Content analysis*

Indirect observations can be made of various media: books, films, TV, CDs, etc. Such observations are 'indirect' because they are observations of the communications produced by people.

The process involved is similar to any observational study:

1. Decisions about a sampling method. (what material to sample and how frequently).
2. Decisions about coding units.

*Note: content analysis is not required in the AQA 'A' AS

An example of content: analysis using lonely hearts ads

Evolutionary psychologists propose that men and women seek different things in a partner because of the basic differences between eggs and sperm. Women produce relatively few eggs, each at a physiological cost, so a female seeks a male partner who has 'resources' (such as being wealthy) to enhance her reproductive success. Men produce millions of sperm and should therefore seek youth and fertility in a partner to enhance the reproductive success of their genes. Features that are regarded as attractive in women are often things that are signs of health and youth (firm breasts, small waist, symmetrical face).

Various studies have analysed the contents of lonely hearts ads to see if what men and women advertise, and also what they seek, fits evolutionary predictions. For example, Waynforth and Dunbar (1995) analysed nearly 900 ads from 400 American newspapers. They looked at three behaviours: individuals seeking resources, seeking attractiveness and offering attractiveness. Age was also taken into account. Some of their findings are shown on page 71.

Naturalistic observation versus natural experiment

Both involve naturally occurring variables that have not been manipulated by the researcher. Both may involve an IV, but in a natural experiment the researcher is measuring a dependent variable (DV).

Qs 36

1. Explain in what way a content analysis is a form of observation.
2. Suggest **one** advantage of doing this kind of research.
3. How might observer bias affect the findings of a content analysis?
4. Identify **one** advantage of a natural experiment as contrasted with a naturalistic observation.
5. Identify **one** advantage of a naturalistic observation as contrasted with a natural experiment.

Advantages ☺ and disadvantages ☹ of
Naturalistic observations

Content analysis

Evaluating naturalistic observations

Advantages

- What people say they do is often different from what they actually do so observations are more valid than questionnaires/interviews.

- The method offers a way to study behaviour when there are objections to manipulating variables, such as arranging for a child to spend time apart from his or her parent.

- Gives a more realistic picture of spontaneous behaviour. It is likely to have high ecological validity.

- A means of conducting preliminary investigations in a new area of research in order to produce hypotheses for future investigations.

Disadvantages

- There can be little or no control of extraneous variables.

- The observer may 'see' what he/she expects to see. This is called observer bias. This bias may mean that different observers 'see' different things, which leads to low **inter-observer reliability**.

- There are a number of ethical problems such as lack of **informed consent** and invasion of **privacy**.

- The method requires observer preparation and training.

Activity 19 — DIY Content analysis

Many studies using content analysis consider the content of advertisements. For example, Lewis and Hill (1998) examined the ads for food that were shown between children's TV shows. They found that over half of the ads shown were for food products, most being for foods of 'dubious' nutritional value. The ads were designed to engage attention (e.g. used animation) and to produce an emotional response.

In order to replicate this study, you should:

1. Design an appropriate coding system/checklist. This might include the following sections, which need to be operationalised:
   - Product, e.g. cereals, sweets, savoury products.
   - Tone of advertisement, e.g. humour, fun, happiness, mood alteration.
   - Central character, e.g. man, woman, boy, girl (could rate these in terms of how 'stereotypical' they are).

2. Other design decisions: decide on when you will sample the ads, for how long and using what sampling method.

3. Divide the class to cover different channels, times and days.

4. Display your findings using one or more graphs.

37

Task 1

On the right are a variety of graphs. For each one, identify the type of graph and describe one or more conclusions that could be drawn from the graph.

Task 2

A psychology class conduct a study on memory. Each student does a memory test first thing in the morning and then again in the afternoon. The table below shows how many items they got correct each time.

Student	1	2	3	4	5	6	7	8	9	10
Morning test	18	20	17	16	19	22	21	19	15	13
Afternoon test	20	18	15	12	18	20	16	16	17	14

(a) Calculate the mean, median, mode and range for each data set.

(b) What measure of central tendency would be most suitable to use to describe this data? Explain your answer.

(c) What measure of dispersion would be most suitable to use to describe this data? Explain your answer.

(d) Draw both a histogram and a scattergraph to represent the data from this study.

(e) From studying your graphs, what conclusions could you draw about this data?

Task 3

In this book, we have covered seven methods of research. Now let's see what you can remember!

When writing about strengths and weaknesses, try as far as possible to state a strength/weakness that is particular to the method, not one that could be applied to any method.

Research method	Two strengths	Two weaknesses	Two possible ethical issues
Lab experiment			
Field experiment			
Natural experiment			
Questionnaire			
Interview			
Investigation using a correlational analysis			
Naturalistic observation			

Task 4

You may recall that, right at the beginning of the book, there was a note on how learning about research methods was a bit like learning a foreign language – you have to learn a new set of words and what they mean. The best way to do this is to *use* your new language. The exercises throughout this book were intended to help you do this.

Write down now all the new words you have learned (those you can remember) and then check through your Research Methods Booklet to see what words you have forgotten. You might also check to see which terms were commonly forgotten. In fact, there's lots of scope for further analysis!

You might work with a partner and, when you have finished, get another pair to check your list. See who in the class can correctly identify the most terms. You could even record the results in a bar chart!

Task 5

Test a friend on the key terms (or other terms). Read out a definition and see whether your friend can give the right term, You can do this using your AQA student workbook or the glossary at the end of this book. Or you can even make a game by constructing cards with the definitions on one side and the term on the reverse. (See 'Supplementary materials' on the Nelson Thornes website (www.nelsonthornes.com/researchmethods) for a Word file of the glossary.)

Task 6

Now that you have (just about) finished research methods, you could look back to the topic you found most challenging. To help you understand this better, create something memorable (for you and your class mates). It could be a PowerPoint® presentation, a mobile, a poster for your classroom, a cartoon strip, a poem or even a rap.

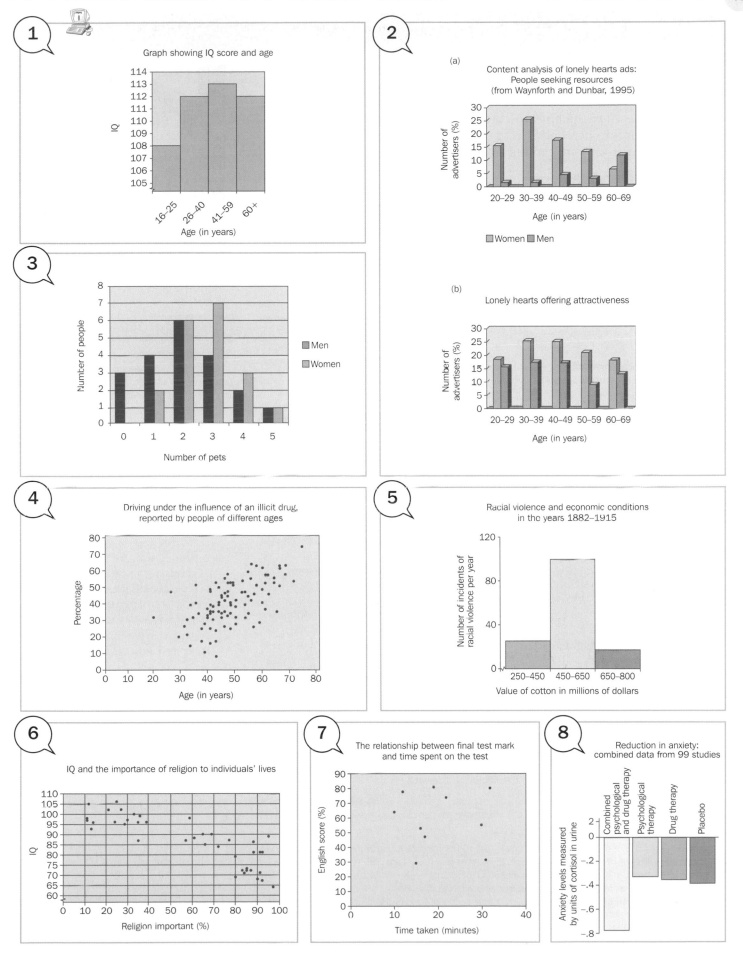

1

Graph showing IQ score and age

2

(a) Content analysis of lonely hearts ads:
People seeking resources
(from Waynforth and Dunbar, 1995)

Women ■ Men

3

(b) Lonely hearts offering attractiveness

4

Driving under the influence of an illicit drug,
reported by people of different ages

5

Racial violence and economic conditions
in the years 1882–1915

6

IQ and the importance of religion to individuals' lives

7

The relationship between final test mark
and time spent on the test

8

Reduction in anxiety:
combined data from 99 studies

A few other things

This book (and the AS specification) only covers some of the research methods and some of the designs that are used by psychologists. On this page, we will very briefly mention some other methods and designs. These are the ones you are likely to encounter when you read about research in psychology, and it is useful to know something about them and their plus and minus points.

Cross-cultural study

Psychologists quite often compare behaviours in different cultures and make comparisons across cultures. This is a way of seeing whether cultural practices affect behaviour. It is a kind of **natural experiment** in which the IV is, for example, child-rearing techniques in different cultures and the DV is some behaviour, such as attachment. This enables researchers to see if the DV is due to child-rearing techniques.

☹ There are many limitations to such studies. For example, researchers may use tests or procedures that have been developed in the US and are not valid in the other culture. This may make the individuals in the other culture appear 'abnormal' or inferior. The term that is used to describe this is an *imposed etic* – when a technique or psychological test is used in one culture even though it was designed for use in another culture.

☹ A second limitation is that the group of participants may not be representative of that culture, yet we make generalisations about the whole culture – or even the whole country.

38

In each of the following, identify the research method and, where relevant, the research technique(s) or design.

1. Scores from a questionnaire 'How good is your memory' are related to GCSE results.

2. A male or female confederate stands by the roadside with broken-down car to see if people are more likely to help a male or female.

3. Psychology A level results from two classes are compared to see if Teacher A's teaching style was better than that of Teacher B.

4. Children are shown two films: one that shows a child being helpful and another that shows a child not being helpful. They then are given free play time to see if they are more helpful.

5. Students are asked to explain what methods they find most successful for revision.

6. Interactions between first-time mothers and their newborn babies are compared with the interactions of mothers having a second baby.

7. A study on gambling is based around the experiences of one individual.

Longitudinal and cross-sectional designs

When the same participants are studied repeatedly over a long period of time, a study is said to have a **longitudinal design** (it's long!). Such studies aim to be able to observe long-term effects and make comparisons between the same individual at different ages.

An alternative way to do this (which takes a lot less time) is to use a **cross-sectional design**. In this design, one group of participants of a young age are compared with another, older group of participants at the same moment in time.

☹ The problem with a cross-sectional study is that the two groups of participants may be quite different. The **participant variables** in a cross-sectional design are not controlled in the same way that they are not controlled in an independent groups design (in fact a cross-sectional design is an **independent groups design**, and a longitudinal design is a **repeated measures design**). This means that, in a cross-sectional design, differences between groups may be due to participant variables rather than the IV.

In Zimbardo's classic study of obedience and conformity, participants were required to play the roles of prisoners or guards (Zimbardo *et al.*, 1973).

Role Play

In some investigations, participants are told to take on a certain role and their behaviour can then be observed as if it were real life. For example, they might be asked to imagine that they are lying, or to pretend that they are a prison guard. This is a form of **controlled observational study**.

☺ This enables researchers to control certain variables so real-life behaviour can be studied that might otherwise be impractical or unethical to observe.

☹ The question is whether people really do act as they would in real life. In Zimbardo's study, the participants acting as guards might have been following what they *thought* was guard-like behaviour, as seen in films. If they had been real-life guards, they might have acted more in accordance with personal principles rather than according to social norms.

Case study

A case study is a research investigation that involves the detailed study of a single individual, institution or event.

☺ Case studies concern unique individuals or cases. The opportunity to study one case permits us to record rich details of human experience.

☹ It is, however, difficult to generalise from such individual cases and hard to uncover what did actually happen in the past.

OTHER TERMS

Case study
Cross-cultural study
Cross-sectional design
Longitudinal design
Role play

Multiple choice questions

1. **Observation is a**
   a. Research method.
   b. Research technique.
   c. Form of experiment.
   d. Both a and b.

2. **The key feature of a naturalistic observation is that**
   a. No set categories are used to record behaviour.
   b. Behaviour is observed.
   c. There is an IV.
   d. Everything has been left as it normally is.

3. **A coding system is a method used in observational research for**
   a. Sampling behaviours.
   b. Making systematic observations.
   c. Analysing the findings.
   d. All of the above.

4. **Which of the following is *not* a method of sampling observations?**
   a. Continuous observation.
   b. Event sampling.
   c. Microscopic sampling.
   d. Time sampling.

5. **Event sampling involves**
   a. Noting what a target individual is doing every 30 seconds.
   b. Keeping a count of each time a target behaviour occurs.
   c. Making notes on all behaviours that occur.
   d. Noting what everyone is doing at a point in time.

6. **A disclosed observation is where**
   a. Observers do not participate in the study.
   b. Observers are also participants in the study.
   c. Participants know they are being observed.
   d. Participants do not know they are being observed.

7. **When observations are made from data in a newspaper, this is called**
   a. Direct observation.
   b. Indirect observation.
   c. Content analysis.
   d. Both b and c.

8. **The reliability of observations may be affected by:**
   a. Lack of agreement between several observers when observing the same thing.
   b. Lack of agreement between observations made by one observer on several occasions.
   c. Lack of agreement between several observers when observing different things.
   d. Both a and b.

9. **The validity of observations may be affected by**
   a. Observer bias.
   b. Low inter-observer reliability.
   c. Limited sample of participants.
   d. All of the above.

10. **Low reliability can be dealt with by**
    a. Using more than one observer.
    b. Conducting observations in varied settings with varied participants.
    c. Training observers to use the coding system.
    d. Both a and b.

11. **Low validity can be dealt with by**
    a. Using more than one observer.
    b. Conducting observations in varied settings with varied participants.
    c. Training observers to use the coding system.
    d. Both a and b.

12. **Inter-observer reliability is the extent to which**
    a. Two or more observers produce the same observations.
    b. Observers are not biased in the judgements they make.
    c. Observers do not drop out during an observational study.
    d. Both a and b.

13. **Which of the following ethical issues is *not* likely to be a problem in a naturalistic observation?**
    a. Informed consent.
    b. Privacy
    c. Confidentiality.
    d. Protection from psychological harm.

14. **Which of the following is *not* a weakness of a naturalistic observation?**
    a. Provides a less realistic picture of behaviour.
    b. Data are difficult to collect.
    c. Cannot investigate cause and effect.
    d. The method requires careful training.

15. **Role play is a kind of**
    a. Naturalistic observation.
    b. Controlled observation.
    c. Field experiment.
    d. Natural experiment.

16. **A case study may concern**
    a. A single individual.
    b. An institution.
    c. An event.
    d. All of the above.

17. **Longitudinal design is like**
    a. A repeated measures design.
    b. An independent groups design.
    c. A matched pairs design.
    d. Counterbalancing.

18. **Which of the following is a non-experimental research method?**
    a. Naturalistic observation.
    b. Interview.
    c. Investigation using correlational analysis.
    d. All of the above.

19. **Which method makes it easier to obtain data from a large sample?**
    a. Experiment.
    b. Questionnaire.
    c. Naturalistic observation.
    d. All of the above.

20. **Which of the following has an IV and a DV?**
    a. Experiment.
    b. Questionnaire.
    c. Naturalistic observation.
    d. Investigation using a correlational analysis.

Answers are on page 77

Exam-style question 7

A dental school was interested to find out what factors might reduce anxiety in dental patients. In one study, the focus was on anxiety level before the patients even got to see the dentist – looking at how the waiting room environment might affect anxiety. For example, some dentists have fish tanks in their waiting rooms, whereas others play soft music to help patients feel less anxious.

A naturalstic observation was designed involving a number of different dental practices. In each practice, observations were made of how anxious each patient was. These observations were recorded by the dental receptionist so that the participants were not aware that they were being observed. The observations were used to produce an anxiety score.

Some of the findings are shown in the graph below.

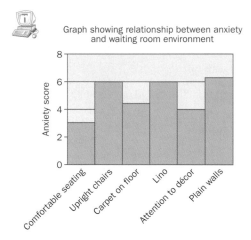

Graph showing relationship between anxiety and waiting room environment

(a) Explain why it is a good idea to carry out a pilot study when doing a naturalistic observation. (3 marks)

(b) Explain why it was important that the participants were not aware that they were being observed. (2 marks)

(c) Explain what is meant by validity. (2 marks)

(d) (i) Describe **two** factors that could affect the validity of this study. (2 marks + 2 marks)

(ii) Explain how you could deal with one of these factors. (2 marks)

(e) (i) Identify the kind of graph that was used to display the findings. (1 mark)

(ii) What conclusion could you draw from the graph? (2 marks)

(f) Explain the difference between a naturalistic observation and an experiment. (3 marks)

(g) (i) Describe the aim(s) of this study. (2 marks)

(ii) The researchers decide to conduct an experiment to investigate the same aims. Write a suitable operationalised experimental hypothesis. (2 marks)

(iii) What experimental design would you use in this experiment? (1 mark)

(iv) Using the design identified in (iii), outline the procedures that could be used for this experiment. (6 marks)

Examiner's tips for answering this question

(a) The question does not specify 'one' reason so you can give several reasons if you wish – bearing in mind that three marks are available for this question. Equally, however, you do not need to write too much.

(b) Your answer needs to be contextualised – although it would be difficult to see how you could avoid doing this!

(c) This is one of those straightforward 'definition' questions in which no context is required – although you can always use context as a means of providing detail.

(d) (i) Don't overlook the fact that 'two' factors are required.

(d) (ii) Make it clear which factor you are dealing with, otherwise the examiner will presume it is the first factor.

(e) (i) It is obviously not a scattergraph, but is it a bar chart or a histogram?

(e) (ii) The question requires only one conclusion for 2 marks so keep your answer fairly brief but do include *some* detail and do provide a conclusion and not just a finding (although it is OK to start with a finding and say '*This suggests that …*').

(f) This is not that simple a question. You must address the question of 'difference' rather than just defining both terms. One way to do this might be to dcfine the terms and then point out the difference. The word 'one' is not used so you may explain the distinction by referring to several differences.

(g) (i) The aims can virtually be lifted from the stimulus material – but make sure you are writing aims and not a hypothesis.

(g) (ii) You may write a directional or non-directional hypothesis.

(g) (iii) It's **RIM** again! Any of the three answers would be acceptable.

(g) (iv) Having identified your experimental design in (iii), you would get zero marks in (iv) if you used a different design.

This part of the question is worth 6 marks so ensure that you spend sufficient time on your answer. Think about all the different aspects of experimental design that you have studied.

Exam-style question 8

A group of psychology students were interested in non-verbal behaviour and decided to conduct a naturalistic observation of people's behaviour when chatting up the opposite sex, i.e. 'flirting behaviour'. They decided to observe the body signals of women when they were talking to a man. To do this, each member of the class had the task of locating a target individual in a suitable public place (such as a pub or club) and observing the woman's behaviour for 10 minutes.

(a) Describe **two** advantages of a naturalistic observation.

(2 marks + 2 marks)

(b) (i) Identify the method used to select participants in this study.

(1 mark)

    (ii) Name **one** other method of selecting participants.   (1 mark)

    (iii) Describe **one** disadvantage of the method identified in part (i) in the context of this study.   (2 marks)

(c) Identify **two** methods of operationalising 'flirting behaviour'.

(1 mark + 1 mark)

(d) Explain how you would collect the data for this study.   (3 marks)

(e) (i) What is meant by reliability?   (2 marks)

    (ii) Identify **one** way in which you could check the reliability between the different observers, and explain how you might put this into practice.   (3 marks)

(f) Describe **one** way in which you could minimise the intrusive nature of your observations.   (2 marks)

(g) Explain **two** features of the study that might affect the validity of the data being collected.   (2 marks + 2 marks)

(h) (i) Identify **one** way in which the students ensured that this study would be carried out in an ethically acceptable manner.

(1 mark)

    (ii) Describe **one** limitation to this approach.   (2 marks)

    (iii) Name **one** other ethical issue that might arise in this study and explain how you would deal with this.   (3 marks)

Examiner's tips for answering this question

(a) It is more usual to be asked for one advantage and one disadvantage of a research method or design, but you could be asked for 'two'. Remember that, when giving advantages (or disadvantages), it is important to try to state advantages of this method in comparison to other methods as far as possible.

(b) (i) Notice that you are asked for a method of selecting participants and not of selecting observations.

(b) (ii) Given the question for part (iii), you might think carefully about what answer to use in part (ii).

(b) (iii) Again remember to explain any comparative terms such as 'longer' – longer than what?

(c) Instead of being asked to explain what is meant by the term operationalisation, you are required to use your knowledge of the term to answer the question. Anything is OK as long as you show an understanding of 'operations' (which would form the basis of a coding system or a behaviour checklist).

(d) Here is your chance to write about sampling/selecting observations, as well as any other considerations you can think of. You need to write 3 marks' worth, but don't write too much.

Note that you need to say what you would do; there is no credit for explaining *why*.

(e) (i) No context is required here.

(e) (ii) Note that there are two parts to this question, although one statement may answer both parts.

(f) Disguising yourself as a table would clearly be unrealistic, but any realistic answer would be given credit.

(g) There are a large number of possible answers here – they could be related to internal or external validity. Start with the definition of validity in your head and then work out what may threaten this.

(h) (i) There is a clue in the stimulus material.

(h) (ii) It is legitimate for you to be asked about advantages/disadvantages or strengths/limitations of any area of research methods – such questions are asking why instead of how.

(h) (iii) Like question (e) (ii), this question has two parts. Candidates often lose marks because they do not provide sufficient detail of how they would deal with ethical issues (what they would actually *do*).

Model answer for question 7

(a) Explain why it is a good idea to carry out a pilot study when doing a naturalistic observation. (3 marks)

Doing a pilot study means you can check your design and make improvements if you see there are problems. In an observational study, you can try out a behaviour checklist to see if it works and you might see if the receptionist can use the coding system without it being too obvious.

(b) Explain why it was important that the participants were not aware that they were being observed. (2 marks)

If participants know they are being watched, then they may behave in a different way.

(c) Explain what is meant by validity. (2 marks)

Validity refers to the legitimacy of a study and includes both internal validity (the extent to which you are measuring what you intended to measure) and external validity (the extent to which the findings can be generalised).

(d) (i) Describe **two** factors that could affect the validity of this study. (2 marks + 2 marks)

The data collected might not be valid because of the coding system that was used; it may have missed out some categories of behaviour.

Or it might be that the observers were not sufficiently trained, and therefore the data they collected were not consistent.

(ii) Explain how you could deal with one of these factors. (2 marks)

The coding system could be checked in a pilot study to make sure that valid data are collected.

(e) (i) Identify the kind of graph that was used to display the findings. (1 mark)

A bar chart.

(ii) What conclusion could you draw from the graph? (2 marks)

It appears that people feel less anxious in more comfortable surroundings (e.g. easy chairs and carpets).

(f) Explain the difference between a naturalistic observation and an experiment. (3 marks)

In a naturalistic observation, you are not investigating a causal relationship so the effects of the IV on the DV are not observed , whereas they are in an experiment. Also, in a naturalistic observation everything is left as it normally is, whereas this is not true in experiments where some control is exerted, even in a natural experiment.

(g) (i) Describe the aim(s) of this study. (2 marks)

The aim was to see if the décor of a dentist's waiting room was related to anxiety levels.

(ii) The researchers decide to conduct an experiment to investigate the same aims. Write a suitable operationalised experimental hypothesis. (2 marks)

Waiting rooms that are nicely decorated produce lower anxiety than poorly decorated waiting rooms.

(iii) What experimental design would you use in this experiment? (1 mark)

Repeated measures.

(iv) Using the design identified in (iii), outline the procedures that could be used for this experiment. (6 marks)

I would identify a suitable group of participants using an opportunity sampling method – I'd just use some participants who happened to be in a dentist's waiting room. I would assess their anxiety levels (the DV) and then I would get them to sit in a different (less attractive room) and again assess their anxiety levels.

In order to avoid an order effect, I would counterbalance the conditions so that some participants started in the less attractive room and had the more attractive room second, and vice versa for the other participants.

I would also consider the ethical issue of lack of informed consent (because you couldn't tell them beforehand), so I would fully debrief them after they had seen the dentist.

Examiner's comments

(a) The answer must be contextualised, and this answer starts out talking about pilot studies in general. Fortunately, the second sentence places the answer in context.

(b) This answer is sufficiently clear for 2 marks. An answer worth 1 mark might simply say, 'It would change behaviour.'

(c) This is really a 3-mark answer that the candidate might have had ready in case the question was worth 3 marks. It might take longer to edit the answer than simply writing the longer answer – but even the definition of internal validity alone is worth 2 marks.

(d) (i) If the candidate had simply written 'because of the coding system', this would only get 1 mark because there would be insufficient detail. The second factor is related to inter-observer reliability, which affects validity.

(d) (ii) There is no penalty for making the same point twice (here and in part (a)).

(e) (i) It is a bar chart because there is no true zero on the horizontal axis and the data are in categories and not continuous.

(e) (ii) Note that the conclusion is about 'people' and not 'participants', and it is a general statement rather than a note of particular findings – although some particular findings have been included for extra detail.

(f) This is a lengthy answer, more than necessary, but it does show that it would be permissible to describe more than one difference.

(g) (ii) You must make sure you operationalise the IV and DV for the full 2 marks. Just saying 'Different waiting rooms produce different anxiety levels' (a non-directional hypothesis) would only get 1 mark.

(g) (iii) It might make better sense to use an independent groups design.

(g) (iv) Various aspects of design have beendiscussed as appropriate for a 6-mark question. Other considerations might have been the control of extraneous variables, the method of assessing the DV and how you would decorate the different rooms (the IV).

Model answer for question 8

Examiner's comments

(a) Describe **two** advantages of a naturalistic observation.

(2 marks + 2 marks)

One advantage is that you can study things in a more natural setting where people behave as they would in real life. A second advantage is that people often don't behave as they think they *do*, so observing them gives a more realistic picture.

(b) (i) Identify the method used to select participants in this study. (1 mark)

Opportunity sample.

(ii) Name **one** other method of selecting participants. (1 mark)

Random sample.

(iii) Describe **one** disadvantage of the method identified in part (i) in the context of this study. (2 marks)

A disadvantage in this study would be that you would only get a certain kind of person – the people who go to discos.

(c) Identify **two** methods of operationalising 'flirting behaviour'.

(1 mark + 1 mark)

Lowering eyes, body facing towards the man.

(d) Explain how you would collect the data for this study. (3 marks)

The students need to agree on a sampling method, such as event sampling, where they draw up a list of behaviours and keep a count of each time they see the behaviour over the set time period. The list would be on a piece of paper.

(e) (i) What is meant by reliability? (2 marks)

Reliability refers to the consistency of measurements, within a set of measurements (internal) or between them (external).

(ii) Identify **one** way in which you could check the reliability between the different observers, and explain how you might put this into practice. (3 marks)

You could calculate the extent of inter-observer reliability, which you would do by collecting the observations from two or more observers who had used the same coding system and correlating their answers.

(f) Describe **one** way in which you could minimise the intrusive nature of your observations. (2 marks)

You could work out a coding system with numbers, so you just note down a number for every observation so that it could be done without much fuss.

(g) Explain **two** features of the study that might affect the validity of the data being collected. (2 marks + 2 marks)

1. If participants knew they were being observed, they wouldn't behave naturally.

2. If the observers couldn't properly see the people they were observing, they might not make an accurate record of what was happening.

(h) (i) Identify **one** way in which the students ensured that this study would be carried out in an ethically acceptable manner. (1 mark)

They chose to conduct the observations in a public place, which means they weren't invading privacy.

(ii) Describe **one** limitation to this approach. (2 marks)

Even though it is a public place, people may not think it is acceptable for a psychology student to note down their behaviour.

(iii) Name **one** other ethical issue that might arise in this study and explain how you would deal with this. (3 marks)

Informed consent could also be a problem. This could be dealt with by debriefing participants after making the observations and asking them if they would like to withhold their data.

Examiner's comments

(a) The advantages are similar but sufficiently different. If the first answer was just '*study things in a more natural setting*', this would only get 1 mark because it is too general and applies to many other research methods. The second part of the answer provides more detail – although it still applies to, for example, a natural experiment. However, for 2 marks this is sufficient.

(b) (ii) Any sampling method other than 'opportunity' would *not* be acceptable.

(b) (iii) The answer is contextualised. If you just gave a disadvantage of opportunity sampling, you would only get 1 mark.

(c) Any behaviour related to 'flirting' that is relatively easy to observe would be creditworthy – but saying '*The girl appears to be thinking she likes the boy*'' would not be acceptable because it is not observable.

(d) A clear and detailed answer focusing on how not why.

(e) (i) Saying 'consistency' on its own is sufficient for 1 mark.

(e) (ii) You do not have to give the precise details of how inter-observer reliability is calculated but just explain how you would get the data to do this.

(f) You would be credited with any answer that reduced how likely it was that the participants would notice your presence, such as saying that '*I'd sit with a friend appearing to be deeply engaged in conversation.*'

(g) These answers are sufficiently detailed for 2 marks.

(h) (i) This was the obvious ethical consideration mentioned in the stimulus material.

(h) (ii) Another limitation would be that justifying privacy does not overcome confidentiality.

(h) (iii) Remember that debriefing is not an issue – lack of informed consent is the issue.

1d	2d	3b	4c	5b	6c	7d	8d	9d	10c
11d	12a	13d	14a	15b	16d	17a	18d	19d	20a

Contents

pages 80–81

Selecting a topic

Designing the study (including the project brief)

Collecting data

Writing the report

Possible ways to justify your choice of test

An abbreviated version of the coursework marking scheme

pages 82–87

Example 1: The matching hypothesis

Grade A example of coursework with examiner's comments

pages 88–93

Example 2: Conformity

Grade C example of coursework with examiner's comments

pages 94–98

Inferential statistics:

Chi-square

The sign test

Spearman's rank correlation test

The Mann–Whitney U test

The Wilcoxon matched pairs signed ranks test

Coursework

There are three guiding principles in producing your coursework:

1. Marks are awarded only for the report, not for the time spent designing and conducting it.

2. Simple projects are more likely to get full marks. This is because simple projects produce simple data that can be easily analysed and discussed.

3. You want to get full marks. The coursework is worth 15% of your final A level mark. This is potentially a gift from the exam board because you can get nearly all the marks if you listen to advice.

Where do you begin?

Selecting a topic

Don't just dream up a hypothesis. Your starting point should be looking at previous research in a particular area. Such research (theories and/or studies) should enable you to select a possible hypothesis to test.

Your project should ideally be related to the sub-sections you are studying (so you get a double benefit from the work). You are required to choose a topic on the specification, but research design is on the specification therefore it is acceptable to do any experiment, questionnaire, etc.

Your teacher may select the topic and do most of the design. In this case, you lose 3 marks for A1 (see the marking scheme on page 81). The only gain (other than immense personal satisfaction) from designing the project yourself is these 3 marks. Candidates who design their own research often lose marks in other parts of the report so, overall, gain little in terms of exam credit. If you have genuinely adapted a previous study (changed not just the stimulus material but some aspect of the design), you may get 3 marks for A1.

If you have designed the project (or adapted an existing study) with a small group of students, you get 2 marks for A1, and just 1 mark if a teacher has advised you about your design.

You are allowed to work in a group of up to four people and share your data (without losing any marks), **but you must write your reports individually**. You are, however, permitted to pool your data with more than four researchers, but then you get zero for A1 and zero for A2 (a total loss of 6 marks)

Designing your own study

If you are keen to design your own study, remember the following:

- Do not re-invent the wheel. You can still get the full 3 marks for A1 if you *adapt* a previous design.
- Make sure you show the project brief to your teacher before you start to collect the data.

Collecting data

In a repeated measures design 12 participants are usually sufficient, and for an independent groups design 24 participants are a minimum.

It may be helpful to record any comments made by participants when they are debriefed because such qualitative data may be relevant to the discussion you write in the report.

Writing the report

In the following section, we look at two reports: one a grade A report (full marks on all sections, see pages 82–87), the other a grade C report, see pages 88–93. The grade A report is annotated with instructions about what should be included and how the report is marked. You do not need full marks for a grade A but a loss of about 8 marks might result in a grade B. The grade C report has a coursework moderator's comments about where marks were lost.

Designing the study

- Select a method (e.g. field experiment, naturalistic observation) and design (e.g. repeated measures).
- Identify potential problems (e.g. bias and confounding variables).
- Identify ethical issues and consider how you will deal with them.
- Decide on a method of sampling.
- Consider what apparatus and/or materials will be necessary. Can you adapt these from material used in previous studies or will you have to design them yourself?
- Write down the standardised procedures and standardised instructions (briefing and debriefing).
- Consider conducting a small pilot study.
- Choose an inferential test beforehand. Any of the tests below will be acceptable, depending on your design and data. Tests designed for ordinal data are recommended and can be used with any data.

| Design/data | Non-parametric | | Parametric |
	Nominal data	Ordinal data	Interval data
Correlation/association	Chi-square (see page 94)	Spearman's (see page 96)	Pearson's
Independent samples	Chi-square	Mann–Whitney (see page 97)	Independent *t*-test
Repeated measures (including matched pairs)	Sign test (see page 95)	Wilcoxon (see page 98)	Related *t*-test

Possible ways to justify your choice of test

In the results section of the report, you are required to justify your choice of inferential test. Below are a variety of possible justifications for your choice of inferential test. In each case, full reference to the data has been made as well as mentioning other important criteria for deciding which test to use.

If you use chi-square

As the data have been put into **categories**, they are classified as **nominal data**. The results are *independent* in each cell, and the *expected* frequencies in each cell are greater than 4. The appropriate inferential test to use is therefore a chi-square test.

If you use the sign test

A test of difference is required because the hypothesis predicts a **difference** between the two groups. The data are **nominal** because they are just yes/no*. This means we should use the sign test.

If you use Spearman's rho

A test of correlation is needed as the hypothesis predicted a **correlation**. The data involved ratings made by participants and these are **ordinal data***. This means we should use a non-parametric test so Spearman's rho is chosen.

If you use Mann–Whitney

A test of *difference* is required because the hypothesis predicts there will be a **difference** between the two groups. The design is **independent groups**, and the data were scores on a test* (**ordinal data**). Therefore the Mann–Whitney test is suitable (test of difference, independent groups, non-parametric).

If you use Wilcoxon

A test of *difference* is required because the hypothesis predicts there will be a **difference** between the two conditions. The design is **repeated measures** as all participants were tested* more than once. The data were reaction times, which are **interval data*** (a true zero), but it is acceptable to use a non-parametric test with such data so a Wilcoxon test was chosen.

*You must fill in a description of your own data.

An abbreviated version of the coursework mark scheme

Project brief

PB1	**Statement of hypothesis**	**PB2**	**Explanation of direction of hypothesis**	**PB3**	**Identification of research design/method**
	No marks given here	1	Appropriate explanation	1	Correctly identified
		0	Inappropriate	0	None or wrongly identified

PB4	**Identification of advantage(s) and disadvantage(s) of chosen research method**	**PB5**	**Identification of bias/confounding variables**	**PB6**	**Explanation of plans for control of bias/confounding variables**
2	Strengths and weaknesses identified	2	Identified and relevant to study	2	Full explanation of procedures (in context)
1	Partially identified	1	An attempt to identify some relevant sources	1	Partial explanation
0	None or incorrect	0	Inappropriate or incorrect	0	Ineffective or missing

PB7	**Statistical significance**	**PB8**	**Identification of ethical considerations**
1	Suitable	3	Issues fully identified and suitable steps to deal with issues
0	Unsuitable	2	Some issues identified and suitable steps
		1	Possible issues identified but inadequate steps
		0	Issues identified are inappropriate or absent

Report

A1	**Implementation: candidate's contribution**	**A2**	**Implementation: design decisions**	**B**	**Abstract**
3	An individual, original design/adaptation	3	Appropriate and competent	3	Clear, concise, covers aims/methods/ results/conclusions
2	Small group, original design/adaptation	2	Appropriate, minor exceptions	2	Fair, key points covered but some lack of clarity or conciseness
1	With teacher support	1	Weakly applied	1	Lacking clarity, minimal information
0	No student input	0	Inappropriate	0	None or inappropriate

C1	**Psychological literature**	**C2**	**Aims/hypothesis: formulation**	**C3**	**Aims/hypotheses: statement**
5	Relevant, concise, carefully selected	3	Clear, logical progression	2	Easily testable, clear
4	Relevant, concise, minor omission/lack of selectivity/coherence carefully, selected but some omissions	2	Some logical progression	1	Lacked clarity or difficult to test
3	Relevant but some omissions lacked selectivity	1	Partial/Inadequate progression	0	Incorrect/missing
2	Important omissions	0	No logical progression		
1	Minimal support				
0	No support				

D	**Reporting of method**	**E1**	**Results: techniques**	**E2**	**Results: presentation**
4	Full replication possible	4	Appropriate, fully justified, significance given/explained	4	Precise and clear
3	Replication reasonable, sufficient detail for replication	3	Substantially appropriate, no reference to data	3	Precise and clear, with minor exceptions
2	Replication difficult, lacking detail	2	Partially appropriate/justified, significance given	2	Some deficiencies
1	Replication very difficult, fundamental omissions	1	Minimal use/justification, inappropriate significance	1	Serious deficiencies
0	Replication impossible, information lacking	0	Inappropriate/absent	0	Irrelevant/incorrect

F1	**Discussion: explanation of findings**	**F2**	**Discussion: background research/ theory**	**F3**	**Discussion: limitations and modifications**
3	Appropriate, coherent	3	Thorough discussion	3	Most mentioned and appropriate
2	Appropriate, coherent with minor exceptions	2	Reasonably coherent discussion	2	Some limitations and modifications
1	Lacking appropriateness and/or coherence	1	Limited discussion	1	Partial awareness, occasional limitations/modifications
0	None made/irrelevant	0	None/irrelevant/incorrect	0	None/inappropriate

F4	**Discussion: implications and suggestions**	**G**	**References**	**H**	**Report style**
3	Appropriate, discussed thoroughly	2	Full, in conventional manner	3	Concise, logical, good quality of language
2	Some, discussed reasonably coherently	1	In conventional manner but omissions	2	Scientific style, logical structure, adequate expression of ideas
1	Appropriate suggestion and/or limited implication	0	None or none meeting normal conventions	1	Lacked structure, inappropriate scientific style, poor expression of ideas
0	None/irrelevant			0	Little psychological basis

COURSEWORK

Example 1: The matching hypothesis

Grade A project: The project brief

**PSYCHOLOGY
PROJECT BRIEF
PROPOSAL FORM**

Title of work
Matching hypothesis

PB1: Identify the aims of the research and state the experimental/alternative
hypothesis/es. *(credited in the report mark scheme)*
Aim: To replicate the work of Murstein (1972) on the theory of the
matching hypothesis.
Alternative hypothesis: There is a positive correlation in the
attractiveness ratings given to the partners in a long-standing romantic
relationship.

PB2: Explain why a directional or non-directional experimental/alternative
hypothesis/es has been selected. *(1 mark)*
A directional hypothesis was chosen because past research suggests
that there will be a positive correlation.

PB3: Identify the chosen research method (experimental, survey, observation
or correlational research) and, if appropriate, the design used. *(1 mark)*
This was a correlational study.

PB4: Identify the advantage(s) and disadvantage(s) of the chosen research
method and/or design. *(2 marks)*
Advantage: This method allows you to investigate variables that cannot
be directly manipulated.
Disadvantage: Does not demonstrate cause-and-effect relationships.

PB5: Identify potential sources of bias in the investigation and any possible
confounding variables. *(2 marks)*
Researcher bias: It could be that the researcher makes unconscious
suggestions to participants about what scores to give the photographs.
Participant bias: Boys may be reluctant to give high ratings to
photographs of men.

PB6: Explain what procedures will be adopted to deal with these. *(2 marks)*
Researcher bias could be dealt with by giving all participants
standardized instructions to read so they do not interact with the
researcher.
Participant bias could be dealt with by asking participants to rate only
opposite-sex photographs.

PB7: Select an appropriate level of statistical significance to be reached
before the experimental/alternative hypothesis will be retained. *(1 mark)*
5%

PB8: Identify any relevant ethical issues and discuss steps to be taken to deal
with these. *(3 marks)*
Informed consent: It will not be possible to inform participants of the true
aims of the study beforehand, but they will be debriefed afterwards, given
this information and offered the right to withdraw their data. They will be
informed beforehand what the task involves (judging photos for
attractiveness).

Deception: It is felt that this is acceptable as no harm is involved and the
deception is minor.

Privacy: The photographs that are used will be taken from magazines. This
is presumed not to be an invasion of privacy because people have agreed
to place their photographs in the public domain.

The hypothesis gets no marks here. It receives credit in the report.

It is not appropriate simply to restate the direction, i.e. 'The hypothesis is directional because I have said which direction the results will go in.' This is a description rather than an explanation of the direction.

The question is why you have used a directional rather than a non-directional hypothesis. The answer is usually because previous research (theory and/or studies) has suggested the findings will occur in the stated direction.

If you use a non-directional hypothesis, it is acceptable to say that previous research has been inconclusive.

If you have used an experimental *method*, you must state the design (repeated measures, independent groups, matched pairs). Otherwise, it is sufficient to name the method chosen.

Take care that you identify the method. For example, you might conduct an experiment using a questionnaire to collect the data. The method is nevertheless an experiment and not a questionnaire survey.

One advantage and one disadvantage, even if rather brief, should earn you the full 2 marks. They must, however, be specific advantages of the method (or design) as opposed to rather general advantages of all research methods, such as saying 'You can collect lots of data.'

You may describe sources of bias, confounding variables or both. These must be set in the context of your study rather than being very general problems such as 'experimenter bias' or 'noise'.

It is sufficient to identify only two problems – but you do need at least two.

Some students say what they would do to deal with the problems – and then do not do this! Make sure that you deal with the problems as planned when you conduct your study.

The 5% level of significance is usually selected for psychological research because such research is not related to 'life and death matters', which require greater certainty (e.g. the 1% level).

Type II errors occur when the significance level chosen is too stringent (e.g. 1%), leading one to reject findings that are 'true'. Type I errors occur when the significance level chosen is too lenient (e.g. 10%), leading one to accept findings that are not true. The 5% level represents a good compromise.

For full marks, you are required to identify possible ethical issues and state how you would deal with each. If certain ethical issues (such as privacy) are not a problem, explain why you do not have to deal with them.

Grade A project: Title page and abstract

Title

The Matching Hypothesis

Psychology A level coursework
by Rosie Setter

TABLE OF CONTENTS

Abstract	1
Introduction	2
Method	4
Results	6
Discussion	8
References	9
Appendices	10

The marks for A1 and A2 are not derived from the content of the report. Your teacher decides on an appropriate mark for A1 and A2 based on your contribution to the design and the quality of the design.

This candidate has been given 3 marks for A1 and 3 marks for A2. This is because:

- It is an adaptation of a previous study, designed by one candidate:
- Design decisions were applied appropriately and competently.

Page 1 of the report

Abstract

The matching hypothesis states that people are attracted to members of the opposite sex who are similar in terms of physical attractiveness rather than seeking the most physically attractive mate. This study aims to test this hypothesis by selecting a set of photographs of married couples and asking participants to rate the attractiveness of each of the partners (females rate male photos and males rate female photos). Forty-eight participants from the sixth form at our school (24 girls and 24 boys) took part and were asked to rate the physical attractiveness on a scale of 1 to 10 (10 = highly attractive). The correlation was not significant ($p = 0.05$, critical value = 0.65, observed value = 0.44, null hypothesis accepted). This suggests that, when looking for a partner, people do not try to match their own physical attractiveness; instead, they may be influenced by a variety of other factors.

Marks for B   *(3 marks)*

You will get 3 marks if you describe the main aims, methods, results and conclusions drawn from the investigation.

The abstract should be clear and concise, ideally about 150 words in length – although some abstracts may have to be slightly longer because the project is more complex.

You should write the abstract after you have written the report, although it is usually placed at the beginning of the report so that readers can get an overview of the study.

This abstract is 150 words long.

COURSEWORK

Page 2 of the report

Introduction

Relationships start with interpersonal attraction. Psychologists have proposed various explanations for interpersonal attraction. One view is that we seek partners who are physically attractive, possibly because this is evidence of their good reproductive potential (evolutionary theory). Features that are considered physically attractive, such as a good complexion and white teeth, suggest that the possessor is healthy and has good genes. Mating with such an individual will help to maximise your own reproductive success.

An alternative view is the matching hypothesis, which suggests that we actually seek a partner whose physical attractiveness matches our own physical attractiveness. This is likely because even though we find physically attractive people most attractive, we go for a compromise when selecting a potential partner in order to avoid rejection. We do not select a partner who is much less physically attractive because this would limit our reproductive success. We can do better and maximise our reproductive success.

Walster et al. (1966) tested this hypothesis in a study called the 'Computer Dance experiment'. About 400 students were invited to a freshers' week dance and told they would be paired with a similar partner (they were in fact paired randomly and judges rated each student in terms of physical attractiveness). At the end of the dance, students were all given questionnaires including a question about whether they would like to see their partner again. Walster et al. found that students were most likely to want to see a physically attractive partner again rather than one who was more of a match.

However, this study was criticised because it did not relate very well to real-life relationships. When Walster and Walster (1966) repeated the study, they found support for the matching hypothesis, probably because this time the participants spent time together beforehand and were given a choice of whom to partner. This time they preferred someone who matched their own perceived physical attractiveness. This makes sense as matching is likely to occur if you are seeking a relationship rather than rating someone you have been paired with. In the latter case, there was no opportunity for selection so matching would not have taken place.

Further support for the matching hypothesis has been found in studies of real-life couples. Silverman (1971) conducted an observational study of couples in public places (such as bars and theatres). The couples were between 18 and 22 and unmarried. Observers independently rated the couples on a 5-point scale and found high similarity between members of a couple. The observers also noted that the more similar the attractiveness, the happier the couple were rated in terms of the degree of physical intimacy (e.g. holding hands).

Murstein (1972) asked couples who were engaged or going steady to rate their own and their partners' attractiveness on a 5-point scale. Independent judges also rated the participants' attractiveness. The similarity ratings for couples were compared with ratings made of randomly paired couples. Murstein found that real couples were significantly more similar than the randomly paired couples.

All these studies support the matching hypothesis in a variety of different settings and in relation to couples in varying stages of a relationship.

Formulation of aims

The aim of this study is to replicate Murstein's research, adapting the original design. Instead of actually asking participants to rate their own attractiveness, this study will use photographs of strangers and require participants to rate the attractiveness of the people in the photographs. We would expect couples to be similar (matching) in attractiveness because they have chosen each other. People should go for someone of a similar level of attractiveness rather than someone who is much more or much less physically attractive.

Statement of alternative hypothesis

There is a positive correlation between the attractiveness ratings given to the partners in a long-standing romantic relationship.

Statement of null hypothesis

There is no correlation in the attractiveness ratings given to the partners in a long-standing romantic relationship.

Marks for the introduction are divided into C1, C2 and C3

C1 Support from psychological literature
(5 marks)
C2 Formulation of aims/hypotheses (3 marks)
C3 Statement of aims/hypotheses (2 marks)

C1 Support from psychological literature

The introduction should provide relevant, concise and carefully selected psychological 'literature' (i.e. theories and/or studies). There should be no *obvious* omissions.

The introduction should contain the studies that you originally looked at before formulating the hypothesis. Two or three studies is often sufficient. No student should say, 'I don't know what to put in my introduction' – if that is true, where did your hypothesis appear from?

→ Do not copy an apparently relevant chunk out a textbook.

→ 500–600 words is about right for the whole introduction.

Be focused, like a funnel

Start with a broad statement of the research area.

Narrow down to the specific topic.

Leading logically to your hypothesis.

C2 Formulation of aims/hypotheses

The aims should show a clear and logical progression from the background literature.

→ Clunk click: The background research should buckle neatly into the aims.

→ Use a subheading 'Formulation of aims'.

C3 Statement of aims/hypotheses

The hypothesis should be clearly stated and easily testable, i.e. it should be operationalized.

→ You need only provide the alternative hypothesis, but it makes sense to include the null hypothesis for drawing statistical conclusions (you either accept or reject the null hypothesis).

This introduction is just over 600 words long, perhaps slightly longer than strictly necessary, but it is carefully selected.

Page 4 of the report

Method

Method and design
This study involved a questionnaire to collect ratings of photographs and used a correlational analysis to assess the data.

Researchers
One A level student collected data.

Target population and sample
An opportunity sample (24 males and 24 females) was taken from sixth form students at our school. Those students who were available at the time of the study were asked to participate. Some individuals declined to take part.

Apparatus/materials
Photographs of 10 married couples were selected from magazines and photocopied, labelling them A to J. All photographs were selected according to certain criteria: the faces of each partner were about the size of a passport photograph and looking straight at the camera; both partners were aged between 20 and 30 (otherwise age might have been a feature of attractiveness rating). Race was also controlled. Only photographs of white Europeans were used.

The male and female photographs were cut out separately and pasted onto a sheet of male photographs and a sheet of female ones. The photographs were placed randomly on each sheet so they were not in the same order (i.e. photo 1 for females was from couple C, whereas photo 1 on the male sheet was from couple J).

An example of the photographs is shown in Appendix 1. (The Appendices have not been included in this book.)

Page 5 of the report

Standardised procedures
Each participant was taken to a separate room to complete the task, away from the distractions of other students.

The standardised briefing instructions were read to the participant (see Appendix 2) and consent was given.

Female participants were shown the male photos, and male participants were shown the female photos. They were asked to rate each photograph on a scale of 1 to 10, where 10 was extremely physically attractive. Participants wrote their ratings on a piece of paper with spaces for 10 answers (see Appendix 2). No names were asked for.

Afterwards, participants were thanked and given the standard debriefing (see Appendix 3), advising them that they would be told further details of the study when all the participants had been tested.

Controls
Researcher bias was minimised by using standardised instructions and not watching participants as they completed the task to avoid participant reactivity.

Participant bias was avoided by asking participants to rate members of the opposite sex because, in a pilot study, boys felt uncomfortable rating men in terms of physical attractiveness.

Differences between photographs were minimised because otherwise this would act as a confounding variable (e.g. age or race).

Ethics
Partially informed consent was sought – participants were told what the task would involve them doing, that they had the right to withdraw at any time and that their answers would remain anonymous.

The minor deception (the aim of the study) was dealt with by debriefing participants at the end of the study.

D Reporting of method
(4 marks)

The main criterion for awarding marks in this section is whether you have provided sufficient detail for your study to be replicated (repeated) by someone else.

The method is like writing a recipe for a cake. You need to provide every detail so that someone else could do the same thing; this is replication.

It is not just a matter of whether someone could do a *similar* study but whether they could do *exactly* the same study. The reason for this is because if one simply varies small details, such as the kind of participant, this may cause the findings to differ. Therefore replication must be as far as possible identical in order to validate the original findings.

→ 500–600 words is about right for the method section

Useful subheadings to use include: method and design, researchers, target population and sample (including sampling procedure), apparatus/materials (actual examples to be placed in the appendix and described/referenced here), standardised procedures (including how participants were allocated to conditions), controls and ethics.

Methodological details to put in the appendix (as appropriate) are: standardized instructions (briefing and debriefing), examples of materials, and maps.

This is about 450 words, a short 'method' section because the study is very straightforward. There is sufficient detail for full replication.

Grade A project: The results

Page 6 of the report

Results: Descriptive statistics

Summary tables of the data for female and male participants are shown below. For each photograph, the 12 ratings given to the photograph were added together and divided by 12 to give a mean rating. A scattergraph was used to display these results visually. The raw data are given in Appendix 4.

Ratings of female photographs	
Photograph	Mean rating
A	4.9
B	4
C	5.8
D	7.3
E	4.4
F	3.2
G	6
H	6.1
I	3.1
J	5.5

Ratings of male photographs	
Photograph	Mean rating
A	5.2
B	5.8
C	7.1
D	7
E	3.1
F	6
G	6.5
H	4.9
I	4.2
J	5.5

Scattergraph to show correlation between ratings of male and female members of a couple

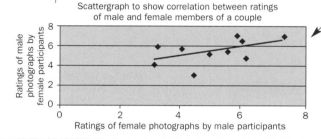

Scattergraph to show correlation between ratings
of male and female members of a couple

Page 7 of the report

Results: Inferential statistics

The scattergraph indicates a weak positive correlation (the line of best fit was produced by Excel). In order to determine whether this positive correlation was significant, we used an inferential statistical test.

We choose to use Spearman's rank correlation test because:

- We needed a test of correlation.
- The data used were ratings made by participants, which are ordinal data.
- This means we should use a non-parametric test.

The statistical calculations are shown in Appendix 5.

Level of significance

The level of significance selected was 5%, the hypothesis was directional, and therefore a one-tailed test is required, N = 10.

The <u>observed value</u> of rho = 0.44.

The <u>critical value</u> of rho = 0.65 (p = 0.05).

As the observed value is less than the critical value, we retain the null hypothesis, which is 'There is no correlation in the attractiveness ratings given to the partners in a long-standing romantic relationship.'

E1 Results: Selection and application of techniques used for analysis *(4 marks)*

E1 is concerned with both the descriptive and inferential statistics.

→ Descriptive statistics allow us to 'eyeball' the data and draw some preliminary conclusions.

→ Inferential statistics allow us to determine whether the data are statistically significant (i.e. are unlikely to have arisen from chance factors).

→ Raw data must be placed in an appendix.

It is not strictly speaking appropriate to use the mean to average ratings because these are not interval data. A rating scale may, however, be regarded as quasi-interval or 'plastic interval' (see page 94) so the mean can be used.

There are seven criteria for E1:

- Selection of appropriate descriptive techniques.
- Application of appropriate descriptive techniques.

Two examples of appropriate descriptive statistics are sufficient, for example, using summary tables and a scattergraph. There is credit for selection and application. The clarity is credited in E2.

- Selection of an appropriate inferential statistical test.
- Application of an appropriate inferential statistical test.
- The use of an inferential test was justified with full reference to the data collected.

In addition to descriptive statistics, you must use an inferential statistical test. In the body of the report, you should provide a full justification of why you chose this test (see page 80 for details of tests and how to justify them), and then include appropriate calculations in an appendix.

If you have used a computer package, you will only need to show the raw data and the number calculated (the calculated or observed value).

- Appropriate level of statistical significance applied.
- Full explanation of the actual level of significance.

In the project brief, the level of significance was identified.

To identify the critical value, you need to know the required level of significance, whether you require a one- or two-tailed test and the number of participants.

E2 Results and appendices: presentation of data *(4 marks)*

The second mark for the results section relates to the clarity of presentation rather than what is there.

- Descriptive statistics were presented precisely and clearly.
- Inferential statistics were presented precisely and clearly.
- Presentation of raw data in an appendix was clear.
- Presentation of calculations in an appendix was clear.

If you want help with inferential tests, see pages 94–98.

Page 8 of the report

Discussion

> The main factors for gaining marks for your discussion are to *discuss* the issues raised and to be thorough. It is more about quality than quantity.

Explanation of findings

The hypothesis predicted a positive correlation between the ratings of physical attractiveness between the male and females members of a couple. The scattergraph showed a weak positive correlation, but this was found to be non-signifcant at the 5% level when using the inferential test. Some couples did have very similar ratings. The means for couple J were identical and those for couples A, D and G very similar. There were, however, large differences for some other couples. Taken together, this suggests that matching for physical attractiveness is not a general phenomenon when selecting a partner.

Relationship to background research

Murstein's findings 30 years ago found a 'definite tendency' for couples to be of a similar level of attractiveness, in contrast to these findings. The historical period may be significant: it is possible that there were different social norms 30 years ago. Physical attractiveness may have been a more important criterion when selecting a partner then, whereas, for example, intelligence may be a more important factor now. A further factor may be that young people did not judge attractiveness in Murstein's study whereas they did here. This may affect the way in which ratings are given.

Other research has found that couples match in terms of criteria other than physical attractiveness. Newcomb (1961), for example, found that similarity in attitudes was important. Also, evolutionary theory predicts that women are more interested in resources than physical attractiveness so they may match physical attractiveness for resources in a male. So if a partner has other attractive qualities, that counts as a way to compensate physical attractiveness in their partner.

Page 9 of the report

Limitations and modifications

The study was limited in a number of ways. Most importantly, the photographs were taken from magazines, and it may be that only certain kinds of couple were represented in such photographs. People in magazines have often done something unusual and therefore may not be typical. One way to deal with this is to get photographs of couples who are known to have more typical relationships.

A further problem is that the judges were only sixth formers and may not see physical attractiveness in the same way as members of a couple do. This means that it may be more appropriate to ask members of a couple to rate themselves and each other in order to see a person as his/her partner does.

Implications and suggestions for future research

The implications of these findings are important in evaluating the matching hypothesis, which may operate only in certain circumstances. If it were shown that matching is important in long-term relationships, this could be used by dating agencies to work out the most successful criteria for matching prospective partners.

Further research might be done on comparing couples who have separated with those who have remained together to see whether there is closer matching in the couples who stay together. Comparisons could also be made between how older and younger people rate attractiveness in photographs.

References

Murstein (1972) in M. Cardwell & C. Flanagan (2003) *Psychology A2: The Complete Companion.* Nelson Thornes. Page 4.
Newcomb (1961) in M. Cardwell & C. Flanagan (2003) cited above. Page 8.
Silverman (1971) in R. Gross (1990) *Key Studies in Psychology* (1st edition). Hodder and Stoughton, p. 87.
Walster and Walster (1966) in M. Cardwell & C. Flanagan (2003) cited above. Page 5.
Walster et al. (1966) in M. Cardwell & C. Flanagan (2003) cited above. Page 4.

Grade A project: The discussion

> **Marks for the discussion are divided into F1, F2, F3 and F4**
>
> F1 Explanation of findings (*3 marks*)
> F2 Relationship to background research (*3 marks*)
> F3 Limitations and modifications (*3 marks*)
> F4 Implications and suggestions for further research (*3 marks*)
>
> → 500–600 words is about right for the discussion section.

> **F1 Explanation of findings**
>
> The outcome of the investigation should be explained in terms of the hypothesis(es) and/or aim(s) in ways that are appropriate and coherent.
>
> → Do more than state the findings: try to explain them. It may help to discuss some particular examples.
> → Relate the findings to the aim(s)/hypothesis(es).
> → Explain other findings, e.g. comments from participants.

> **F2 Relationship to background research**
>
> There should be a thorough discussion of the outcome of the investigation in terms of relevant background research.
>
> This is an example of a discussion that is not thorough:
>
> *Murstein's original study found the same thing. It may be because the study was done 30 years ago. There may have been different social norms then. Newcomb (1961) found that similarity was a factor in interpersonal attraction. Also, women are less interested in physical attractiveness and more interested in resources.*

> **F3 Limitations and modifications**
>
> Most limitations of the investigation should be reported and appropriate modifications suggested.
>
> When does a modification (F3) become a suggestion for future research (F4)? If you are testing a new hypothesis, it is a suggestion. If you are making a relatively minor alteration to the design, it is a modification.

> **F4 Implications and suggestions for further research**
>
> Appropriate suggestions for further research should be mentioned and implications of the findings thoroughly discussed.

This discussion is about 500 words long.

> **G References**   (*2 marks*)
>
> All references should be provided in a conventional way for both sources used and studies quoted in the text. References may be presented as shown here or written out in full, for example:
>
> Murstein, B.I. (1972) 'Physical attractiveness and marital choice'. *Journal of Personality and Social Psychology*, 22, 8–12.
>
> **H Report style**   (*3 marks*)
>
> The report should be concisely written, in an appropriate scientific style, using a broad range of specialist terms, logically organised into sections and characterised by the adequate expression of ideas. There should be no, or only minor, errors in grammar, punctuation and spelling.

We have not included the various appendices from the report in this book, but they would have to be present and complete to receive full marks.

TOTAL MARKS
60/60

Example 2: Conformity

**PSYCHOLOGY
PROJECT BRIEF
PROPOSAL FORM**

Title of work
Conformity in ambiguous and unambiguous conditions

PB1: Identify the aims of the research and state the experimental/alternative hypothesis(es). *(credited in the report mark scheme)*
Participants conform more when answering an ambiguous rather than an unambiguous question.

PB2: Explain why a directional or non-directional experimental/alternative hypothesis(es) has been selected. *(1 mark)*
This is a directional hypothesis because I have predicted the direction that the results will go. I have said that conformity will be higher when the questions are ambiguous.

PB3: Identify the chosen research method (experimental, survey, observation or correlational research) and, if appropriate, the design used. *(1 mark)*
The method used was an experiment.

PB4: Identify the advantage(s) and disadvantage(s) of the chosen research method and/or design. *(2 marks)*
An advantage of this method is that cause and effect can be measured. The effect of one variable is manipulated, and the effects of this are measured. A disadvantage of this method is that it may create an artificial situation. People may act differently from normal.

PB5: Identify potential sources of bias in the investigation and any possible confounding variables. *(2 marks)*
Instructions may vary, leading to experimenter bias.

PB6: Explain what procedures will be adopted to deal with these. *(2 marks)*
The experimenter will give each participant the same set of instructions in a written form to ensure that there is no variation. The experimenter will avoid communicating in any way with participants except by what is written in a script.

PB7: Select an appropriate level of statistical significance to be reached before the experimental/alternative hypothesis will be retained. *(1 mark)*
5%

PB8: Identify any relevant ethical issues and discuss steps to be taken to deal with these. *(3 marks)*
Participants will be assured of confidentiality and told not to put their names on the question sheet.
Participants will also be informed of their right to withdraw and that they do not have to answer the questionnaire.
Participants will be debriefed about the aims of the study.
Participants will not be given any feedback on their scores nor those of any other participant.

Grade C project: The project brief

Project brief marks

	Max mark	Mark given	Moderator's comments
PB2 Hypothesis	1	0	This is not a justification of why a directional hypothesis was chosen. It is a description of how the hypothesis is directional.
PB3 Method/design	1	0	If the method used is an experiment, you must identify the design (in this case, repeated measures).
PB4 Advantages/disadvantages	2	2	There are flaws in the advantages and disadvantages described (e.g. it is not the effects of a variable that are manipulated, and experiments are not always artificial), but there is sufficient here for 2 marks.
PB5 Bias/variables	2	1	This answer is very brief and not really set in the context of the study and there is only one source of bias, as required in this part of the project brief. The answer is not, however, irrelevant or wrong and therefore gets a very generous 1 mark.
PB6 Control of bias/variables	2	2	This is a full explanation (2 marks) rather than a partial explanation (1 mark) of procedures. Both written and verbal instructions have been considered.
PB7 Statistical significance	1	1	It is difficult to see how anyone could get this wrong – but some candidates do. For example, 0.05% is incorrect; 5% is correct and 0.05 is correct. Or you could use the 1% or 10% level.
PB8 Ethical considerations	3	2	The first two issues are fine. Debriefing is not an issue, it is a means of dealing with the issue of deception – in this case the issue has not been identified. The final issue is again not identified, and it is not clear why participants should not be given feedback.

Total mark for project brief = 8/12

This is a relatively low mark for a section on which it is fairly easy to score full marks. Take advice from your teacher about where you have lost marks and put your answers right if you are given a second chance.

Grade C project: Title page and abstract

Conformity

in ambiguous and unambiguous conditions

Psychology coursework
By Lucy Pointer

Table of contents

Abstract	1
Introduction	2
Method	4
Results	6
Discussion	8
References	9
Appendices	10

Page 1 of the report

Abstract

The area of study was conformity. The aim of the experiment was to find out if people are more likely to conform when given an unambiguous or an ambiguous question. This is related to various studies of conformity which have found that people conform even in unambiguous situations and not just ambiguous ones. The hypothesis for the study was that participants conform more when answering an ambiguous rather than an unambiguous question.

The research method was an experiment, and a questionnaire was used to collect the answers. The design was repeated measures. There were 15 participants, both males and females, aged 16 to 18. The participants were chosen using opportunity sampling.

The results were that more people conformed when answering ambiguous questions ($p < 0.05$).

The conclusion drawn is that people conform more to ambiguous questions.

Title page and abstract marks

	Max mark	Mark given	Moderator's comments
A1 Implementation: candidate's contribution to design	3	1	The candidate designed this study with a small group of other students with significant help from the teacher.
A2 Implementation: design decisions	3	3	The study was well designed; there were no major flaws.
B Abstract	3	2	This abstract is about the right length, but there is too much on aims and too little on other points. Not all the main points (aims, methods, results and conclusions) have been adequately covered. The method is not clear, and the results lack precision. Still, it's better than 'lacking clarity, minimal information' (the criteria for 1 mark).

This abstract is 135 words long.

Grade C project: The introduction

Page 2 of the report

Introduction

Background
Conformity is defined as yielding to group pressure. The pressure can come from the physical presence of others or from social norms. There are three types of conformity: compliance, which is where people conform in their given answer but do not actually change their opinion; internalisation, which is where someone goes along with the views of others because they come to believe in them; and identification, which is when you conform to a role in society and behave as you think is appropriate for that role.

Previous research
One of the first major studies was by Sherif (1935). In this study, participants had to look at a stationary light in the dark that appeared to move. This is the autokinetic effect. The participants were asked to estimate how far the dot moved. They were first tested on their own and then in groups of three. When they were tested on their own, they developed their own personal norm. When they were placed with others, their judgements became much more similar. Therefore the group norm replaced the individual norm, thus showing social influence. When participants were tested again individually, they gave answers more similar to the group norm than their own.

Asch (1951) did a study to find out whether participants conformed when the answer was obvious. He showed participants three lines of different lengths and then a fourth line and asked which line matched the fourth line. The participants had to give their answers out loud after a number

Page 3 of the report

of other participants (who were in fact confederates) had given their answers. On most trials the confederates gave the correct answer, but on certain 'critical' trials they gave the wrong answer. Asch found that true participants also gave the wrong answer on 37% of the trials. 75% conformed at least once. This is surprisingly high because, in a control experiment, only 0.7% gave a wrong answer.

Crutchfield (1954) did a study to see if people conformed when other people were not physically present. In this study, the participants sat in individual cubicles and asked a series of questions. They saw the answers that other participants had given and thought they were the last to answer. In half the trials, Crutchfield found that 30% conformed to Asch's line test, 40% conformed to a question on area and 37% agreed to the statement 'I would make a good leader' when they said they would when asked on their own.

People are said to conform because of normative and informational social influence. Normative social influence occurs when a person wants to be accepted, and informational social influence occurs when people are unsure and look to others for the answer.

These studies looked at social influence and how it affects people when others are present or not. I want to find out whether group pressure still exists even when other people are not present. In Asch's and Crutchfield's studies, people conformed when the answer was unambiguous.

Statement of hypothesis
Participants conform more when answering an ambiguous rather than an unambiguous question.

Introduction marks

	Max mark	Mark given	Moderator's comments
C1 Introduction: support from psychological literature	5	4	There are no important omissions from the background literature (criteria for 2 marks), but, on the other hand, the literature has not all been carefully selected (criteria for 5 marks). At the beginning and end of the introduction, material has been included about conformity in general, which is not directly relevant. The 'previous research' reads somewhat as if the studies have been selected because they are studies of conformity rather than ones that are specifically relevant to this piece of coursework. Students often do this – copy an appropriate chunk from a textbook without shaping the material to the specific study they are going to conduct. Nevertheless, the material could not be described as 'lacking selectivity' so gets 4 marks.
C2 Introduction: formulation of aims/hypotheses	3	2	The lack of 'shaping' inevitably means a loss of marks for C2 because the introduction does not lead logically into the aims/hypotheses. In this report, the student has not provided a section entitled 'formulation of aims', but the aims are provided in the last paragraph of the 'previous research'.
C3 Introduction: statement of	2	2	The alternative hypothesis is adequately operationalised and can easily be tested. The lack of a null hypothesis is not penalised.

This introduction is about 500 words long, an appropriate length.

Grade C project: The method

Page 4 of the report

Method

Method and design

This study was a field experiment because it was conducted in a natural environment although participants were aware that they were taking part in a psychology experiment. An independent variable was manipulated. The design was repeated measures because each participant took part in both conditions. The study used a questionnaire to collect data.

In the study, participants were deceived about the true nature of the study. To overcome this, they were debriefed at the end. The fact that they may sometimes have known the answer but felt confused because it was not the one shown may have caused them some slight stress.

Participants

There were 15 participants, a mixture of males and females aged between 16 and 18 from our school sixth form. The participants were selected using an opportunity sampling method. The researchers were both girls in the sixth form who were studying psychology.

Materials

The study was done using a questionnaire. This questionnaire (which is shown in Appendix I) consisted of 20 questions. After each question, there was space for 10 answers, and the first four answers had been filled in ('fake' answers). Some of the questions were ambiguous, such as a photograph of a woman asking you to estimate her age. Other questions were unambiguous, such as asking for the next number in a number sequence.

Page 5 of the report

We did not give all wrong answers because that might have made participants suspicious. On the other hand, it would not make sense to have wrong answers to too many unambiguous questions. So we mixed them up.

Procedures

Before doing the study, we had to decide what questions to use. We tried out a number of different questions on people in a pilot study and divided them into ambiguous and unambiguous depending on how many answers were always the same.

We gave the questionnaire to the participants and read out standardised instructions (see Appendix II). The standardised instructions told participants that they would be answering simple questions that had already been asked to others. They should ignore the previous answers.

After they completed the questionnaire, a standard debrief was read (see Appendix III). This was so they could be informed about the deception. They were also asked whether they wished their data to be withheld from the study.

When the questionnaires were completed, we checked to see where the participants had conformed to the wrong answers on the sheet. These were the only answers that showed that participants had conformed.

	Max mark	Mark given	Moderator's comments
Method marks			
D Reporting of method	4	3	It is not necessary to include details of the design that have already been credited on the project brief, as has been done here.

Some important factors have not been clearly explained. For example, were the fake answers already on the questionnaire always unanimous? If they were not, how many were the same? Also, how many of the questions were given mainly right answers or mainly wrong answers?

The actual procedures described are incomplete. Where were the participants tested? How much time were they allowed to complete the questionnaire? Were they prevented from discussing the questionnaire with others?

There is sufficient detail for reasonable replication – assuming that the questionnaire in the appendix is complete, including the 'fake' answers. Not including the questionnaire would have been a fundamental omission and would have reduced the mark to 1 out of 4. |

This method section is about 400 words, on the short side because it is a relatively straightforward study.

Page 6 of the report

Results: Descriptive statistics

The data in the table show how many times participants conformed on questions that were ambiguous or not ambiguous. The graph below that shows the scores for each participant.

Participant	Number of unambiguous questions where participant conformed	Number of ambiguous questions where participant conformed
1	3	2
2	5	4
3	2	4
5	2	2
6	2	1
7	4	2
8	3	5
9	5	5
10	1	3
11	0	3
12	3	2
13	2	1
14	1	4
15	3	1

	Ambiguous	Unambiguous
Mean	2.47	2.87
Median	2	3
Mode	2 and 3	2 and 4

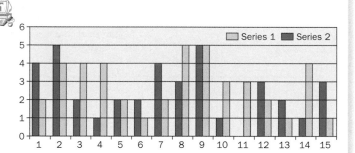

Page 7 of the report

Results: Inferential statistics

The data collected in this study were interval data and were related measures. Since a test of difference was required, we chose to do the Wilcoxon test.

The calculations for the test are shown in Appendix IV. The result was that $T = 15$. As our observed value is less than the critical value for 5% level, this means our results are significant and we can accept the alternative hypothesis.

Grade C project: The results

Results marks

	Max mark	Mark given	Moderator's comments

E1 Results: selection and application of techniques used for analysis

	Max mark	Mark given	Moderator's comments
Selection of appropriate descriptive techniques	4	2	The table of actual results belongs in the appendix. The mean is a useful descriptive statistic but the median and mode are unnecessary. The bar chart (comparing participants) does not actually make sense. It would have been more useful to see how many participants got a higher score on the unambiguous condition and how many a higher score on the ambiguous condition. The graph on the left shows this.

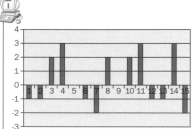

	Max mark	Mark given	Moderator's comments
Application of appropriate descriptive techniques	4	4	Fine.
Selection of appropriate inferential statistical test	4	4	Fine.
Application of appropriate inferential statistical test	4	4	In the appendix.
The use of an inferential test was justified with full reference to the data collected	4	3	It is stated that the data are interval, but what makes these data interval (equal intervals) is not fully explained.
Appropriate level of statistical significance applied	4	4	Yes.
Full explanation of the actual level of significance	4	3	This is not clearly explained. It would be better to say, 'The observed value of T is 15. The critical value for N = 14 (because there is one zero value), is 21 (for a one-tailed test, 5% significance level).'

Overall, E1 averages out to a score of 3 out of 4

E2 Results and appendices: presentation of data

	Max mark	Mark given	Moderator's comments
Descriptive statistics were presented precisely and clearly	4	2	The bar chart has no labels for the x and y axes, nor a title, and 'Series 1' and 'Series 2' are not explained; there are therefore some deficiencies.
Inferential statistics were presented precisely and clearly	4	4	Yes (in the appendix).
Presentation of raw data in an appendix was clear	4	0	No, the raw data are in the wrong place. They are on page 6 of the report.
Presentation of calculations in an appendix was clear	4	4	Yes.

Overall E2 averages out to a score of 3 out of 4

Page 8 of the report

Discussion

Explanation of findings

In this study, the results support the alternative hypothesis. Participants conformed more to questions that were ambiguous rather than unambiguous. However, it is interesting to look at the actual data. This shows that the difference between ambiguous and unambiguous questions is rather small. Almost the same number of participants conformed more to ambiguous rather than unambiguous questions. Six participants gave more wrong answers to the unambiguous questions, whereas seven participants gave more wrong answers to the ambiguous questions. This is not a very big difference. The reason the results were significant was perhaps because those who did conform more to the unambiguous conditions did so by a greater amount.

Relationship to background research

These findings relate to earlier research. Sherif found that people conform in unambiguous situations. Asch found that a surprisingly high number of people conform to an incorrect answer even if it is unambiguous. But Asch's study involved face-to-face contact with other participants, whereas Crutchfield found more conformity to ambiguous questions than ambiguous ones. So even if participants do conform to unambiguous questions, as they did here, they conform *more* to ambiguous questions. This shows informational social influence rather than normative social influence because participants were not face to face.

Page 9 of the report

Limitations and modifications

One limitation of this study was that the participants may not have taken the experiment seriously since they were tested in a relaxed setting in the student common room. A second limitation was that although participants were asked to fill in the questionnaire separately, there was a bit of discussion, again not leading to serious answers. There is also the problem of age range. It is difficult to generalise from a study involving just 16–18-year-olds.

The way to improve this is to isolate each participant during the experiment and also extend the experiment to a wider sample.

Implications and suggestions for future research

One implication of conformity research is for advertising and how people decide what brands to buy. Most decisions to purchase something are related to ambiguous situations so advertisers can use informational and normative social influence to change this.

Further research might look at ambiguous and unambiguous communications in advertising to see how much people change their minds.

References

Sherif, M. (1935) A study of some factors in perception.
Asch, S.E. (1956) Studies of independence and conformity: A minority of one against a unanimous majority. *Psychological Monographs*.

Grade C project: The discussion

Discussion marks	Max mark	Mark given	Moderator's comments
F1 Discussion: explanation of findings	3	3	The outcome has been related to the hypothesis, and the results are explained coherently, so this is sufficient for full marks.
F2 Discussion: relationship to background research	3	2	This is a discussion of important points but it does not go that much beyond material already credited in the introduction. Only a few further insights are offered. However, as the discussion is 'reasonably coherent' rather than 'limited', 2 marks are awarded.
F3 Discussion: limitations and modifications	3	2	Suggesting that participants did not take the experiment seriously raises the question of design. Either a mark should be deducted from the design (A2) or the limitation identified should receive minimal credit (partial awareness of the limitations). Since a modification is mentioned, the candidate can gain 2 marks rather than just 1.
F4 Discussion: implications and suggestions for further research	3	2	One implication and one suggestion for future research have been made so the candidate must receive 2 marks. For the full 3 marks, a more thorough discussion of one or both of these is needed.

This discussion is just over 350 words, somewhat on the short side.

References and report style marks	Max mark	Mark given	Moderator's comments
G References	2	1	The references are not complete (Crutchfield has been omitted and not all details for Sherif have been given), nor are they in alphabetical order.
H Report style	3	3	The report was concisely written, in an appropriate scientific style, using a broad range of specialist terms, logically organized into sections and characterised by the adequate expression of ideas. There were a few errors of grammar, punctuation or spelling but not enough to affect the overall mark.

We have not included the various appendices here.

TOTAL MARKS 44/60

Inferential statistics

Chi-square (x^2)

When to use the chi-square test

The hypothesis predicts a *difference* between two conditions or an *association* between variables.

The sets of data must be *independent* (no individual should have a score in more than one 'cell').

The data are in frequencies (*nominal* – see facing page for an explanation).

Note
This test is unreliable when the *expected* frequencies fall below 5 in any cell, i.e. you need at least 20 participants for a 2×2 contingency table.

Critical values of chi-square (x^2) at the 5% level

df	One-tailed test	Two-tailed test
1	2.71	3.84
2	4.60	5.99
3	6.25	7.82
4	7.78	9.49
5	9.24	11.07

The observed value of x^2 must be **equal to** or **exceed** the critical value in this table for significance to be shown.

Source: abridged from R.A. Fisher and F. Yates (1974) *Statistical tables for biological, agricultural and medical research (6th edition)*. Longman.

How to do the chi-square test: Example 1

Alternative hypothesis: Belief in the paranormal (believing or not believing) is related to a correct assessment of coincidence (non-directional, two-tailed)
Null hypothesis: There is no association between belief in the paranormal and correct assessment of coincidence

STEP 1 Draw up a contingency table (right)
In this case it will be 2×2 (rows first, then columns)

Assessment of chance	Belief in the paranormal		Totals
	High	Low	
Right	5 (cell **A**)	12 (cell **B**)	17
Wrong	10 (cell **C**)	9 (cell **D**)	19
Totals	15	21	36

STEP 2 Find the observed value by comparing observed and expected frequencies for each cell

	Row × column/ total = expected frequency (E)	Subtract expected value from observed value, ignoring signs $|(E-O)|$	Square previous value $(E-O)^2$	Divide previous value by expected value $(E-O)^2/E$
Cell A	17×15/36 = 7.08	5 – 7.08 = 2.08	4.3264	0.6110
Cell B	17×21/36 = 9.92	12 – 9.92 = 2.08	4.3264	0.4361
Cell C	19×15/36 = 7.92	10 – 7.92 = 2.08	4.3264	0.5463
Cell D	19×21/36 = 11.08	9 – 11.08 = 2.08	4.3264	0.3905
Adding all the values in the final column gives you the observed value of x^2				1.984

STEP 3 Find the critical value of chi-square

Yates's correction is advised for 2×2 contingency tables

- Calculate degrees of freedom (*df*): calculate (rows – 1) × (columns – 1) = 1
- Look up the value in a table of critical values (on the left)
- For a two-tailed test, *df* = 1, and the critical value of x^2 ($p \leq 0.05$) = 3.84
- As the observed value (1.1448) is less than the critical value (3.84), we must retain the null hypothesis and conclude that there is no association between belief in the paranormal and the correct assessment of coincidence.

How to do the chi-square test: Example 2 (a larger contingency table)

Alternative hypothesis: Certain parental styles are associated with greater turmoil in adolescence (non-directional, two-tailed)
Null hypothesis: There is no association between parental style and greater turmoil in adolescence

STEP 1 Draw up a contingency table (right)
In this case, it will be 3×2 (rows first, then columns)

Parental style	Adolescent turmoil		Totals
	High	Low	
Authoritarian	10 (cell **A**)	4 (cell **B**)	14
Democratic	5 (cell **C**)	7 (cell **D**)	12
Laissez-faire	8 (cell **E**)	2 (cell **F**)	10
Totals	23	13	36

STEP 2 Find the observed value of x^2 by comparing observed and expected frequencies for each cell

	Row × column/total = expected frequency	Subtract expected value from observed value, ignoring signs $|(E-O)|$	Square the previous value $(E-O)^2$	Divide the previous value by the expected value $(E-O)^2/E$
Cell A	14×23/36 = 8.94	10 – 8.94 = 1.06	1.1236	0.1257
Cell B	14×13/36 = 5.06	4 – 5.06 = –1.06	1.1236	0.2221
Cell C	12×23/36 = 7.67	5 – 7.67 = –2.67	7.1289	0.9294
Cell D	12×13/36 = 4.33	7 – 4.33 = 2.67	7.1289	1.6464
Cell E	10×23/36 = 6.39	8 – 6.39 = 1.61	2.5921	0.4056
Cell F	10×13/36 = 3.61	2 – 3.61 = –1.61	2.5921	0.7180
Adding all the values in the final column gives you the observed value of x^2				4.0472

STEP 3 Find the critical value of x^2

- Calculate degrees of freedom (*df*): calculate (rows – 1) × (columns – 1) = 2
- Look up the critical value in a table of critical values (on the left)
- For a two-tailed test, *df* = 2, and the critical value of x^2 ($p \leq 0.05$) = 5.99
- As the observed value (4.0472) is less than the critical value (5.99), we must retain the null hypothesis and therefore conclude that there is no association between parental style and greater turmoil in adolescence.

The sign test (S)

> You can remember these using the acronym NOIR.

When to use the sign test

The hypothesis predicts a *difference* between two sets of data or when you have an answer with only two possible values (e.g. yes/no, plus/minus) response for each participant.

The two sets of data are pairs of scores from one person (or a matched pair) = *related*.

The data are nominal or reduced to *nominal* data, e.g. + and − (as in the table on the right).

What are nominal, ordinal, interval and ratio data?

Nominal The data are in separate categories, as when grouping people according to their favourite football team (e.g. Liverpool, Inverness Caledonian Thistle, etc.).

Ordinal Data are ordered in some way, for example asking people to put a list of football teams in order of liking. Liverpool might be first, followed by Inverness and so on. The 'difference' between items is not the same, i.e. the individual may like the first item a lot more than the second, but there might be only a small difference between the items ranked second and third.

Interval Data are measured using units of equal intervals, such as when counting correct answers or using any 'public' unit of measurement. Many psychological studies use 'plastic interval scales' in which the intervals are arbitrarily determined so we cannot actually know for certain that there are equal intervals between the numbers. For the purposes of analysis, however, such data may be accepted as interval.

Ratio There is a true zero point, as in most measures of physical quantities.

Critical values of S at the 5% level

N	One-tailed test	Two-tailed test
5	0	
6	0	0
7	0	0
8	1	0
9	1	1
10	1	1
11	2	1
12	2	2
13	3	2
14	3	2
15	3	3
16	4	3
17	4	4
18	5	4
19	5	4
20	5	5
25	7	7
30	10	9
35	12	11

The observed value of S must be **equal to** or **less than** the critical value in this table for significance to be shown.

Source: F. Clegg (1982) *Simple statistics*. Cambridge University Press. With permission from the publishers.

How to do the sign test

Alternative hypothesis: People sleep more after a day of heavy exercise rather than a day spent resting. (directional, one-tailed).

Null hypothesis: There is no difference in the amount of sleep after a a day of heavy exercise rather than a day spent resting.

STEP 1 Count the number of each sign

Participant	1	2	3	4	5	6	7	8	9	10	11	12
Hours of sleep after a day of heavy exercise	8	8	7	7	8	8	9	9	7.5	7	8	8
Hours of sleep after a day spent resting	7	8.5	8	9	9.5	7.5	8	9.5	7	7.5	8.5	9
Difference	+	−	−	−	−	+	+	−	+	−	−	−

There are 4 pluses and 8 minuses.

STEP 2 Find the observed value of S

S = the less frequently occurring sign, in this case 4

STEP 3 Find the critical value of S

- N = 12
- Look up the critical value in a table of critical values (on the left).
- For a one-tailed test, N = 12, and the critical value of S = 2.
- As the observed value (4) is greater than the critical value (2), we must retain the null hypothesis and conclude that there is no *difference* between amount of sleep after a day of heavy exercise and amount of sleep after a day spent resting.

Probability of snow – 20%

Probability of warm barn – 2%

Spearman's rank correlation test (*rho*)

When to use Spearman's rank correlation test

The hypothesis predicts a *correlation* between two variables.

The two sets of data are pairs of scores from one person or thing = *related*.

The data are *ordinal* or *interval* (see page 95 for an explanation).

*Charles Edward Spearman
(1863–1945)*

How to do Spearman's rank correlation test

Alternative hypothesis: Participants recall on a memory test is positively correlated to their GCSE exam performance (directional, one-tailed).

Null hypothesis: There is no correlation between recall on a memory test and GCSE exam performance.

STEP 1 Record the data, rank each co-variable and calculate the difference

Rank A and B separately, from low to high (i.e. the lowest number receives the rank of 1).

If there are two or more scores with the same number (tied ranks), calculate the rank by working out the mean of the ranks that would have been given.

Participant	Memory score (A)	GCSE score (B)	Rank A	Rank B	Difference between rank A and rank B (d)	d^2
1	18	8	10	2.5	7.5	56.25
2	14	16	5.5	9	−3.5	12.25
3	17	10	9	5	4.0	16.0
4	13	9	4	4	0	0
5	10	15	3	8	−5.0	25.0
6	8	14	1	7	−6.0	36.0
7	15	12	7	6	1	1.0
8	16	8	8	2.5	5.5	30.25
9	9	17	2	10	−8.0	64.0
10	14	5	5.5	1	4.5	20.25
N = 10					Σd^2 (sum of differences squared) =	261.0

STEP 2 Find the observed value of *rho*

$$rho = 1 - \left(\frac{6\Sigma d^2}{N(N^2 - 1)} \right)$$

$$= 1 - \frac{6 \times 261.0}{10 \times (100 - 1)} \qquad = 1 - 1566/990 \qquad = 1 - 1.58 \qquad = -0.58$$

STEP 3 Find the critical value of *rho*

- N = 10
- Look up the critical value in a table of critical values (on the right)
- For a one-tailed test, N = 10, and the critical value of *rho* = 0.564
- As the observed value (0.58) is greater than the critical value (0.564), we can reject the null hypothesis and conclude that participants' recall on a memory test is positively correlated to their GCSE exam performance.

**Critical values of *rho*
at 5% level**

N	One-tailed test	Two-tailed test
4	1.000	
5	0.900	1.000
6	0.829	0.886
7	0.714	0.786
8	0.643	0.738
9	0.600	0.700
10	0.564	0.648
11	0.536	0.618
12	0.503	0.587
13	0.484	0.560
14	0.464	0.538
15	0.443	0.521
16	0.429	0.503
17	0.414	0.485
18	0.401	0.472
19	0.391	0.460
20	0.380	0.447
21	0.370	0.435
22	0.361	0.425
23	0.353	0.415
24	0.344	0.406
25	0.337	0.398
26	0.331	0.390
27	0.324	0.382
28	0.317	0.375
29	0.312	0.368
30	0.306	0.362

The observed value of *rho* must be **equal to** or **greater than** the critical value in this table for significance to be shown.

Source: J.H. Zhar (1972) Significance testing of the Spearman rank correlation coefficient. Reproduced from the *Journal of the American Statistical Association*, **67**, 578–80. With kind permission of the publisher.

The Mann-Whitney *U* test

How to do the Mann–Whitney test

Alternative hypothesis: Male participants interviewed on a high bridge give higher ratings of the attractiveness of a female interviewer than those interviewed on a low bridge (directional, one-tailed).

Null hypothesis: There is difference in the ratings of attractiveness between those interviewed on a high or low bridge.

STEP 1 Record the data and allocate points

Attractiveness ratings given by high-bridge group	Points	Attractiveness ratings given by low-bridge group	Points
7	1.5	4	0
10	0	6	0.5
8	1	2	0
6	1.5	5	0.5
5	2.0	3	0
8	1	5	0.5
9	0.5	6	0.5
7	1.5	4	0
10	0	5	0.5
9	0.5	7	1.0
		9	0.5
		3	0
		5	0.5
		6	0.5
$N_1 = 10$	9.5	$N_2 = 14$	5

To allocate points, consider each score one at a time

Compare this score with all the scores in the other group

Give 1 point for every higher score

Give ½ point for every equal score

STEP 2 Find the observed value of *U*

U is the lowest total number of points

STEP 3 Find the critical value of *U*

- N_1 = number of participants in one group
- N_2 = number of participants in other group
- Look up the critical value in a table of critical values (on the right)
- For a one-tailed test, $N_1 = 10$ and $N_2 = 14$, and the critical value of $U = 41$
- As the observed value (5) is less than the critical value (41), we can reject the null hypothesis and conclude that participants interviewed on a high bridge give higher ratings of attractiveness to a female interviewer than those interviewed on a low bridge.

When to use the Mann-Whitney test

The hypothesis predicts a *difference* between two sets of data.

The two sets of data are from separate groups of participants = *independent groups*.

The data are *ordinal* or *interval* (see page 95 for an explanation).

Critical values of *U* at the 5% level for a one-tailed test

		N_1													
		2	3	4	5	6	7	8	9	10	11	12	13	14	15
N_2	2				0	0	0	1	1	1	1	2	2	2	3
	3		0	0	1	2	2	3	3	4	5	5	6	7	7
	4		0	1	2	3	4	5	6	7	8	9	10	11	12
	5	0	1	2	4	5	6	8	9	11	12	13	15	16	18
	6	0	2	3	5	7	8	10	12	14	16	17	19	21	23
	7	0	2	4	6	8	11	13	15	17	19	21	24	26	28
	8	1	3	5	8	10	13	15	18	20	23	26	28	31	33
	9	1	3	6	9	12	15	18	21	24	27	30	33	36	39
	10	1	4	7	11	14	17	20	24	27	31	34	37	41	44
	11	1	5	8	12	16	19	23	27	31	34	38	42	46	50
	12	2	5	9	13	17	21	26	30	34	38	42	47	51	55
	13	2	6	10	15	19	24	28	33	37	42	47	51	56	61
	14	2	7	11	16	21	26	31	36	41	46	51	56	61	66
	15	3	7	12	18	23	28	33	39	44	50	55	61	66	72

For any N_1 and N_2, the observed value of *U* must be **equal to** or **less than** the critical value in this table for significance to be shown.

Source: R. Runyon and A. Haber (1976) *Fundamentals of behavioural statistics (3rd edition)*. Copyright 1976. Reproduced with kind permission from McGraw-Hill Education.

Critical values of *U* at the 5% level for a two-tailed test

		N_1													
		2	3	4	5	6	7	8	9	10	11	12	13	14	15
N_2	2							0	0	0	0	1	1	1	1
	3				0	1	1	2	2	3	3	4	4	5	5
	4			0	1	2	3	4	4	5	6	7	8	9	10
	5		0	1	2	3	5	6	7	8	9	11	12	13	14
	6		1	2	3	5	6	8	10	11	13	14	16	17	19
	7		1	3	5	6	8	10	12	14	16	18	20	22	24
	8	0	2	4	6	8	10	13	15	17	19	22	24	26	29
	9	0	2	4	7	10	12	15	17	20	23	26	28	31	34
	10	0	3	5	8	11	14	17	20	23	26	29	33	36	39
	11	0	3	6	9	13	16	19	23	26	30	33	37	40	44
	12	1	4	7	11	14	18	22	26	29	33	37	41	45	49
	13	1	4	8	12	16	20	24	28	33	37	41	45	50	54
	14	1	5	9	13	17	22	26	31	36	40	45	50	55	59
	15	1	5	10	14	19	24	29	34	39	44	49	54	59	64

For any N_1 and N_2, the observed value of *U* must be **equal to** or **less than** the critical value in this table for significance to be shown.

Source: R. Runyon and A. Haber (1976) *Fundamentals of behavioural statistics (3rd edition)*. Copyright 1976. Reproduced with kind permission from McGraw-Hill Education.

The Wilcoxon matched pairs signed ranks test (*T*)

When to use the Wilcoxon test test

The hypothesis predicts a *difference* between two sets of data.

The two sets of data are pairs of scores from one person (or a matched pair) = *related*.

The data are *ordinal* or *interval* (see page 95 for an explanation).

How to do the Wilcoxon test

Alternative hypothesis: There is a difference in the score on a short-term memory test when it is taken in the morning or in the afternoon (non-directional, two-tailed).

Null hypothesis: There is no difference in the score on a short-term memory test when it is taken in the morning or in the afternoon.

STEP 1 Record the data, calculate the difference between the scores and rank them

Rank the numbers from low to high, ignoring the signs (i.e. the lowest number receives the rank of 1)

If there are two or more of the same number (tied ranks), calculate the rank by working out the mean of the ranks that would have been given

If the difference is zero, omit this from the ranking and reduce *N* accordingly

Participant	Score on test taken in morning	Score on test taken in afternoon	Difference	Rank
1	15	12	3	8
2	14	15	−1	2
3	6	8	−2	5.5
4	15	15	omit	
5	16	12	2	5.5
6	10	14	−4	9
7	8	10	−2	5.5
8	16	15	1	2
9	17	19	−2	5.5
10	16	17	−1	2
11	10	15	−5	10
12	14	8	6	11

STEP 2 Find the observed value of *T*

T = the sum of the *ranks* of the less frequent sign

In this case, the less frequent sign is plus, so *T* = 8 + 5.5 + 2 + 11 = 26.5

STEP 3 Find the critical value of *T*

- *N* = 11
- Look up the critical value in a table of critical values (on the right)
- For a two-tailed test, *N* = 11, and the critical value of *T* = 10
- As the observed value (26.5) is greater than the critical value (10), we can retain the null hypothesis and conclude that there is no difference in the score on a short-term memory test when it is taken in the morning or in the afternoon.

Critical values of *T* at the 5% level

N	One-tailed test	Two-tailed test
5	T ≤ 0	
6	2	0
7	3	2
8	5	3
9	8	5
10	11	8
11	13	10
12	17	13
13	21	17
14	25	21
15	30	25
16	35	29
17	41	34
18	47	40
19	53	46
20	60	52
21	67	58
22	75	65
23	83	73
24	91	81
25	100	89
26	110	98
27	119	107
28	130	116
29	141	125
30	151	137
31	163	147
32	175	159
33	187	170

The observed value of T must be **equal to** or **less than** the critical value in this table for significance to be shown.

Source: R. Meddis (1975) *Statistical handbook for non-statisticians*. Copyright 1976. Reproduced with kind permission from McGraw-Hill Education.

If you want help with inferential tests that we have not covered here or need further suggestions about coursework, consult M. Cardwell & H. Coolican (2003) *A–Z psychology: coursework (2nd edition)*. *Handbook*. Hodder.

Review exercises

The intention of this chapter is to provide ideas and materials to enable you to practise your knowledge throughout the course. You will have spent a short period covering the basics of research methods in the first four chapters of the book. It is equally important to continue to rehearse and gain greater understanding as you progress through your AS year.

Contents

pages 100–105

1 Quizzes

Write your own quizzes

A bank of quizzes:

Quiz 1   Variables and other things

Quiz 2   Aims and hypotheses

Quiz 3   Sampling

Quiz 4   Validity and reliability

Quiz 5   Experimental control

Quiz 6   Data analysis

Quiz 7   The relationship between researchers and participants

Quiz 8   Methods of conducting research

Quiz 9   Ethical issues and other things

Quiz 10 General review

page 106

2 Research methods key terms

pages 107–109

3 Using star studies to revise research methods

4 Marking exercises

pages 110–120

Past exam questions, each with some guidance about how to answer the questions and two student answers for you to mark

May 2002

January 2003

May 2003

January 2004

May 2004

Marks for student answers to exam questions

pages 121–123

5 More exam style questions

Questions 9–14

Task 1 Quizzes

Write your own quizzes

Look at the specification in Appendix I (pages 124 and 125). You will see that it is divided into three sections, and these are further sub-divided. Divide your class into groups and give each group a part of the specification. Their task is to write some quiz questions on their part of the specification. These can be MCQs, fill-in-the blank or exam-style questions.

If each student writes 10–15 questions (and answers), you can then pool the questions and take the quizzes.

Swap quizzes between groups and see which group gets the highest percentage score on their quiz.

You may decide that some questions are not legitimate, but that's all part of studying for the research methods exam.

A bank of quizzes

Keep your own score

There are an assortment of quizzes on the following pages, loosely related to specific topics. Students might take one quiz every 2 weeks, and keep a running score of how they do.

One way to mark the quizzes is to ask other students to mark the answers.

You can use the following mark schemes:

2 marks	Accurate and sufficiently detailed
1 mark	Muddled, not sufficiently clear
0 marks	Wrong

3 marks	Accurate and detailed
2 marks	Not worth 3 marks but also not 1 mark! Not enough detail
1 mark	Muddled, not sufficiently clear
0 marks	Wrong

Quiz no:	1	2	3	4	5	6	7	8	9	10	TOTAL
My score											
Total possible	50	50	50	50	50	50	50	50	50	50	500

QUIZ 1

Variables and other things

1. What do the letters IV and DV stand for? [2]

2. In the following list, which is the IV and which the DV?

   (a) In an experiment to test the relationship between imagery and memory, the two variables are performance on a memory test and instruction about how to process the stimulus words (rehearsal or imagery). [2]

   (b) In an experiment to see if physical attractiveness makes a person more likeable, the two variables are the attractiveness of a person's photograph and whether they are rated as more or less likeable. [2]

   (c) In an experiment to find out if people think blondes are less intelligent, the two variables are an estimate of IQ and a photo of a person in a blonde or a brunette wig. [2]

3. Explain the difference between an IV and a DV. [3]

4. What is an extraneous variable? [3]

5. What is a confounding variable? [2]

6. What is the difference between a confounding variable and an extraneous variable? [3]

7. Explain in what way a confounding variable acts like an independent variable. [2]

8. What is an experiment? [3]

9. Explain how a laboratory experiment differs from a natural experiment. [3]

10. *A psychologist aims to investigate context-dependent recall by arranging for students to be given a lesson on Freud in their normal classroom and then assessing their recall of this material in their teaching room or in the examination hall.*

    (a) Identify the IV and DV in this study. [2]

    (b) How could you operationalise the DV? [2]

    (c) Think of at least **one** extraneous variable that should be controlled. [3]

    (d) How might you control this extraneous variable? [2]

11. *In a research study, psychologists showed participants a set of photographs and then asked them a week later to identify the photographs they had seen out of a larger set of photographs. The original set consisted of photographs of people and of scenery. They expected to find that participants were more likely to remember the photographs of people.*

    (a) Identify the IV and DV in this study. [2]

    (b) Think of at least **one** extraneous variable that should be controlled. [3]

    (c) How might you control this extraneous variable? [2]

12. Why are standardised instructions needed in a study? [3]

13. What are co-variables? [2]

14. *A research study looked at the relationship between mother's age and length of time breastfeeding.*

    What are the co-variables in this study? [2]

QUIZ 2

Aims and hypotheses

1. What are the 'aims' of a study? [2]

2. Define the term 'hypothesis'. [2]

3. What is the difference between an experimental hypothesis and an alternative hypothesis? [2]

4. Why would a psychologist choose to use a directional hypothesis? [2]

5. When would a non-directional hypothesis be appropriate? [2]

6. Explain the difference between a directional and a non-directional hypothesis. [3]

7. In the examples below, state whether the hypothesis is directional or non-directional.

   (a) Men have a better recall of words than women. [1]

   (b) In STM memory, words are recalled acoustically rather than semantically. [1]

   (c) STM and LTM differ in the way in which memory is encoded. [1]

   (d) The presence of cues affects recall. [1]

8. Write a suitable alternative hypothesis for the following research ideas or questions:

   (a) A psychologist wishes to find out whether Therapy A is better than Therapy B for treating patients with depression. [2]

   (b) Do older people sleep more or less than young people? [2]

   (c) Do children perform better on intelligence tests if they have done some practice tests? [2]

9. Select **one** research study you are familiar with.

   (a) State the aims of the study. [2]

   (b) State a suitable hypothesis for this study. [2]

   (c) Is this hypothesis directional or non-directional? [1]

   (d) Write a different hypothesis (directional or non-directional). [2]

10. *A team of psychologists decide to conduct research into the effects of eating sweets on children's heath. Previous research suggests that children who eat more sweets have more illness than children who eat fewer sweets so they decide to use a directional hypothesis for their study.*

    (a) What is meant by the phrase a 'directional hypothesis' in the context of this study? [2]

    (b) Write a suitable directional hypothesis suitable for a correlational analysis. [2]

    (c) Why did they choose a directional hypothesis rather than a non-directional one? [2]

    (d) Write a suitable non-directional hypothesis for this study. [2]

11. For each of the following behaviours, suggest **two** ways in which they could be operationalised:

    (a) Hunger [2]

    (b) Embarrassment [2]

    (c) Being stressed [2]

    (d) Anger [2]

    (e) Memory [2]

    (f) Affection [2]

QUIZ 3

Sampling

1. What is a target population? [2]

2. Why is it desirable to obtain a representative sample for a research study? [2]

3. What is a random sample? [2]

4. How would you obtain a random sample? (State at least **two** steps that would be involved.) [2]

5. What is an opportunity sample? [2]

6. How would you obtain an opportunity sample? (State at least **two** steps that would be involved.) [2]

7. What is a volunteer sample? [2]

8. How would you obtain a volunteer sample? (State at least **two** steps that would be involved.) [2]

9. Give **one** advantage and **one** disadvantage of each of the three sampling methods named above. [6]

10. Why do very few studies use random sampling as a method, whereas the other two methods are more common? [3]

11. Why might a volunteer sample be preferable to an opportunity sample? [2]

12. What is the difference between a random sample and a systematic sample? [3]

13. How can a systematic sample be turned into a random sample? [2]

14. Why might an opportunity sample be preferable to a volunteer sample? [2]

15. Identify the sampling method used in each of the following examples.

    (a) A group of psychology students interview shoppers in a local shopping centre about attitudes towards dieting. [1]

    (b) Psychology students advertise for people willing to fill out their questionnaire. [1]

    (c) The researchers post questionnaires to pupils in a school by selecting the first five names in each class register. [1]

    (d) Participants for a memory test are obtained by placing the names of everyone in the school in a box and selecting 30 names. [1]

16. *In an observational study, the research question is 'To what extent do primary school children behave helpfully?'*

    (a) Suggest **two** suitable behavioural categories that could be used to record how helpful children are. [2]

    (b) The researchers have to decide on a sampling technique for collecting their data. There are three observers. Suggest **one** suitable method of observing children in a playground and explain how you would do it. [2 + 2]

    (c) Suggest **one** advantage and **one** disadvantage of using this method. [2 + 2]

    (d) What is the advantage of using more than one observer? [2]

QUIZ 4

Validity and reliability

1. Explain what is meant by validity and reliability. [3 + 3]

2. Distinguish between internal and external validity. [3]

3. Distinguish between internal and external reliability. [3]

4. *A psychologist conducts interviews with mothers about their attitudes towards day care.*

    (a) Describe **two** features of the study that might affect the validity of the data being collected. (Try to identify one thing that would affect internal validity and one that would affect external validity.) [2 + 2]

    (b) Explain how you could improve the validity of the study. [2]

5. *A psychologist conducts a study to see if students do more homework in the winter or spring term. To do this, he asks students to keep a diary of how much time they spend on homework each week.*

    (a) Describe **two** features of the study that might affect the validity of the data being collected. [2 + 2]

    (b) Explain how you could improve the validity of the study. [2]

6. *A psychologist wishes to discover what factors are associated with bullying on the school playground. To do this, he observes primary school children during their playtimes for 1 month.*

    (a) Describe **two** features of the study that might affect the validity of the data being collected. [2 + 2]

    (b) Explain how you could improve the validity of the study. [2]

7. *A psychologist intends to use a repeated measures design to test participants' memories in the morning and afternoon. He uses two tests of memory.*

    (a) Suggest how he can ensure that both tests are measuring the same thing (internal reliability). [2]

    (b) Suggest **one** way in which investigator effects might threaten the validity of this research study. [2]

    (c) Explain how you could deal with this problem. [2]

8. *A psychologist interviews teenage girls about their dieting.*

    (a) Outline **one** way in which she could check the reliability of the data she collects in her interviews with the girls. [2]

    (b) Suggest **one** factor that could affect the validity of the interviews with the girls. [2]

    (c) Explain how you could deal with this problem. [2]

9. *Some psychology students plan to conduct an observational study on the effects of different dress styles – to see if men look more at girls dressed casually or smartly.*

    (a) Identify **two** ways in which you could operationalise 'being dressed casually'. [2]

    (b) Identify **one** way in which you could ensure reliability between the different observers. [2]

    (c) Explain how you would put this into practice. [2]

    (d) Explain **one** feature of the study that might affect the validity of the data being collected. [2]

QUIZ 5

Experimental control

1. Explain the difference between an experimental group and a control group. [3]

2. Explain the difference between an experimental group and an experimental condition. [3]

3. What are standardised instructions? [2]

4. In what way are standardised procedures important for experimental control? [2]

5. What is it that the standardised procedures are controlling? [2]

6. Why are controls important in an experiment? [3]

7. Explain the difference between a confounding variable and an extraneous variable. [3]

8. Suggest **two** ways in which an experimenter might allocate participants to experimental groups. [2 + 2]

9. Why is counterbalancing used? [2]

10. Describe **one** way of counterbalancing conditions. [3]

11. Name **three** kinds of experimental design. [3]

12. In what way do experimental designs provide a form of control? [2]

13. Which experimental design(s) avoid order effects? [1]

14. Which experimental design(s) control participant variables? [1]

15. Which experimental design(s) avoid participants guessing the purpose of the study? [1]

16. Name **two** order effects. [2]

17. *A psychological study investigates how caffeine affects memory. The researcher gives participants a memory test before and another one after drinking a cup of coffee. Each test consists of a list of 20 five-letter words. All the words in the lists were equally common.*

    (a) What kind of design was this? [1]

    (b) Which was the experimental condition, and which was the control condition? [2]

    (c) The experimenter used words that were all of similar length and frequency. Give **one** reason why. [2]

    (d) Identify **one** order effect that might affect the result. Explain how. [2]

    (e) Suggest an alternative experimental design that would avoid this. [1]

18. *In an experiment, participants are given two word lists to compare whether it is easier to learn 'concrete' or 'abstract' nouns.*

    (a) The experimenter wants to ensure that the word lists (one of concrete nouns and one of abstract nouns) are equivalent. Suggest **two** methods of doing this. [2]

    (b) If a repeated measures design were used, how could the experimenter counterbalance the lists? [3]

QUIZ 6

Data analysis

1. Explain the difference between a bar chart and a histogram. [3]

2. Susan Morgan asks 20 people to take part in a memory and imagery experiment. Ten participants are tested in Condition A (they are told to just rehearse the words to be recalled) and 10 in Condition B (they are asked to form an image of each word). The number of words remembered in each condition were:

   Group A (rehearsal)   4 5 5 7 6 4 6 6 3 8

   Group B (imagery)   6 5 9 6 5 8 7 6 9 7.

   Mary drew two graphs to show her findings

   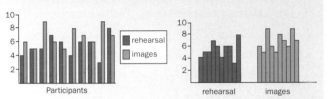

    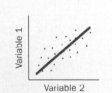

   (a) Which graph is meaningless? Why? [3]

   (b) What information is missing from both charts? [3]

   (c) Are these bar charts or histograms? [1]

   (d) What can you conclude from the graphs? [3]

   (e) Using the raw data, calculate the mean, mode and median for each experimental group. [3]

   (f) Draw a bar chart of the means alone. Do you think this is a better way to represent the data? Why or why not? [3 + 3]

3. Label the scattergraphs below as positive, negative or zero. [3]

   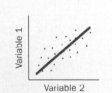

   a)   (b)   (c)

4. What is a correlation coefficient? [2]

5. What is the difference between a correlation and a correlation coefficient? [3]

6. What does a correlation coefficient tell you about a set of data? [2]

7. Give an example of a positive correlation coefficient and a negative correlation coefficient. [2 + 2]

8. Explain what the following correlation coefficients mean:

   (a) +1.00   (d) −0.60

   (b) −1.00   (e) +0.40

   (c) 0.00   (f) +0.10   [2 each]

9. In a study with 30 participants, would a correlation of +0.30 be a weak, moderate or strong correlation? [1]

10. Give **one** advantage and **one** disadvantage of a study using a correlational analysis. [2 + 2]

QUIZ 7

The relationship between researchers and participants

1. Explain why participant reactivity is likely to happen in a study. [2]

2. How could a single-blind design overcome the problem of participant reactivity? [2]

3. How could a double-blind design overcome the problem of participant reactivity? [2]

4. What is a demand characteristic? [2]

5. In what way does a demand characteristic act as a confounding variable? [2]

6. Give an example of demand characteristics from an investigation you have studied (explain why it is a demand characteristic). [3]

7. Explain investigator bias. [2]

8. Describe **one** way to deal with investigator bias. [2]

9. Explain interviewer bias. [2]

10. What is a participant effect? [2]

11. Identify **one** participant effect and say how you could deal with this effect. [3]

12. *A student designed an experiment that used a repeated measures design to investigate obedience to male and female teachers. The student decided to do this by observing how pupils behaved with different teachers. She asked various friends to record teacher behaviours in their classrooms.*

    (a) State a possible directional hypothesis for this study. [2]

    (b) The student thought it would be a good idea to conduct a pilot study. Describe **two** possible things she could achieve in a pilot study. [2 + 2]

    (c) Suggest **one** way in which investigator bias might be a problem for this study. [2]

    (d) Suggest **one** way in which participant effects might be a problem for this study. [2]

    (e) What is **one** disadvantage of using undisclosed observation? [2]

13. *Rob Jones designs a set of questions to collect data about people's attitudes about smoking.*

    (a) Explain how he might deal with the problem of response bias when choosing the questions. [2]

    (b) Suggest **one** advantage and **one** disadvantage of presenting the questions in writing rather than conducting face-to-face interviews. [2 + 2]

    (c) Why would standardised instructions be necessary? [2]

    (d) What is participant reactivity? [2]

    (e) In what way might might participant reactivity be a problem in this study? [2]

    (f) How might demand characteristics be a problem in this study? [2]

QUIZ 8

Methods of conducting research

1. Explain the difference between:

    (a) A research method and a research design. [3]

    (b) A field experiment and a natural experiment. [3]

    (c) A naturalistic observation and an experiment. [3]

    (d) An investigation using a correlational analysis and an experiment. [3]

    (e) An interview and a questionnaire. [3]

2. Explain why natural experiments are 'quasi-experiments'. [2]

3. Explain why a natural experiment may or may not have greater ecological validity than a laboratory experiment. [3]

4. What is a controlled observation? [2]

5. Explain the particular characteristics of a naturalistic observation. [3]

6. In what way can cross-cultural studies be classified as natural experiments? [3]

7. Give **one** advantage and **one** disadvantage of using interviews as a way of collecting data. [2 + 2]

8. The person conducting the interviews may have a set of questions that he or she will ask. What kind of interview is this (a structured or unstructured interview)? [1]

9. If you were going to collect data about day care experiences using a questionnaire, write **one** question that would collect quantitative data and **one** question that would elicit qualitative data. [2 + 2]

10. If you wanted to find out about attitudes towards dieting, why would it be preferable to conduct an questionnaire rather than an interview? [3]

11. Why might it be better to conduct an interview rather than a questionnaire? [3]

12. In the following list, state what research method could be used:

    (a) A researcher records the behaviour of male and female birds during courtship. [1]

    (b) An investigation to demonstrate that rats in a maze without food will learn the layout as quickly as rats that receive food. [1]

    (c) A study of newborn infants to see if they looked longer at a black or a chequered square. [1]

    (d) A researcher uses a charity-collecting tin to see whether people will give more money if the researcher has a child with him. [1]

    (e) An investigation to look at the relationship between IQ and age. [1]

    (f) A study using the exam results from two schools to see whether streaming (used in School A) was better than no streaming (used in School B). [1]

    (g) A researcher approaches pedestrians and asks them questions about local shopping facilities. [1]

QUIZ 9

Ethical issues and other things

1. What is 'debriefing'? [3]

2. What ethical issue(s) can be resolved by debriefing? [3]

3. Consider the star studies you have learned about. Can you think of one which raises no ethical issues? Explain why. [3]

4. For each of the following, identify **one** ethical issue that might have arisen in this study and suggest how the researcher might have dealt with it.

   (a) A correlation of pupil IQ scores and GCSE results. [3]

   (b) Interviewing teenage girls about their dieting habits. [3]

   (c) An observational study of the way in which children cross the road going to and from school. [3]

   (d) A psychologist decides to conduct a field experiment to see whether people are more likely to obey someone wearing a uniform or dressed in a casual suit. [3]

   (e) A school decides to conduct a natural experiment to see if the students doing a new maths programme do better in their GCSE maths exam than a group of students using the traditional learning methods. [3]

   (f) An experiment to test the effect of self-esteem on performance. Participants are given a self-esteem questionnaire and then given a false score (told they either have high or low self-esteem). [3]

   (g) A teacher asks her students to take part in a research project, telling them it is about eating habits whereas it is really about eating disorders. [3]

5. For each item in the following list, think of an appropriate psychological term to explain behaviour. [Answers are: demand characteristics, double blind, experimental realism, experimenter bias, investigator effect, mundane realism, observer bias, participant effect, placebo, single blind.]

   (a) The expectations that an experimenter has may bias the way in which participants will behave in the experiment. [2]

   (b) In some laboratory experiments, participants feel so involved that they act as they would normally. [2]

   (c) The expectations that an observer has influences what they 'see'. [2]

   (d) Some participants were told they were given a drug when in fact it was sugar water. [2]

   (e) Participants were not told the purpose of the experiment in case their expectations affected their behaviour. [2]

   (f) A participant's performance may be influenced by the experimenter's behaviour. [2]

   (g) The experimenter was not told the purpose of the study in case his expectations influenced the behaviour of participants, who were themselves unaware of the condition they were participating in. [2]

   (h) Some aspects of the experimental situation provide cues about how participants should behave. [2]

   (i) The extent to which an experiment mirrors real life. [2]

   (j) The participant's search for cues about how to behave. [2]

QUIZ 10

General review

1. What is research? [3]

2. Why do psychologists conduct research? [3]

3. Which variable is manipulated by the experimenter – the independent or the dependent variable? [1]

4. Do longitudinal or cross-sectional studies control participant variables? [1]

5. In an experiment, what should be the only thing that affects the behaviour of the participant? [1]

6. Explain the difference between qualitative and quantitative data. [3]

7. Give **one** advantage and **one** disadvantage of using qualitative data. [2 + 2]

8. Give **one** advantage and **one** disadvantage of using quantitative data. [2 + 2]

9. You are conducting research on eating disorders. Give **one** advantage of collecting quantitative data *in the context of this study* and **one** disadvantage of collecting qualitative data *in the context of this study*. [2 + 2]

10. In the context of this study, why might it be preferable to collect quantitative data? [2]

11. Is content analysis, an example of qualitative or quantitative analysis? [1]

12. How can 'leading questions' be a problem in interviews or questionnaires? [3]

13. Give an example of a leading question and explain why it is 'leading'. [2]

14. What is the 'social desirability bias'? [2]

15. *A psychological study looked at the effect of different teaching styles on children's ability to learn. To do this, children were given a lesson, using either traditional or more pupil-centred teaching methods, on how the moon was formed. The children were tested the day before the lesson and again a week later using the same test to see how much they knew about the moon. Participants were drawn from three different year groups and randomly assigned to experimental conditions.*

   (a) What is the experimental design of this study? [1]

   (b) Give **two** advantages of using this experimental design. [2 + 2]

   (c) Why was it desirable to give the tests a week apart? [2]

   (d) Why did the experimenter choose classes from three different year groups? [3]

   (e) What were the two experimental conditions in this study? [2]

   (f) What does 'randomly allocated to experimental conditions' mean? [2]

   (g) Think of **one** way in which the experimental conditions might have differed from what the experimenter intended. [2]

2 Research methods key terms

An exam question may occasionally require you to 'simply' define or explain a term such as 'validity' or 'laboratory experiment' (rather than using your knowledge of such terms to answer contextualised questions). Questions that require a definition or explanation are likely to be worth 2 or 3 marks.

It pays to be ready with an answer to such questions, and learning such definitions should increase your understanding.

For each key term, you should record three points that you need to remember. Three points should provide you with sufficient information to write 3 marks' worth.

Produce a table like the blue one below and record three points for each of the key terms in the purple box below that. There is a third column for additional information that might be useful to remember. You can find the full version of the blue table in the supplementary material on the Nelson Thornes website www.nelsonthornes.com/researchmethods.

Key term	Three points describing each term	Additional information, such as
		• Advantages and/or disadvantages • How might a researcher deal with this problem? • How would you do it?
Validity	• • •	

Key terms you need to know
Note that some of these are very simple concepts and you will not be able to write 3 marks' worth.

Aims	External validity	Matched pairs design	Positive correlation
Bar chart	Extraneous variable	Measures of central tendency	Qualitative data
Correlational analysis	Field experiment	Measures of dispersion	Quantitative data
Correlation coefficient	Histogram	Natural experiment	Random sampling
Demand characteristics	Independent groups design	Naturalistic observation	Reliability
Dependent variable	Independent variable	Negative correlation	Repeated measures
Directional hypothesis	Internal validity	Non-directional hypothesis	Research design
Ethical issue	Interview	Operationalisation	Scattergraph
Experimental/alternative hypothesis	Investigator effects	Opportunity sample	Volunteer sample
Experimental design	Laboratory experiment	Pilot study	

3 Using star studies to revise research methods

In the AS specification, there are a group of key studies (they have been called 'star studies' in *The AS Complete Companion*). For each key study, you need to know the aims, procedures, findings, conclusions and one or two criticisms. You can use these as a way of revising research methods, revising your star studies at the same time!

Go through the star studies and for each of them:

- Identify the research method that was used (note that a study may involve observations or questionnaires as a way of collecting data but the method may be an experiment because there is an IV/DV; or, if there isn't an IV/DV, the method is an observation, questionnaire or interview).

- If it is an experiment, state the IV and DV.

- You should also state the hypothesis and indicate whether this is directional or non-directional.

- Finally, you should note any special design considerations (for experiments, you should state whether they are repeated measures, independent groups or matched pairs).

Fill in a table that looks like the one below. The first entry has been filled in for you. (A copy of the full table for you to fill in is given in the supplementary material at www.nelsonthornes.com/researchmethods.)

One thing you will discover is just how few studies fall into a neat category!

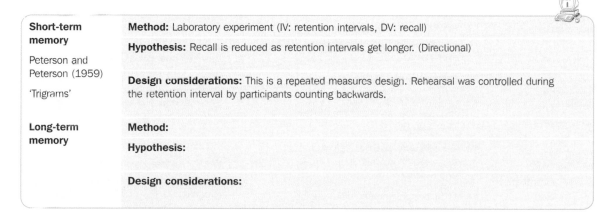

Short-term memory Peterson and Peterson (1959) 'Trigrams'	**Method:** Laboratory experiment (IV: retention intervals, DV: recall) **Hypothesis:** Recall is reduced as retention intervals get longer. (Directional) **Design considerations:** This is a repeated measures design. Rehearsal was controlled during the retention interval by participants counting backwards.
Long-term memory	**Method:** **Hypothesis:** **Design considerations:**

Revising ecological validity (or internal validity, external validity, reliability)

You can choose your own star studies to use in this table. The ones in this table have been selected from the chapter on Social Psychology in *The AS Complete Companion*.

For each of the studies below, present arguments about whether it has high or low ecological validity.

Study	Arguments about why it may have high ecological validity	Arguments about why it may have low ecological validity
Asch (1956)		
Moscovici *et al.* (1969)		
Milgram (1963)		
Hofling *et al.* (1966)		
Bickman (1974)		

Some questions about selected star studies

The full references for these studies can be found in *The AS Complete Companion*.

Peterson and Peterson – a study into the nature of STM

1. What variable did they manipulate/alter directly (i.e. what is the IV)?
2. How did they measure the effects of this manipulation (i.e. what is the DV)?
3. Why was it necessary to count backwards during the retention interval?
4. Explain why you might suggest that this study lacked ecological validity?
5. What sampling method might they have used to obtain the participants in this study?
6. In what way could the sampling method affect validity?
7. What factors may have threatened the internal validity of this study?
8. What factors may have threatened the external validity of this study?

Ainsworth et al. – a study of individual differences in attachment

1. In what way is the Strange Situation a controlled observation?
2. In what way is the Strange Situation better described as an experiment?
3. What observational techniques were used in the Strange Situation?
4. How could event sampling be used in the Strange Situation?
5. What was the behaviour checklist that was used in the Strange Situation?
6. Describe the **two** conflicting values that led to an ethical issue in this study.
7. Do you think this means that the study should not have been conducted?
8. How might this ethical issue have been resolved?
9. If you were going to conduct a study using the Strange Situation procedure, what would you tell the parents beforehand in order to obtain their informed consent?
10. Do you think that asking for their informed consent might affect their behaviour during the study in any way? How?
11. If seeking informed consent may affect behaviour, can you think of an alternative way of dealing with the participants' right to know what they are letting themselves in for?

Baddeley – a study into the nature of LTM

1. When testing encoding in LTM, why was it necessary to have four conditions?
2. What experimental design was used?
3. Describe **one** advantage and **one** disadvantage of this design in the context of this study.
4. What was the IV?
5. How was the IV operationalised?
6. What method was used to select participants?
7. How could you allocate participants to conditions?
8. How could investigator effects have threatened the validity of this study?
9. How might the researcher have dealt with such investigator effects?

Van Ijzendoorn and Kroonenberg (1988) – a study of cross-cultural variations in attachment

1. In what way is this study a natural experiment?
2. Identify the IV and DV in this study.
3. Describe **one** advantage of using this research method in the context of this study.
4. Describe **one** disadvantage of using this research method in the context of this study.
5. Is the design repeated measures or independent groups?
6. What is a meta-analysis?
7. Describe **one** advantage and **one** disadvantage of conducting a meta-analysis.
8. What is a cross-cultural study?
9. Describe **one** advantage and **one** disadvantage of conducting cross-cultural studies.
10. Infant behaviour was assessed using the Strange Situation. What research technique was involved?
11. How could you check the reliability of the Strange Situation?

Loftus and Palmer – a study into the role of leading questions in EWT

1. Identify the IV and DV in this study.
2. There were five experimental groups. Describe the key characteristic of each group.
3. Is this a repeated measures design or an independent groups design?
4. Give **one** advantage and **one** disadvantage of this design in this study.
5. How could participants have been allocated to conditions?
6. Describe any demand characteristics that may have occurred in this study.
7. What other threats to validity might have been present?
8. Identify **one** ethical issue that may have arisen in this study and describe how it could be dealt with.

Hodges and Tizard – a study to the effects of privation

1. Explain in what way this study is a natural experiment.
2. Describe **one** advantage of using a natural experiment in the context of this study.
3. Describe **one** disadvantage of using a natural experiment in the context of this study.
4. Identify the IV and DV in this study.
5. Write a suitable hypothesis for this study.
6. Is your hypothesis directional or non-directional?
7. Explain why you choose a directional or non-directional hypothesis.
8. The study by Hodges and Tizard is a longitudinal design. Are longitudinal studies repeated measures or independent groups designs?
9. Why do psychologists conduct longitudinal studies?
10. An alternative design to use when comparing age groups is to use a cross-sectional design. Are cross-sectional studies repeated measures or independent groups designs?
11. What sampling method was used in this study?
12. Describe **one** disadvantage of this sampling method in the context of this study.

Kiecolt-Glaser et al. – a study into the relationship between stress and the immune system

1. State a suitable alternative hypothesis for this study.
2. Is your alternative hypothesis directional or non-directional?
3. Justify your choice.
4. Explain in what way this study is a matched participants design.
5. Describe **one** advantage and **one** disadvantage of using this design in the context of this study.
6. How do you know that it was a volunteer sample in this study?
7. Why might this sampling method lead to a sample bias?
8. Suggest another way in which they might have obtained their sample.
9. Explain why this study is a natural experiment.
10. Describe **one** reason why this study might be thought to have low validity.
11. Participants rated stress on a '10-point perceived stress scale'. How could you assess the validity of this scale?

Rahe et al. – a study into life changes as a source of stress

1. What are the co-variables in this study?
2. How were the co-variables operationalised?
3. Why is 0.118 significant in this study, whereas in another study it might not be?
4. What kind of correlation were they expecting to find?
5. What kind of graph would be used to represent the data from this study?
6. What sampling method was used in this study?
7. Describe **one** advantage and **one** disadvantage of using this method in the context of this study.
8. Why might it have been useful to conduct a pilot study?
9. Life changes were assessed using the SRRS. How could you assess the reliability of this measure?
10. How could you replicate this study?
11. What would be the value of replicating this study?

Marmot et al. – a study into workplace stressors

1. Describe the **two** hypotheses that were investigated in this study.
2. Describe **one** reason why this study might be thought to have low validity.
3. How was stress operationalised in this study?
4. Why did they test the participants after 5 years (instead of 1 year or 10 years)?
5. What was the experimental design in this study?
6. Describe **one** advantage and **one** disadvantage of using this design in this study.
7. Identify **two** possible ethical issues that might have arisen in this study and say how the researcher could have dealt with them.
8. A questionnaire was used to collect data. Describe **two** factors that might have affected the validity of this questionnaire.
9. How could the researcher deal with these problems?
10. Is this a field experiment or a natural experiment? Explain your answer.

Asch – a study into conformity

1. Why did Asch debrief his participants?
2. Do you think debriefing was sufficient to deal with the possible harm he may have caused?
3. Describe **one** factor that might affect the internal validity of this study.
4. Describe **two** factors that might affect the external validity of this study.
5. Why were confederates used in this study?
6. Why was it necessary to have some trials that were not 'critical'?
7. What was the IV and DV in this study?
8. What kind of experiment is this?
9. State a suitable hypothesis for this study.
10. Describe **one** advantage and **one** disadvantage of using this kind of experiment.
11. What method of graphical representation would be suitable for the findings of this study? Explain your answer.

Moscovici et al. – a study into minority influence

1. The consistent and inconsistent conditions could be seen as an IV. What was the DV in this study?
2. What is the experimental design?
3. There were six people in each group. Why do you think they used this number of people?
4. Identify **two** possible ethical issues that might have arisen in this study and say how the researcher could deal with them.
5. What possible extraneous variables might affect the validity of the findings?
6. Suggest how you might deal with **one** of these extraneous variables.
7. How could the relationship between the researcher and participants have affected the validity of this study?
8. Suggest **one** way of dealing with researcher/participant effects.
9. What would be a suitable kind of graph to use for findings of this study?
10. Sketch the graph and put in appropriate labels and a title.
11. Write a suitable hypothesis.

Milgram – a study into obedience to authority

1. Explain why this could be seen to be a laboratory experiment.
2. Describe **one** advantage of using a laboratory experiment in the context of this study.
3. Describe **one** disadvantage of using a laboratory experiment in the context of this study.
4. Describe **two** possible threats to the validity of this study.
5. Suggest how you could deal with these problems.
6. What sampling method was used in this study?
7. Describe **one** advantage and **one** disadvantage of this sampling method in the context of this study.

Make up your own You can make up your own question cards for the other star studies, as well as other research covered in your course, to help revise the studies and research methods. Just writing the questions is a good way to revise.

4 Marking exercises: May 2002

A team of psychologists was interested in studying the effects of alcohol on people's reaction times. Earlier research suggested that the increase in reaction time was either due to the alcohol itself or due to people's expectations.

The psychologists recruited two groups of volunteers (an independent groups design) from a local university. Each participant's reaction time was measured by using a computer game. They were then given a drink. The first group received a drink containing a large measure of strong alcohol; the second group received an identical drink without alcohol, but with a strong alcoholic smell.

Finally, all participants were required to play the computer game again to assess their reaction time. Once they had completed the task, they were then thanked for their time and allowed to leave.

The results from the study are shown in the table below:

Table 1: Table to show *increase* in reaction time in milliseconds.

Group 1 (with alcohol)	Group 2 (without alcohol)
16	12
17	12
18	12
18	13
19	15
20	16
20	19
21	20
23	21
47	23

(a) (i) Give an appropriate experimental/alternative hypothesis for this study. *(2 marks)*

   (ii) State whether your hypothesis is directional or non-directional and justify why you choose this form of hypothesis. (3 marks)

(b) (i) Identify the sampling method used in this study. (1 mark)

   (ii) Explain **one** limitation of this method of sampling. (2 marks)

(c) Suggest **one** advantage and **one** disadvantage of using an independent groups design in this study. (2 marks + 2 marks)

(d) What measure of central tendency is most suitable to describe the data in Table 1? Explain your choice of measure of central tendency. (3 marks)

(e) Consider what the data in Table 1 seem to show about the effect of alcohol on reaction time. (6 marks)

(f) Identify **one** ethical issue that the researchers do not appear to have considered. Explain how this ethical issue could have been dealt with. (3 marks)

(g) Other than ethical issues, explain **two** ways in which the design of this study might have been improved. (3 marks + 3 marks)

Marking scheme

For 3 mark questions:

3 marks	Accurate and informed description.
2 marks	Limited, generally accurate but less detailed.
1 mark	Brief or muddled description.
0 marks	No reason given or incorrect description.

(a) (i) For 2 marks, need a clear IV and DV.

   (ii) Appropriate direction plus some mention of previous research plus what it told us.

(b) (i) Correct method (volunteer or self-selecting).

   (ii) Must be only one limitation. Should say, for example, likely to be biased *and* therefore cannot generalise.

(c) Advantage/disadvantage needs to be contextualised.

(d) Median; to explain this, state that it is suitable when there are extreme scores because it is not affected by such scores.

(e) Both groups showed an increase in reaction time (i.e. reaction time became slower), which suggests that the thought of having alcohol has an affect. Group 2 showed less of an increase, which suggests that mere belief is not the main effect on slower reaction time. However, the difference was not that big, which indicates quite a large psychological component to effect reaction time. Could note individual differences.

(f) Debriefing is not an issue. Must name an acceptable issue and then deal with it, e.g. informed consent is the issue; ask for informed consent *and* state what this might entail.

(g) Could use a better sample, could use a control group with no alcohol, matched pairs design. For each, state details and why.

MARKING EXERCISES

Student Answer 1

(a) (i) Alcohol will have an effect on reaction time.

   (ii) This is a non-directional hypothesis since it says there will be an effect but it does not state which direction the effect will take.

(b) (i) Random sampling.

   (ii) One limitation is that it is only representative of that population; thus the findings of this research could not be applied to a wider population.

(c) An advantage of using an independent groups design is that there are no order effects and the findings are not influenced by practice or fatigue, which can be seen in repeated measures.

   One disadvantage of using an independent measures design is that participant variables may be an influencing factor. The group who have alcohol may show differences from other groups in terms of sex, intelligence, age and so on.

(d) The measure of central tendency that would be most suitable in Table 1 would be the mean. This is because it takes all the values into account.

(e) The data in Table 1 show that the increase in reaction time for Group 1 was greater in the beginning than for Group 2. However, the rate of reaction time increased in Group 1 less than in Group 2. Group 1's reaction time is consistently more than Group 2's, suggesting that alcohol did indeed have an effect on people's reaction time. However, towards the end the reaction times are pretty similar for both groups, implying that there was little difference between the two groups. The only significant difference is the last reaction time, in which case Group 1's reaction time is much more than Group 2's.

(f) One ethical issue is that the participants were deceived. They believed they were being given a drink of alcohol but some were not. This could have been addressed by a full debriefing afterwards.

(g) This study could have been better if reaction time had not been tested using a computer game. Some of the volunteers might have been used to using computers, whereas others might not have been. A better way of measuring reaction time could have been trying to catch a ruler when dropped from a certain height.

   Another way in which the study might have been improved is using a matched pairs design instead of independent groups. They could have been matched for age, intelligence, etc., thus limiting the participant variables as possible confounding variables.

Student Answer 2

(a) (i) An experimental hypothesis for this study would be 'The reaction time for people who have an alcoholic drink will be slower than the reaction time of people who have no alcohol'.'

   (ii) My hypothesis is directional. I selected this because previous research suggested that this might be the case.

(b) (i) The sampling method used is opportunity sampling.

   (ii) A limitation of this kind of sampling technique is that it is not very likely to give a representative sample of the population as the majority would refuse to be involved in an experiment.

(c) One advantage of using an independent groups design in this study is that one group will be able to have a drink while the others will not as there was a group of participants for each situation. One group is expected to do both conditions, which would make it very difficult to achieve a valid result.

   A disadvantage of this design is that it uses a lot of people and therefore is time consuming and possibly expensive as alcohol would have to be bought so so everybody involved got the same amount.

(d) I think the median would be the best measure of central tendency because in group 2 there is only a small range of scores but in group 1 there is an outlying score that could affect the mean if it were used, and it would make research invalid, but if the median is used the outlying score is ignored. It's also easier to work the median out.

(e) In general the data in this table suggest that alcohol increases reaction time as the median in the non-alcoholic group is 16 but in the alcoholic group it is 20, an increase of 4 milliseconds. However, the reaction time difference is only very small so the table shows that although reaction time does increase if alcohol is consumed in measured quantities, the effects are similar and one could almost say irrelevant.

(f) One ethical issue that the researchers do not appear to have considered is that people might in fact have been forced into the experiment if they were with their friends and chose not to drink alcohol but might have felt forced to in the presence of others to save face. A way of overcoming this would be to check with participants on their own to ensure that they were comfortable with the experimental situation.

(g) The design of the study might have been improved by the use of a more representative sample as students do not represent the whole population; in fact students are known for their ability to consume large amounts of alcohol so they might be more resistant to its effects than 'normal' people.

   Another way they might have improved this study is to have used a test-retest measure to ascertain the validity of the study so that people could be sure that the findings were true and not just results of the type of person; a happy person might feel the effects more than a sad person. This would mean that the responses of a happy person would be different from those of a sad person.

See page 120 for suggested marks.

Marking exercises: January 2003

A local authority was concerned about the amount of under-age drinking in the area. As part of a long-term strategy to try and eliminate this activity the local authority asked a group of psychology students to help design a questionnaire to be used to survey local school children in the area.

The following is an extract from the questionnaire:

-2-

4. Do you drink alcoholic drinks?   Yes/No
5. How many units of alcohol do you consume, on average, each week? ☐
6. What age can you legally buy alcohol in a pub?   ☐
7. Why did you start consuming alcoholic drinks?
    ....
    ....
8. For what reasons do you consume alcoholic drinks?
    ....
    ....
    ....

(a) Outline **one** advantage and **one** disadvantage of using a questionnaire.   (2 marks + 2 marks)

(b) Explain **one** reason why a pilot study should have been carried out in the context of this survey.   (3 marks)

(c) (i) Identify **one** question in the extract above that would provide qualitative data.   (1 mark)

    (ii) With reference to the question you have identified in part (i), explain why this question would produce qualitative data.   (3 marks)

(d) (i) Identify **one** sampling method that could have been used in this survey.   (1 mark)

    (ii) In the context of this survey, explain **one** reason for using the sampling method you have identified in (i).   (2 marks)

(e) (i) The questions in the extract above can be criticised. Select **one** question and give **one** criticism of it.   (2 marks)

    (ii) Re-write the question you selected so that it overcomes the criticism you identified in (i).   (2 marks)

(f) Describe **two** ways of making sure that this survey would be carried out in an ethically acceptable way.   (3 marks + 3 marks)

(g) Following the survey it was decided to conduct an observational study into under-age drinking. Outline procedures for carrying out such an observation.   (6 marks)

Marking scheme

For 3 mark questions:

3 marks	Accurate and informed description.
2 marks	Limited, generally accurate but less detailed.
1 mark	Brief or muddled description.
0 marks	No reason given or incorrect description.

(a) No context is required. Must provide detail. 'Cheaper' counts as zero, whereas 'cheaper than' counts as 1 mark. Two marks for comment that is exclusive to a questionnaire.

(b) Not 'what is a pilot study' but why would you do one here. Only first answer credited. Must be in context.

(c) (i) Question 7 or 8.

    (ii) Answers must be contextualised with examples to gain marks, but examples alone would not be credited. Could say that all answers will be different, which makes analysis more difficult.

(d) Must explain why selected rather than define the method. If there were zero marks for (i), there will be zero for (ii).

(e) (ii) The new question must be able to produce the same data as the original if reproduced.

(f) Marks here for how you would deal with the problem, not a description of the issue, e.g. how exactly would you get informed consent.

(g) Must reflect an understanding of how observational research is conducted, e.g. what kind of observation, what does the observer usually do during observation, what location, how many observers, how would one check reliability, how record data, how present data, ethical considerations?

Student Answer 1

(a) One advantage of using questionnaires is that they enable researchers to cover a wide sample of people in a less time-consuming way than other methods.

One disadvantage of using questionnaires is that people may not take them seriously and give unhelpful answers.

(b) One reason a pilot study should have been carried out is to test the design format and find out if people have understood and answered properly.

(c) (i) Question 8: For what reasons do you consume alcoholic drinks?

(ii) This question would not only give information about how people drink but give more insight into the reasons for under-age drinking and how this affects drinkers.

(d) (i) Random sample.

(ii) I would have put all the names in a hat.

(e) (i) How many units of alcohol do you consume? This question assumes that everyone who drinks, drinks weekly.

(ii) How often do you drink? Once a week? Daily? 2 or 3 times a week?

(f) I would write a short paragraph as an introduction to the questionnaire stating what I was investigating to allow for informed consent.

I would also make the questionnaire anonymous so that there would be no fear on the respondent's behalf.

(g) I would choose a covert study with one person of a similar age as the observation group who would observe how much they drink, what they drink, how they behave and how frequently they drink. They would then report back their findings as do others at least three times for increased reliability.

Student Answer 2

(a) Advantage: Qualitative and quantitative data can be gained using questionnaires so that the researcher can gain in-depth material for analysis.

Disadvantage: People are not always honest when filling out questionnaires. They may not want people to know the truth or may want to make themselves look better, or aim to please the researcher.

(b) A pilot study is a good idea because you are able to deal with problems that may arise and then can get rid of these problems for the actual study. In the context of this survey, the problems might be that some people don't understand the questions, and it may be helpful to change the words around to make it more understandable for the audience that it is aimed at.

(c) (i) Question 7.

(ii) The question asks the child 'why' they first started drinking alcohol. This would produce qualitative data because it is open-ended. The participant is able to write freely what their reasons are and this can't be easily categorised as numerical data until it has been interpreted by the researcher.

(d) (i) Opportunity sampling.

(ii) The psychologist needs to aim this research at young people in the school; therefore an ideal method would be to take boys and girls of different ages so that this reflects the distribution of the target population.

(e) (i) Question 5 assumes that the child is familiar with alcohol units and would know how much alcohol constitutes one unit. The answer would be inaccurate as they would either guess or leave the answer blank if they were unsure.

(ii) 'In a week how many alcoholic drinks do you have, on average?' Then ask a second part which is about what kinds of drink they have, for example alcopops, wine, spirits.

(f) Before the questionnaire is given to the children themselves, the researcher could give it to parents to read first, and then give it to the children after obtaining parental permission.

Prior to the children completing the survey, the researchers would need to explain to them that their answers will be used in research and that they have the right to withdraw.

(g) The study could be covert or overt, which means that those being watched may not necessarily know so ethical guidelines need to be respected; for example it is acceptable to observe them in a public place. They might be observed in a playground and then observers might pretend to be a parent looking after a child. Researchers often record their observations afterwards or they might have a video camera or a tape recorder to record observations more reliably. It is important to remember personal safety when carrying out observations. An example of an observational study was Piliavin's study on the subway.

See page 120 for suggested marks.

Marking exercises: May 2003

The teacher in a small secondary school wanted to find out whether there was any truth in her idea that students who used a computer regularly for their homework achieved higher exam grades than those who did not.

She decided to interview a sample of 30 students taken from across the school. She tape-recorded all the interviews. She later obtained their end of year exam grades from their reports.

(a) (i) Name **two** different methods that the teacher might have used to select her sample. (2 marks)

(ii) Explain how she would have carried out one of the methods of selection named in part (i). (2 marks)

(b) (i) Outline **one** advantage of using interviews in psychological research. (2 marks)

(ii) Outline **one** weakness of using interviews in psychological research. (2 marks)

(c) Outline **one** way in which the teacher could check the reliability of the data concerning computer use that she collected from the interviews with the students. (2 marks)

(d) What is meant by the term validity in the context of research? (2 marks)

(e) Give **one** factor that could affect the validity of the interviews with the students. (2 marks)

(f) Identify **one** ethical issue that the teacher might have considered and explain how she might have dealt with it. (1 mark + 2 marks)

(g) (i) Identify **one** appropriate measure of central tendency for the time students spent on the computer each week and explain how you would calculate it. (2 marks)

(ii) Outline **one** disadvantage of the measure of central tendency you have identified in (i). (2 marks)

(h) The teacher decided to conduct an experiment to see whether giving students more time using computers would improve their grades.

(i) Suggest a non-directional hypothesis for this experiment. (2 marks)

(ii) Identify an appropriate design. (1 mark)

(iii) Using the design identified in (i) outline the procedures that could be used for this experiment. (6 marks)

Marking scheme

For 3 mark questions:

3 marks	Accurate and informed description.
2 marks	Limited, generally accurate but less detailed.
1 mark	Brief or muddled description.
0 marks	No reason given or incorrect description.

(a) A context is required in (ii).

(b) Only take the first answer. For full marks, it must be specific to an interview (as opposed to any other research method) or be sufficiently elaborated.

(c) Some form of test-retest, e.g. students are re-interviewed a month later to see if their answers are the same. Testing reliability of the measuring tool.

(d) Could discuss internal and/or external validity. Multiple answers are OK.

(e) The answer may be same as for (b) (ii). Must be contextualised.

(f) Debriefing is not an issue.

(g) One mark for naming it. The disadvantage must be more than 'because of outliers'.

(h) (i) Must be stated in the form of a hypothesis (not 'to see if …'). Full marks only if fully operationalised (e.g. 'time spent on computers'). No marks for (iii) if (ii) is incorrect or absent. Also no marks for (iii) if no mention is made of the design in (ii).

Student Answer 1

(a) (i) The teacher may have used a random sample of students in their final year or a systematic sample using every 10th student in their final year.

(ii) By using systematic sampling, the teacher would have compiled a list of students in their final year. Then gone down the list selecting every 10th student and asked them to complete the interview.

(b) (i) One advantage of using interviews is that they are a direct way to collect data; they can be quick and detailed long answers may be given.

(ii) One weakness of using interviews is that participants may feel social desirability where they give the answers they think the experimenter wants to hear. For example, the students might reply that they have a computer at home because they might feel bad if they don't. In most interviews many participants are dishonest.

(c) The teacher could check if this data were reliable by asking the parents to be interviewed as well. The parents are less likely to be dishonest as they have less to lose.

(d) Validity means the extent to which data can be applied to another situation. This would mean ecological in this case. Also, experimental validity is the extent to which the data can be applied to how well they met the aims of the research.

(e) If all students were dishonest, then validity would be low as all answers would be biased.

(f) Informed consent. The teacher may therefore have asked a small sample of students whether they would mind taking part in such an interview. This means she would have obtained presumptive consent before the experiment took place.

(g) (i) The mean. The number of hours the students spent on the computer would all be added together and divided by the number of students who gave data. The answer would be the mean time students spent on computers.

(ii) One disadvantage is that if one student spent a very small amount of time on the computer, the mean would be affected.

(h) (i) Does the use of computers improve exam performance?

(ii) Field experiment.

(iii) I would collect my systematic sample from students in their final year, among schools in the area. I would then ask my sample various questions such as 'Do you own a computer?' and 'How long do you use it each week?'. After this I could compare the grades of the students in the sample to see if I had collected a representative sample. This study would be a natural study, which would provide better validity.

Student Answer 2

(a) (i) Random sampling or opportunity sampling.

(ii) For random sampling you draw all the names out of a hat.

(b) (i) One advantage is that you can collect quantitative data, which are easy to sort out and compare.

(ii) A weakness of using interviews is that participants could answer wrong or the way they think the experimenter wants them to.

(c) The teacher could give them the questions on the interview again after a month and see if they give the same answer.

(d) Validity means whether you get the answer you were looking for. Whether the results are right.

(e) The interview could be asking questions in different ways so that the pupils answered them with different meanings because they misunderstood the question.

(f) An ethical issue would be debriefing. The teacher could deal with this by offering debriefing at the end of the interviews.

(g) (i) The mean number of hours spent on a computer would be an appropriate measure. This could be done by adding everything together and dividing by how many there were.

(ii) One disadvantage of the mean is that if one number is very obscure, it could bring the mean number down, e.g. 5, 5, 6, 6, 7, 9, 10 = 48/10 whereas 1, 5, 6, 6, 7, 9, 10 = 44/10.

(h) (i) A non-directional hypothesis would be that there would be a difference in the results between pupils who had more time on a computer and those who had less time.

(ii) Independent group design.

(iii) The teacher would split the students into two groups randomly and give one group more time on the computers, and the second group would have the same time as before. At the end of the year you could see if there was a difference in the grades scored by the two groups. Before doing the experiment, the teacher should conduct a pilot study to see if there were any difficulties with the design.

See page 120 for suggested marks.

Marking exercises: January 2004

Research has suggested that the content of television programmes can influence a person's mood. If the news is mainly negative people feel depressed after watching it, while if the news is positive they do not.

A team of psychologists from a university tested this idea. They designed two similar news programmes; one contained positive events (e.g. a cure for cancer had been found; unemployment rates were low) and the other contained negative events (e.g. peace talks had failed; earthquake left many dead). Half of the participants watched the positive programme first and the negative programme three weeks later. The other half saw the programmes in the reverse order. A mood questionnaire measured their mood on each occasion. A high score on the questionnaire represented a more positive mood.

The findings are shown below.

Table 1: Table to show increase in reaction time in milliseconds.

	Mean	Standard deviation
Positive news	19.00	2.38
Negative news	15.92	1.26

(a) State the aim of this experiment. (2 marks)

(b) Describe the operationalised independent variable and operationalised dependent variable for this experiment.
(2 marks + 2 marks)

(c) (i) Identify the type of experimental design that was used.
(1 mark)

(ii) Give **one** advantage and **one** disadvantage of this design.
(2 marks + 2 marks)

(d) Explain why the experiment was designed so that half the participants saw the positive programme first and the other half of the participants saw the negative programme first. (3 marks)

(e) (i) Give **one** advantage of using the mean. (2 marks)

(ii) What does the standard deviation tell us about data?
(2 marks)

(f) The researchers summarised their data in the following bar chart:

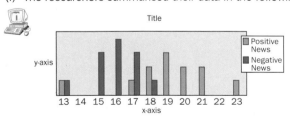

(i) Provide a suitable title for this bar chart. (1 mark)

(ii) Give an appropriate label for the x-axis. (1 mark)

(iii) Give an appropriate label for the y-axis. (1 mark)

(g) Give **one** conclusion that can be drawn from the data (as illustrated in the table and histogram). (3 marks)

(h) This study used the experimental method. Briefly describe how you would use a method other than an experiment to investigate the same aims. (6 marks)

Marking scheme

For 3 mark questions:

3 marks	Accurate and informed description.
2 marks	Limited, generally accurate but less detailed.
1 mark	Brief or muddled description.
0 marks	No reason given or incorrect description.

(a) Must mention positive *and* negative news.

(b) Positive and negative for IV. If DV is just 'mood' then 1 mark; 'mood questionnaire score' for 2 marks.

(c) No need for context, but no marks for (ii) if (i) is incorrect.

(d) Wrong answers: trying to see if there is a difference between seeing the programme first or second, stops participants guessing the aim. Must have context for the full 3 marks.

(e) It is enough to say 'average' for 1 mark. First answer only for (i).

(f) Straightforward.

(g) Any mention of participants gets zero, or if written in the past tense. Full marks if comment on the effect of positive and negative news. News affects mood gets 1 mark. Could elaborate conclusions by referring to findings. Credit first answer only.

(h) No marks for an experiment; no marks for evaluation of method selected.

Student Answer 1

(a) To see whether the content of the TV programme affected mood.

(b) The independent variable is the news programme, whether it is positive or negative. The dependent variable is the score on the mood questionnaire.

(c) (i) The experimental design was repeated measures.

(ii) The advantage of this kind of design is that it eliminates the differences between the groups because one is using the same participants.

The disadvantage is that as they are doing both conditions they may get bored or work out what is expected, and this may cause demand characteristics.

(d) The experimenter is using a method of counterbalancing, which aims to eliminate practice or order effects. By doing this the participants are less likely to work out the aims of the experiment.

(e) (i) The mean uses all of the data and provides us with an average value. It is useful when the data tend to cluster around a central value.

(ii) Standard deviation shows the spread of the data in relation to an average. It shows whether the data cluster around a central value or whether they are widely spread out.

(f) (i) A graph to show how participants scored on a mood questionnaire after watching positive and negative news.

(ii) Score on mood questionnaire.

(ii) Frequency of people.

(g) After watching the positive news programme the participants scored more highly on the mood questionnaire, as opposed to when watching the negative news. The positive news produced higher scores on the mood questionnaire.

(h) I would use a natural observation and watch participants after they had watched a positive and a negative programme. I would do this by observing the behaviour of 40 participants; 20 of them would have watched a positive programme and 20 of them would have watched a negative programme. I would observe their behaviour and record it on a scale. I would give each behaviour a number and categorise the findings. For example, ways of showing depression might include sobbing or comforting others. That would be recorded at one on the scale. Smiling or laughing would be at the other end of the scale.

Student Answer 2

(a) To see if the kind of news (positive or negative) would affect mood.

(b) The independent variable is the news programme, and the dependent variable is the participant's mood.

(c) (i) The design was an experiment.

(ii) The advantage of an experiment is that it can demonstrate cause and effect. The disadvantage is that the high control often makes it artificial.

(d) Doing the experiment this way prevents order effects. This way there can be no influence due to the order in which the participants see the news programmes. It increases the validity of the experiment.

(e) (i) Using the mean ensures that all the data are used so that it gives a more valid result.

(ii) Standard deviation shows the range of the data.

(f) (i) Histogram showing mood after watching certain types of news.

(ii) Mood.

(ii) People.

(g) If the news is positive, more people are likely to have a positive mood after watching it. If the news is negative, then people are likely to have a negative mood.

(h) An interview method could be used instead. Participants might watch the news and then be questioned by the experimenter about how they feel. Also observations could be carried out where people are observed and watched for their behaviour after watching the news. This should show similar results but with people behaving naturally. This makes it a better method to use.

See page 120 for suggested marks.

Marking exercises: May 2004

As part of their coursework, a small group of AS Level Psychology students decided to examine the relationship between stress and physical illness. They designed a scale to measure stress using a list of 20 life events (e.g. exams, driving test, end of a relationship). After getting permission from their Head Teacher and the participants' parents to conduct the study, they obtained a random sample of 15 students from the 6th Form.

They asked the participants to tick any of the life events that they had experienced in the past two years. This was used to establish a stress score between 0 and 20. On this scale a high score indicates a lot of stress. After each participant had completed the stress scale, they were asked how many days they had taken off school through illness that year.

Previous research had led the psychology students to expect a positive correlation between stress and illness.

The results are shown on the scattergraph below.
The correlation coefficient was −0.734.

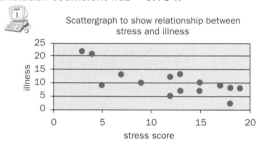

Scattergraph to show relationship between stress and illness

(a) How were the variables 'stress' and 'illness' operationalised by the students who designed the study?   (2 marks + 2 marks)

(b) (i) What is meant by investigator effects?   (1 mark)

   (ii) Give an example of **one** possible investigator effect in this study.   (2 marks)

   (iii) Describe how this investigator effect might be overcome in this study.   (2 marks)

(c) (i) What is meant by the term correlation coefficient?   (2 marks)

   (ii) Using the information from the scattergraph **and/or** the correlation coefficient, describe the relationship between stress and illness that the researchers found in this study.   (2 marks)

   (iii) Give **one** advantage and **one** disadvantage of an investigation using a correlational analysis.   (2 marks + 2 marks)

(d) (i) Explain how the students might have selected their random sample.   (2 marks)

   (ii) Give **one** limitation of random sampling.   (2 marks)

(e) Although the students correctly obtained permission from their Head Teacher and the participants' parents:

   (i) Identify **one** ethical issue that they do not seem to have considered.   (1 mark)

   (ii) Explain how the researchers could have dealt with this ethical issue.   (2 marks)

(f) Due to their unexpected finding the students felt it would be useful to gather some qualitative data about the participants' experience of stress and illness.

   (i) Explain how they could obtain such qualitative data about participants' experiences.   (3 marks)

   (ii) Outline how they could analyse the data collected.   (3 marks)

Marking scheme

For 3 mark questions:

3 marks	Accurate and informed description.
2 marks	Limited, generally accurate but less detailed.
1 mark	Brief or muddled description.
0 marks	No reason given or incorrect description.

(a) For stress, must say score or stress scale and elaborate. For illness, must say number of days off for illness.

(b) (i) Any effect the investigator has on the participant or on the findings.

   (ii) Constructing the life events scale does not count.

   If (ii) is zero, then (iii) is zero.

   (iii) Must deal with the problem in (ii); credit only one way of dealing with the problem.

(c) (i) Need to mention 'number' or 'value' for full marks.

   (ii) Any two of the following: strong, negative, as stress goes up illness goes down.

   (iii) Take only the first answer. May be advantage/disadvantage of doing a correlational study or plotting a scattergraph or calculating a correlation coefficient.

(d) (i) Need to say target population (6th form students) and how.

(e) (i) Debriefing is not an issue.

(f) (i) Just listing methods gets only 1 mark; no marks for explaining *why*. You must say how.

   (ii) Need to turn qualitative data into quantitative data (e.g. categories or themes); then can get credit for using a bar chart.

N.B. The topic of qualitative analysis is no longer on the specification (as from September 2005). Always be cautious when using past papers!

Student Answer 1

(a)   Stress = total of life events, high score on a life event questionnaire.

Illness is number of days off through illness.

(b) (i) Where the appearance, body language and presence of the researcher have an effect on the participants, making them react and therefore changing the results.

(ii) If the investigator was a friend or not. If the participants were more open and shared life events and the truth about days off school.

(iii) By making sure that the experimenter was not a friend of the participant, or keeping questionnaires anonymous so that everyone can tell the truth.

(c) (i) The correlation coefficient is the type of relationship between the two variables being studied. It is numerical, it can be either positive or negative.

(ii) −0.734 indicates a moderate to strong negative correlation.

(iii) Advantage – can compare two variables effectively and gain clear information about how strong the relationship is.

Disadvantage – cannot establish cause and effect and whether one causes the other.

(d) (i) By giving each 6th form student a number and then picking numbers randomly from a hat.

(ii) The participants selected are not always available, which means that the sample size is reduced and the sample may become biased.

(e) (i) Consent from the individuals studied.

(ii) By giving retrospective consent when participants are allowed to withdraw their data after debriefing.

(f) (i) Interviews with open-ended questions where the interviewer prompts the topics that need to be covered (e.g. experience of stress and illness). Or a questionnaire with open-ended questions and a lot of topics and prompts to be included. Both would give qualitative data about individual experiences. Observation would not be appropriate or ethical because the person would be suffering stress or illness at the time.

(ii) Interviews would have to be recorded to keep a record of what was said. Key themes could be picked out to see if there are recurring patterns such as stress makes an individual more determined, or if parents are more observant over illness so children are less likely to take days off through illness. The themes could be further investigated by future interviews.

Student Answer 2

(a)   Illness was operationalised by number of days off school.

(b) (i) Investigator effects refer to the characteristics, e.g. gender, sense of humour and behaviour of the investigator, that affect the behaviour of the participants.

(ii) When participants respond to certain cues in the experiment and change their behaviour.

(iii) The double-blind procedure may be used. This is when neither participant nor experimenter know the aims of the research; therefore the experimenter's expectations cannot affect the behaviour of the participants as the experimenter does not know what to expect.

(c) (i) A correlation coefficient is a figure that represents the relationship between two variables.

(ii) The researchers found that as stress levels increase the amount of illness decreases.

(iii) It enables researchers to investigate variables that cannot be investigated in an experiment. This is an advantage.

A disadvantage would be that there might be a third variable that is causing the relationship, and stress and illness are not directly linked.

(d) (i) They may have obtained a random sample by putting the names in a hat and selecting out 15.

(ii) No good if you only randomly sample everyone who has been ill off school.

(e) (i) Debriefing.

(ii) You would debrief by telling participants the aims of the study, and getting them to sign a consent form.

(f) (i) They would used a guided interview or a questionnaire.

(ii) Look at the answers and observe the relationship between stress and illness, trying to quantify it. Take into account additional factors and a more relevant answer may be achieved.

See page 120 for suggested marks.

Marks for student answers to exam questions

	a	b	c	d	e	f	g	h	Total/30
May 2002 (page 111)									
Answer 1	1 + 1	0 + 0	1 + 2	0	2–	1 + 1	1 + 3		13
Answer 2	2 + 3	0 + 0	0 + 2	3	4	1– and 1+	3 + 2		21
Jan 2003 (page 113)									
Answer 1	2 + 1	1 (several reasons given)	1 + 1	1 + 0	0+ and 0	2 + 1	3		13
Answer 2	1 (true of other methods) + 2	3	1 + 3	1 +	2 + 2–	3 + 2	4 ('less detailed')		25
May 2003 (page 115)									
Answer 1	2 + 2	1 + 2	0	2– (ignore last sentence)	1 (no 'why')	1 + 2	2 + 2–	0 + 0 + 0	17
Answer 2	2 + 1	1 + 0	2	0	2–	0 + 0	1 + 2	1 + 1 + 3	16
Jan 2004 (page 117)									
Answer 1	1	2 + 2	1 + 2 + 2	2 (no context)	2 + 2	1 + 1 + 1	0	4 (mixture of naturalistic observation and natural experiment)	24
Answer 2	2	1 + 1	0 + 0 0 + 0	3	2 + 0	1 + 1 + 0	2 (two conclusions given)	2– (two methods named, credit 'observation')	15
May 2004 (page 19)									
Answer 1	2 + 2	(i) 1 (ii) 2 (iii) 1	(i) 2 (ii) 2 (iii) 0 + 2	(i) 2 (ii) 2	(i) 1 (ii) 2)	(i) 2+ (ii) 2			25
Answer 2	0 + 1	(i) 1 (ii) 0 (iii) 0	(i) 2 (ii) 1 (iii) 2 + 2	(i) 1 (ii) 1	(i) 0 (ii) 0	(i) 1 (ii) 1–			13

More exam-style questions

Question 9

There is a saying that 'hunger is the best cook'. A psychologist decided to test the relationship between hungriness and the tastiness of food. He prepared a dish of scrambled eggs and toast for each participant. Before they started to eat he asked them how long it was since they had last eaten. After they had the meal he asked them to rate the tastiness of the meal on a scale of 1 to 10 where 10 is very tasty.

He plotted his findings as shown below. The correlation coefficient was 0.15.

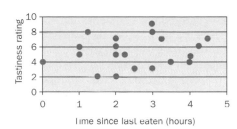

Graph showing the relationship between hungriness and tastiness

(a) Describe the aims of this study. (2 marks)

(b) How were hungriness and tastiness operationalised? (2 marks + 2 marks)

(c) (i) This study uses a correlational analysis. Describe **one** advantage and **one** disadvantage of a study using this method of analysis. (2 marks + 2 marks)

(ii) What is meant by the term 'correlation coefficient'? (2 marks)

(iii) Using the correlation coefficient **and/or** the scattergraph, describe the relationship between the two variables in this study. (2 marks)

(d) (i) Describe **one** possible threat to the validity of this study. (2 marks)

(ii) Explain how the psychologist could deal with this problem. (2 marks)

(e) (i) Explain what is meant by reliability. (2 marks)

(ii) Tastiness was measured using a rating scale. How could you check the reliability of this scale? (2 marks)

(f) Identify **one** ethical issue that might have arisen in this study and suggest how the psychologist might have dealt with this. (3 marks)

(g) (i) The scores for 'hungriness' were 2, 2, 3, 3, 4, 4, 4, 5, 5, 5, 6, 6, 6, 6, 7, 7, 7, 8, 8, 9 (units of time without food). Suggest **one** suitable method of central tendency to use with this data. (1 mark)

(ii) Explain how you would calculate this measure of central tendency. (2 marks)

(iii) Describe **one** advantage of this method of central tendency. (2 marks)

Question 10

A class of students are studying questionnaire design as part of their psychology course. In order to learn about questionnaire design they decide to try to construct their own questionnaire on the value of homework for A level students. The following is an extract from their questionnaire.

3. How many hours of homework do you do on average every week?
None 1 hour 2 hours 3 hours 4 hours 5 hours
6 hours More than 6 hours (Circle your answer)

4. Do you like doing homework? Yes No (Circle your answer)

5. Give one reason in favour of having to do homework.

_____

6. Suggest one reason against doing homework.

_____

7. Write down all your GCSE exam results.

_____

(a) Give **one** advantage and **one** disadvantage of using a questionnaire. (2 marks + 2 marks)

(b) (i) Suggest a suitable method of selecting participants and explain how you would do this. (1 mark + 2 marks)

(ii) Give **one** advantage of the method of selecting participants that you used in (i). (2 marks)

(c) (i) Identify **one** question in the extract that would produce qualitative data. (1 mark)

(ii) With reference to the question you have identified in (i), explain why this would produce qualitative data. (2 marks)

(iii) Suggest **one** disadvantage of using a question such as this. (2 marks)

(d) (i) Suggest **one** criticism of question 4. (2 marks)

(ii) How could you deal with this criticism? (2 marks)

(e) (i) Explain what a pilot study is. (2 marks)

(ii) Describe how a pilot study might have been carried out in this study. (3 marks)

(f) The students decide to ask about GCSE results to see if there is a correlation between average amount of time spent doing homework and GCSE results. For each student they calculate an average score for GCSE results by allocating 10 points for an A star, 9 points for an A and so on, and then adding these up and dividing by the number of GCSE results.

(i) What measure of central tendency did the students use to calculate the average GCSE score? (1 mark)

(ii) Name a suitable graphical method for displaying the results of this correlational analysis. (1 mark)

(iii) Describe how you would label the x-axis and y-axis of this graph. (2 marks)

(iv) State a suitable hypothesis for this part of the study. (2 marks)

(v) Is your hypothesis directional or non-directional? (1 mark)

Question 11

A psychology class wishes to investigate the effects of emotional factors on recall. Some research suggests that emotion leads to better recall whereas other research suggests that recall is less good in emotional situations. In order to investigate whether emotion is associated with better or less good recall they decide to test recall under two emotional conditions. Group 1 will be given a list of words to remember. In order to create emotional arousal, the participants in this group will be asked to run on the spot while learning the list (creates physiological arousal).

Group 2 are given the same list to remember but remain seated during the learning period.

An hour after learning the list, all participants are invited back and asked to write down all the words they can remember. The graph below shows the mean words recalled for each group.

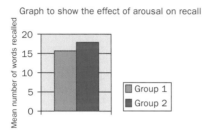

Graph to show the effect of arousal on recall

(a) Identify the independent variable and the dependent variable in this study. (2 marks + 2 marks)

(b) (i) State a suitable non-directional hypothesis for this study.

(2 marks)

    (ii) Explain why it would be appropriate to use a non-directional hypothesis in this study. (2 marks)

(c) (i) What is an experiment? (2 marks)

    (ii) Give **one** advantage of laboratory experiments compared to field experiments. (2 marks)

(d) (i) What was the experimental design that was used in this study? (1 mark)

    (ii) Give **one** advantage of using this design. (2 marks)

    (iii) State an alternative experimental design that could have been used. (1 mark)

    (iv) Explain how you would re-design this study using this new method of experimental design. (3 marks)

(e) (i) Describe the findings shown in the graph. (2 marks)

    (ii) State **one** conclusion that can be drawn from the findings. (2 marks)

(f) (i) Give **one** disadvantage of using the mean as a measure of central tendency. (2 marks)

    (ii) Identify **one** other measure of central tendency. (1 mark)

(g) (i) Describe **one** way that the experimenter might have influenced the participants' behaviour. (2 marks)

    (ii) Describe how the investigator might have dealt with this problem. (2 marks)

Question 12

An A level psychology class decided to study one aspect of minority influence – flexibility. They set up an experiment where one member of a group of 6 participants would be a 'confederate'. The confederate was briefed beforehand about what to do. The group would be asked to decide on compensation for a man injured in a road accident. They would be told that a previous committee had awarded £5,000 compensation for a similar accident involving a younger man.

There were two experimental groups selected from students in A level classes. In one group the confederate (an A level student) was told to start with an extreme position (a very low amount) and stick by it no matter what. In the second group the confederate started with the same extreme position but was told to be prepared to be flexible and move towards the group view.

The group met in an empty classroom. At the start of the experiment each participant was informed that this was a study to investigate determining compensation in accidents. Each participant was asked to record the sum he or she thought was appropriate. The group was then allowed 5 minutes to discuss the case and again each person was asked to individually record what figure they thought was appropriate.

The findings from this study are shown in the table below.

Table 1: Results from study of minority influence

Participant	Group 1 (confederate not flexible) Judgment of compensation (£) Before discussion	After discussion	Group 2 (confederate flexible) Judgment of compensation (£) Before discussion	After discussion
1	£5,000	4,000	5,000	3,000
2	3,000	3,000	4,000	4,000
3	4,000	4,000	5,000	3,000
4	5,000	4,000	4,000	3,000
5	5,000	3,000	4,000	4,000
Mean for group	4,500	3,600	4,500	3,400

(a) (i) Explain what is meant by an 'independent variable'. (2 marks)

    (ii) Identify the independent variable and the dependent variable in this experiment. (2 marks)

(b) Write a suitable directional hypothesis for this experiment. (2 marks)

(c) (i) Is this experiment a repeated measures design or an independent groups design? (1 mark)

    (ii) Give **two** advantages of the design you have identified in part (d). (2 marks + 2 marks)

(d) Identify **one** method for selecting the participant sample and give **one** advantage of this method. (1 mark + 2 marks)

(e) (i) The students calculated the mean estimates for each group. What is meant by 'the mean'? (1 mark)

    (ii) Give **one** strength of using the mean as a measure of central tendency. (2 marks)

(f) From the information given in Table 1, outline **two** conclusions that could be drawn from this investigation. (2 marks + 2 marks)

(g) (i) Identify **one** possible ethical issue that might have arisen in this investigation. (1 mark)

    (ii) Explain how the researchers might have dealt with this issue. (2 marks)

(h) (i) Suggest **two** factors that might threaten the validity of this study. (2 marks + 2 marks)

    (ii) For **one** of the factors that you have identified in (h), explain how the researchers might overcome this problem. (2 marks)

Question 13

A psychologist was interested in why people sleep, and investigated the effects of extra exercise on the amount of sleep people have.

He asked marathon runners to record the number of hours they slept on two different nights. One of the study nights was after running a race and the other was after a rest day.

(a) Identify the independent and dependent variable in this study.
(2 marks)

(b) (i) Explain what an investigator effect is. (2 marks)

    (ii) Explain how an investigator effect might have threatened the validity of this study. (2 marks)

    (iii) Suggest how you might overcome the problem you identified in (ii). (2 marks)

(c) Why might it have been a good idea to conduct a pilot study? (2 marks)

(d) If the psychologist found that each individual slept for about the same length of time on both occasions what might he conclude in terms of his original aims? (3 marks)

(e) (i) Explain why it would be a good idea to collect qualitative as well as quantitative data. (2 marks)

    (ii) How could the researcher collect qualitative data from this study? (2 marks)

(f) The psychologist recorded the numbers of hours slept for each night and calculated the mean and standard deviation for these two data sets as shown below:

	Mean number of hours slept	Standard deviation
Night before the race	7.9	1.2
Night after the race	8.2	2.5

    (i) Which is a measure of dispersion (the mean or the standard deviation)? (1 mark)

    (ii) From the table above what can you conclude about the dispersion of the data? (2 marks)

(g) (i) Explain why this study is a natural experiment. (2 marks)

    (ii) Give **one** advantage and **one** disadvantage of a natural experiment. (2 marks + 2 marks)

    (iii) Name an alternative research method that could be used. (1 mark)

    (iv) Describe how you would design a study to investigate the effects of exercise on sleep using this alternative research method. (3 marks)

Question 14

Research has found that familiar things reduce stress. A recent study investigated this further by seeing whether you could lower the stress levels of sheep by exposing isolated sheep to photos of other sheep (Kendrick et al., 2001).

The team took 40 sheep of a Welsh lowland breed called Clun Forest, and isolated them one at a time. For the first 15 minutes, four identical pictures of a white inverted triangle were projected on to the rear wall. For the next 15 minutes, the animals were shown four photos of an unfamiliar sheep face or shown four pictures of an unfamiliar goat.

As soon as the animals were left alone, their heart rates began to soar and stress hormone levels also increased. The animals seemed to ignore the triangle pictures, but after 15 minutes of simulated sheep company, the animals became calmer. Heart rates fell to pre-isolation levels. Stress hormone levels more than halved, and the number of unhappy bleating noises dropped by 20-fold. The goat photos had no effect.

(a) Identify **two** ways in which stress responses were operationalised in this study. (2 marks)

(b) (i) Write a suitable hypothesis for this study. (2 marks)

    (ii) Is your hypothesis a directional or non-directional hypothesis? (1 mark)

    (iii) Explain why you choose such a hypothesis. (2 marks)

(c) (i) Suggest a suitable sampling method that could have been used in this study. (1 mark)

    (ii) Give **one** advantage of this method in the context of this study. (2 marks)

    (iii) Name **one** other sampling method that is used in psychological research. (1 mark)

(d) (i) Identify the experimental design used in this study. (1 mark)

    (ii) Describe **one** advantage and **one** disadvantage of this experimental design. (2 marks + 2 marks)

(e) (i) Explain what an extraneous variable is. (2 marks)

    (ii) Identify **one** possible extraneous variable in this study. (1 mark)

    (iii) Explain how the researcher might have controlled this extraneous variable. (2 marks)

(f) Explain why the researchers started with an inverted white triangle and why they showed some participants photos of goats instead of sheep. (3 marks)

(g) A subsequent study intends to observe the behaviour of sheep with familiar and unfamiliar sheep. The researchers intend to observe the sheep for signs of stress.

    (i) Describe **one** advantage of a naturalistic observation. (2 marks)

    (ii) Describe how you would conduct this as a naturalistic observation. (6 marks)

Appendix 1 AQA 'A' AS Specification

Specification content	At the end of this topic you should be able to	Possible exam questions
Qualitative and quantitative research methods		
The nature and usage of the following research methods and their advantages and weaknesses, and how they relate to the scientific nature of psychology. The nature and usage of ethical guidelines in psychology • Experiments (including laboratory, field and natural experiments) • Investigations using correlational analysis • Naturalistic observations • Questionnaire • Interviews	• Explain what is meant by a research method • Describe the main research methods used in psychology. This includes being able know how each differs from the other methods • Be familiar with how to conduct studies using each method • Describe at least **one** advantage and **one** weakness of each method • Understand the need for objectivity in research • Describe ethical issues relevant to each method and describe how to deal with such issues	• What is the research method that has been used in this study? • Explain **one** advantage and **one** weakness of this method in the context of this study. • Identify **one** ethical issue that might arise in this study and describe how you would deal with it. • How else could you investigate this behaviour? Describe the aims and procedures of another study.
Research design and implementation		
Aims and hypotheses (including the generation of appropriate aims; the formulation of different types of experimental/alternative hypotheses (directional/non-directional)	• Explain what is meant by research aims, hypotheses, experimental hypothesis, alternative hypothesis, directional and non-directional hypothesis • Identify the aims of a selected study • Write a suitable hypothesis (experimental/, alternative, directional, non-directional) for a selected study	• Describe the aims of this study. • Describe a suitable experimental (alternative) hypothesis. • Identify whether your hypothesis is directional or non-directional. • Describe a suitable directional hypothesis for this study. • Explain why you used a directional (or a non-directional) hypothesis.
Experimental designs: (including independent groups, repeated measures and matched participants) and the design of naturalistic observations, questionnaire and interviews	• Explain what is meant by research design, experimental design, independent groups, repeated measures and matched participants • Describe advantages and disadvantages of each kind of experimental design • Describe and evaluate design decisions that are taken and procedures that are used in experiments, naturalistic observations, questionnaires and interviews	• What kind of research design has been used in this study? • What kind of experimental design has been used in this study? • Give **one** advantage and **one** disadvantage of the experimental design in the context of this study. • In an observational study, how would you sample behaviour? • Describe **one** way in which you could minimise the intrusive nature of observations. • Describe **two** factors in good questionnaire design. • Describe **one** factor that should be taken into consideration when designing an interview. • Describe **one** way in which you could minimise the effects that the interviewer's behaviour might have on an interviewee.
Factors associated with research design, including the operationalisation of the IV/DV; conducting pilot studies; control of extraneous variables; techniques for assessing and improving reliability and internal and external validity. Ethical issues associated with research design.	• Explain what is meant by control, dependent and independent variable, operationalisation of variables, pilot study, extraneous variable, reliability, internal and external validity, ethics • Operationalise variables • Explain why researchers use pilot studies and describe how they are done	• Explain what is meant by reliability and validity. • Identify ways in which you might operationalise a named variable. • Identify the independent variable in this study. • Identify the dependent variable in this study. • Describe **two** reasons for using a pilot study in an investigation.

It is wise to check the most recent version of the specification on the AQA website.

Specification content	At the end of this topic you should be able to	Possible exam questions
Research design and implementation *(continued)*		
	• Explain how extraneous variables can be controlled • Identify threats to reliability and describe how to improve reliability • Identify threats to validity and describe how to improve validity • Identify possible ethical issues and suggest how to deal with them, and the problems associated with these strategies	• Identify **two** variables that might need to be controlled in a study. Explain how you would control these variables. • Explain the term 'extraneous variable'. • How might an extraneous variable be a threat to the design of an experiment? • Identify **one** way to ensure reliability among observers, and explain how you would do this. • Describe **two** features of a study that might affect the validity of the data being collected. • Describe **one** feature of a study that might affect the internal validity of the investigation. • Describe **two** features of a study that might affect the reliability of the data being collected. • Describe **one** ethical issue that might arise in a study and describe one way of dealing with it.
The selection of participants, including random, opportunity and volunteer sampling	• Explain what is meant by random sampling, opportunity sampling and volunteer sampling • Describe and evaluate ways of selecting participants	• Explain what is meant by random sampling, opportunity sampling and volunteer sampling. • Explain how an investigator might have selected a 'random sample' 'volunteer sample' and 'opportunity sample' of participants. • Give **one** advantage and **one** disadvantage of your chosen sampling technique.
The relationship between researchers and participants (including demand characteristics and investigator effects)	• Explain what is meant by demand characteristics and investigator effects • Describe how demand characteristics might influence the results of a study • Explain how you could deal with such effects • Describe how investigator effects might influence the results of a study • Explain how you could deal with such effects	• Explain what is meant by demand characteristics and investigator effects. • Describe how demand characteristics might have been a problem in this study. • Describe how you might deal with such a problem. • Explain **one** way in which an investigator effect might have influenced the results obtained in this study. • How might you overcome this problem?
Data analysis		
The nature of qualitative data including strengths and weaknesses	• Explain what is meant by qualitative data • Describe how to collect qualitative data, and evaluate the use of such data	• Explain what is meant by qualitative data. • Explain how a researcher might have collected some qualitative data in this study. • Give **one** advantage and **one** disadvantage of using qualitative data.
Measures of central tendency and dispersion (including the appropriate use and interpretation of medians, means, modes; range and standard deviations)	• Explain what is meant by measures of central tendency and measures of dispersion • Explain the use of medians, means, modes; range and standard deviations • Describe advantages and disadvantages of means, modes; range and standard deviations	• Identify a suitable measure of central tendency. • Give **one** advantage and **one** disadvantage of the method you have chosen. • Identify a suitable measure of dispersion. • Give **one** advantage and **one** disadvantage of the method you have chosen.
The nature of positive and negative correlations and the interpretation of correlation coefficients	• Explain what is meant by correlational analysis, correlation coefficient, positive and negative correlations, and scattergraphs • Interpret data from a scattergraph • Understand the meaning of a correlation coefficient	• Explain what is meant by the term correlation coefficient and a negative correlation. • Describe the relationship between the co-variables in this study. • Give **one** advantage and **one** disadvantage of using a correlational analysis.
Graphs and charts (including the appropriate use and interpretation of histograms, bar charts and scattergraphs)	• Explain what is meant by bar charts and histograms • Interpret data in a graph • Draw conclusions from data in a table or graph	• Give **one** conclusion that could be drawn from the data in the graph. • Describe suitable labels for a bar chart.

Appendix II How the exam questions are marked and where candidates go wrong

How the exam questions are marked

Research methods is assessed in question 3 on the Unit 3 exam (PYA3) (the other question to be answered on PYA3 will be on the Social Psychology section). This question consists of one piece of 'stimulus material' and a set of questions worth 30 marks in total. The questions are related to the research study described in the stimulus material.

- In research methods, only one question is set.

- The research methods question will consist of 3 **AO1** marks, 6 **AO2** marks and 21 **AO3** marks.

- This means a large emphasis on questions that require candidates to use their knowledge of research methods (**AO3**-style questions) rather than explaining the terms/concepts (**AO1**). Thus, when a question includes the phrase 'in the context of this study', candidates must contextualise their answers.

1. Contextualisation

Many questions on the research methods exam use the phrase 'in this study'. This means that candidates must make reference to the study. Thus, when asked to 'Describe **one** disadvantage of using an independent groups design *in this study*', an answer that said 'Participant variables are not controlled' would receive 1 out of 2 marks, whereas 'Participant variables, such as susceptibility to alcohol, are not controlled' (when the study was about alcohol) would received the full 2 marks.

Most of the research methods questions are assessed in terms of assessment objective 3 (**AO3**) '**design, conduct and report research**'. Therefore, most of the questions require candidates to apply their knowledge to the stimulus material. You must learn to go beyond the specification when answering these questions.

The assessment objectives in the AS exam:

Assessment objective 1 (AO1)
Description (knowledge and understanding of psychology)

Assessment objective 2 (AO2)
Evaluation (assessment and commentary)

Assessment objective 3 (AO3)
To design, conduct and report research

2. Positive marking

In the research methods part of the exam, candidates are credited only for their first answer when the question asks for '**one**' of something. For example, if you are asked for 'one advantage of a laboratory experiment' and you describe **two** advantages ('They are artificial and tend to produce demand characteristics, i.e. participants may respond to the experimenter's cues'), you will only receive credit for the first answer even when the second answer is better.

The positive marking rule does not apply to research methods because candidates are sometimes unsure, for example, of an advantage of using an experiment and list lots of possible advantages, knowing that one of them is right, as shown in the table below.

3. Accuracy and detail

The marking scheme that is used to mark research methods questions is essentially based on the criteria of accuracy and detail.

Questions worth 1 mark		Questions worth 2 marks		Questions worth 3 marks		Questions worth 6 marks	
1 marks	Answer is **appropriate**	2 marks	Answer is **accurate and detailed**	3 marks	Answer is **accurate and detailed**	6–5 marks	Answer is **accurate and detailed**
0 marks	Answer is **incorrect**	1 marks	Answer is **basic, lacking detail** and may be **muddled** and/or **flawed**	2 marks	Answer is **limited**. It is **generally accurate** but **less detailed**	4–3 marks	Answer is limited. It is **generally accurate** but **less detailed**
		0 marks	Answer is **inappropriate** or **incorrect**	1 marks	Answer is **basic, lacking detail** and may be muddled and/or **flawed**	2–1 marks	Answer is **basic, lacking detail** and may be **muddled** and/or **flawed**
				0 marks	Answer is **inappropriate** or **incorrect**	0 marks	Answer is **inappropriate** or **incorrect**

Where candidates go wrong

1. Defining instead of explaining

Very few questions require you to define a term because there are only three **AO1** marks (as stated on the left). Most questions require you to use your knowledge. For example, instead of asking you 'What is meant by control', you would more often be asked to 'Describe how the researcher might have controlled one of the variables in this study.' The focus is on 'how' instead of 'what'.

2. Explaining how instead of why

Questions often ask you to explain *how* a particular problem was dealt with or how a procedure could have been conducted. In order to provide elaboration, candidates often explain *why* the solution was chosen, but such information is irrelevant to the question and thus not creditworthy.

For example:

Question: Explain how qualitative data about participants' experience could be collected.

Answer: The researchers could use open-ended questions. These are better than closed ones for getting qualitative data. [The first sentence is 'how'. The second sentence is 'why' and not creditworthy.]

Question: Outline procedures for carrying out such an observation.

Answer: You would use behavioural categories because these allow easy collection of data. [The material after 'because' is irrelevant.]

3. Better than what?

An advantage or disadvantage of anything is a comparative statement. If you say that the dinner you had last night was good, it implies it was better *than another occasion*. When you say a 'questionnaire is easier', you mean that it is easier than, for example, doing an interview.

You need to go even further and explain why it is easier, or why you can collect more data, or why it is less expensive, or why participants are more honest, or whatever. Don't just make these bold statements that something is easier, quicker, cheaper, better, but say in comparison to what and explain the basis of your claim.

4. Not answering all parts of the question

Some questions contain several parts, such as 'Identify one ethical issue that the researchers do not appear to have considered and explain how this ethical issue could have been dealt with.' Many candidates ignore the first or second part of the question.

5. Hypotheses

The best way to ensure that you get full marks for stating a hypothesis is to make sure you operationalise it, i.e. state the specific operations that will be tested. Remember also that hypotheses should be in the present tense and be about populations and not samples.

6. Findings and conclusions

Candidates are often asked to describe conclusion(s) that could be drawn from a table or graph but then mistakenly describe the findings instead of conclusions.

Findings are facts. Conclusions are an interpretation of the facts – making generalisations.

Findings are part of conclusions and can be used as a platform for giving the conclusions.

Findings concern participants (samples) and are usually given in the past tense, e.g. 'The study found that the male participants conformed more than the female participants.'

Conclusions concern people (populations) and are usually stated in the present tense, e.g. 'The study found that the male participants conformed more than the female participants, which suggests that men are less conformist than women.'

(Findings may lack validity because of low internal validity; conclusions may lack validity because of low external validity.)

 39

Explain what is wrong with these student answers and write a fully correct answer.

1. Question: *Describe one advantage of a correlational analysis.*

   Student answer: They are easy to do and provide information that cannot be obtained in an experiment.

2. Question: *Give an example of an investigator effect.*

   Student answer: An investigator effect is when an investigator affects the behaviour of participants during a study.

3. Question: *Identify one ethical issue and explain how the researcher might have dealt with it.*

   Student answer: Informed consent should be sought in all experiments because it provides a participant with information to make a decision about whether to participate.

4. Question: *State one conclusion that could be drawn from Graph X.*

   Student answer: The study found that age and intelligence are positively correlated.

5. Question: *Describe one advantage of a questionnaire.*

   Student answer: You can collect lots of data.

6. Question: *State an appropriate hypothesis for a study about the effects of noise on memory.*

   Student answer: Participants will do better when it is noisy.

7. Question: *Explain how stress and illness could be operationalised.*

   Student answer: Stress could be operationalised by identifying a set of life events and developing a scale.

8. Question: *Explain how a pilot study might have been carried out in the context of this survey.*

   Student answer: A pilot study is a small-scale trial of a study run to see if there are any things that could be improved.

9. Question: *Give one advantage of using a repeated measures design.*

   Student answer: It means that there are fewer extraneous variables.

Appendix III Ideas for research activities related to the AQA AS specification

The ideas given here are focused on ways to enhance understanding of different research methods in relation to topic areas of the AS specification.

Studies in red are described in detail on pages 130–132.

Details of the emboldened studies can be found in *Psychology AS: The Teacher's Companion* published by Nelson Thornes (ISBN 0-7487-8077-7), available from www.nelsonthornes.com.

Those activities in italics are described in *Psychology AS: The Complete Companion*, Revised Edition, also published by Nelson Thornes (ISBN 0-7487-9463-8). Page numbers are given. Some studies cannot be done as activities (for ethical and/or practical reasons) but might be discussed as examples of particular research methods, as indicated in the table.

	Cognitive	Developmental	Physiological	Individual differences	Social
Laboratory experiment	**Duration of STM (Peterson and Peterson, 1959)** **Encoding in STM and LTM (Baddeley, 1966)** **Levels of processing (Craik and Tulving, 1975)** *Proactive and retroactive interference (p. 19)* **Cue-dependent forgetting (Tulving and Psotka, 1971)** **Leading questions (Loftus and Palmer, 1974)** **Schema and recall (Bransford and Johnson, 1972)** **Demonstration of the effects of schema (Pompi and Lachman, 1967)**	Example: Harlow's monkeys (1959), in *The AS Complete Companion*, p. 54	**Stress task (word search with missing answers) in *The AS Teacher's Companion*** Can be used to relate stress responses and cardiovascular activity (students are given tasks of varying stressfulness; assess the pulse or use biodots to measure skin temperature) Example: animal experiments on the effects of stress on the immune system e.g. Riley (1981), in *The AS Complete Companion*, p. 93	Example: Fichter and Pirk (1995) stared at normal individuals, which caused a change in their hormone and neurotransmitter levels, in *The AS Complete Companion*, p. 147	Conformity using a general knowledge quiz Example: Moscovici *et al* (1969) blue-green slides – comparing consistent and inconsistent conditions, in *The AS Complete Companion*, p. 169
Field experiment	Context-dependent recall (Abernethy, 1940): test some students in room where they were taught and others in a different room, in *The AS Complete Companion*, p. 20		Example: Evans *et al.*'s (1994) students had to give a talk (acute stress) to see the effect on the immune system, compared with chronic stress, in *The AS Complete Companion*, p. 93		**Conformity – beans in a jar (Jenness, 1932)** Example: Hofling *et al.*'s (1966) study of obedience, in *The AS Complete Companion*, p. 178

	Cognitive	Developmental	Physiological	Individual differences	Social
Natural experiment	Very long-term memories: Get students and teacher to list names of their primary school peers. Who remembers more? Lots of flaws in the design. See Bahrick et al., 1975, in *The AS Complete Companion*, pp. 6–7)	Example: Bowlby's 44 thieves (1944), in *The AS Complete Companion*, pp. 55–6 Example: Hodges and Tizard's study of privation (1989), in *The AS Complete Companion* pp. 64–5 Example: day care studies comparing high and low quality care e.g. Burchinal et al. (2000), see *The AS Complete Companion* p. 75.	Example: Kiecolt-Glaser et al. (1995), on the effects of caring for a chronically ill person on the immune system, in *The AS Complete Companion*, pp. 92–3	Example: twin studies of anorexia nervosa and bulimia nervosa (e.g. Holland et al., 1988, in *The AS Complete Companion*, p. 148) – or is this a difference study? Example: Nasser (1986) compared attitudes towards eating in Arab females in Cairo and London, in *The AS Complete Companion*, p. 153	
Questionnaire	**Flashbulb memory (construct your own questionnaire, based on Brown and Kulik, 1977)**	**The love quiz (Hazan and Shaver, 1987), tests the continuity hypothesis** (can relate early and late attachment – a difference study rather than a natural experiment) *Day care questionnaire (p. 68)*	**Devise your own stress or health questionnaire (Homes and Rahe, 1967)** *List of stress warning signals, (p. 113) in The AS Complete Companion.* **Type A questionnaire** *Hardiness questionnaire (p. 115), in The AS Complete Companion.*	Attitudes to abnormality Questionnaire about defining abnormality **Attitudes towards eating disorders**	
Interview	Flashbulb memory	**Day care interviews, interviewing mothers about day care**			Ask people what they think about the use of deception in psychological studies
Study using correlational analysis	Could correlate data from study on very long-term memories	*Day care and GCSE results (Ermisch and Francesconi, 2000; p. 74)*	**A correlation, e.g. health and stress**	**Changing body shapes (Garner et al., 1980): use data on the vital statistics of Miss America**	
Observational study	**War of the ghosts – content analysis (Bartlett, 1932)**	Observe young children and mothers/fathers in a playpark, and note the distance between them at various times (assessing the secure base concept) **Strange Situation role play (Ainsworth et al., 1978)** Example: Robertson and Robertson's observations (1968–73) **Assessing the quality of day care centres (work out a coding system)**	**Give students a mildly stressful task and work out a coding system to record stress-related behaviours**	Make mobiles representing each of the four models and their assumptions	
Other activities (not specifically related to research methods)	**Effect of organization on memory (Mandler, 1967)** Stereotypes and recall (Allport and Postman, 1947) Use picture in *The AS Complete Companion* on p. 29	Conduct a debate for and against the harmful effects of day care Make a leaflet for parents about the value of day care	Create mild stress (tell students they are going to do a test that will count towards their final A level). Then ask them to describe what they were feeling. Provides a list of behaviours associated with ANS arousal	Perform a qualitative analysis on descriptions of anorexia nervosa and bulimia nervosa	**Role play Asch's study(stimulus materials provided)** Role play Milgram's study Role play an ethics committee

Note: The references cited here have not been included in the references in this book but can all be found in *The AS Complete Companion*.

Ideas for research activities

A lab experiment: levels of processing an alternative for activity 2

Step 1: Answer the questions by ringing yes or no

1. SPEECH Is the word in capital letters? YES/NO
2. brush Is the word a something used for cleaning? YES/NO
3. cheek Does the word rhyme with 'teak'? YES/NO
4. FENCE Is the word in small letters? YES/NO
5. FLAME Does the word mean something hot? YES/NO
6. FLOUR Is the word in capital letters? YES/NO
7. honey Is the word in small letters? YES/NO
8. KNIFE Does the word mean a type of furniture? YES/NO
9. SHEEP Is the word a type of farm animal? YES/NO
10. copper Is the word in capital letters? YES/NO
11. GLOVE Does the word rhyme with 'shove'? YES/NO
12. MONK Is the word in small letters? YES/NO
13. daisy Does the word rhyme with 'teak'? YES/NO
14. miner Is the word in small letters? YES/NO
15. cart Does the word rhyme with 'start'? YES/NO16.

16. CLOVE Is the word in capital letters? YES/NO
17. ROBBER Does the word mean a type of flower? YES/NO
18. mast Does the word rhyme with 'rove'? YES/NO
19. fiddle Is the word in small letters? YES/NO
20. CHAPEL Does the word rhyme with 'grapple'? YES/NO
21. SONNET Does the word mean something to wear? YES/NO
22. WITCH Does the word rhyme with 'rich'? YES/NO
23. sleet Is the word a type of weather? YES/NO
24. brake Is the word in small letters? YES/NO
25. twig Does the word rhyme with 'coach'? YES/NO
26. grin Does the word rhyme with 'school'? YES/NO
27. DRILL Does the word mean a kind of fish? YES/NO
28. moan Does the word mean a mode of travel? YES/NO
29. CLAW Is the word a part of an animal? YES/NO
30. singer Does the word rhyme with 'ringer'? YES/NO

Step 2: Cover up the questions in step 1. Then look at the words below. Which of the following words were in the list of 30 questions? Tick the right answers.

Brush	Lamp	Grin	Dance	Cart	Pond	Monk	Wool	Roach
Cheek	Cherry	Drill	Field	Clove	Lane	Chapel	Soap	Rice
Sonnet	Jade	Witch	Sleet	Sheep	Pail	Knife	Boat	Twig
Daisy	Clip	Miner	Juice	Speech	Bear	Brake	Tire	Child
Fence	Rock	Moan	Floor	Robber	Nurse	Fiddle	State	Boy
Flame	Earl	Claw	Glass	Mast	Lark	Honey	Week	Tree
Flour	Pool	Singer	Tribe	Copper	Trout	Glove	Gram	Orange

Step 3: From the table above, tick each of the words you remembered

Shallow	Rhyme	Semantic
Speech	Cheek	Brush
Fence	Glove	Flame
Flour	Daisy	Knife
Honey	Cart	Sheep
Copper	Mast	Robber
Monk	Chapel	Sonnet
Miner	Witch	Sleet
Clove	Twig	Drill
Fiddle	Grin	Moan
Brake	Singer	Claw

Step 4: Draw a bar chart to show your class findings

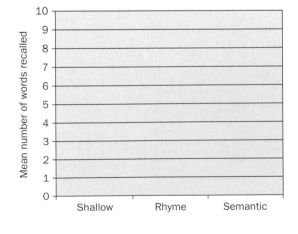

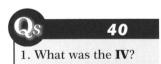

Qs 40

1. What was the **IV**?
2. What was the **DV**?
3. What were the aims of this experiment?
4. Did you guess what the aims were?
5. Were some words more 'memorable' than others? Why?

Background:

Craik and Lockhart (1972) proposed that the reason we remember things over time (i.e. long-term memory) is that we have processed some things more deeply. Processing refers to what you do with information. The more complex the thing you do, the more memorable the information becomes. A classic test of this approach was conducted by Craik and Tulving (1975). You have just replicated their experiment.

A field experiment: Conformity an alternative for activity 6

Fill a jar with beans (or you can use Smarties, pasta shells – whatever) and ask people to provide estimates. The participants in this experiment should not be aware of the aims of the study. You should therefore create a set of standardised instructions, telling people that you are doing a school project on estimating.

Participants should be asked to record their answers on a piece of paper. This piece of paper should be prepared earlier and show some previous answers, supposedly from previous estimates. There need to be two forms of this answer paper: Form H, which has high estimates, and Form L, which has low estimates. You can decide how extreme to make these estimates. The estimates should be hand written to be convincing.

1. Prepare forms H and L. You will need a new form for each participant.

2. Write standardised instructions.

3. Collect data.

4. Calculate a mean of the estimates from each form and show these on a bar chart such as the one below.

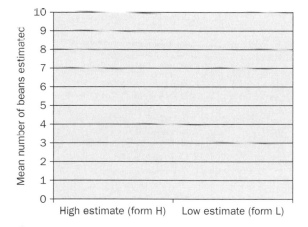

Background

This study is an adaptation of one by Jenness (1932). He asked students to guess how many beans there were in a jar. Then they were given an opportunity to discuss their estimates and, finally, to give their individual estimates again. Jenness found that individual estimates tended to converge to a group norm. It seems reasonable that, in an ambiguous situation (such as this), one looks to others to get some ideas about what is a reasonable answer. Other conformity research has found that people conform even when the material is unambiguous (e.g. Asch's studies).

Qs   41

1. What are the research aims of this experiment?

2. Identify the IV and DV in this experiment.

3. How do you know it is an experiment?

4. How do you know it is a field experiment?

5. Write a suitable hypothesis for this experiment.

6. What method did you use to select your participants?

7. Give **one** advantage and **one** disadvantage of using this method of selecting participants.

8. What was the experimental design that you used?

9. Give **one** advantage and **one** disadvantage of using this experimental design in the context of this study.

10. Can you think of **one** ethical issue raised in this study?

11. How could you deal with this issue?

12. Name a suitable measure of central tendency to use with your data and explain why.

A very shy guy goes into a pub and sees a beautiful woman sitting at the bar. After an hour of gathering up his courage, he finally goes over to her and asks, tentatively, 'Um, would you mind if I chatted with you for a while?'

She responds by yelling, at the top of her voice, 'NO! I won't sleep with you tonight!' Everyone in the bar is now staring at them. Naturally, the guy is hopelessly embarrassed and slinks back to his table.

After a few minutes, the woman walks over to him and apologises. She smiles and says, 'I'm sorry if I embarrassed you. You see, I'm a psychology student, and I'm studying how people respond to embarrassing situations.'

To which he responds, at the top of his voice, 'What do you mean £200?!'

An investigation using a correlation analysis: stress and health
an alternative for activity 15

To investigate this you need:

1. A measure of stress.

   A score can be obtained by writing your own version of a life change scale or daily hassles, or you can use the Survey of Recent Life Experiences, on the right.

2. A measure of health (or illness).

   You need to construct a short questionnaire to assess participants' health (e.g. ask them how many days they had off school for illness in the last month/6 months).
   This will give you a health score.

   To analyse your data follow the instructions on page 48.

Background

Holmes and Rahe (1967) played a key role in developing the idea that life changes are linked to stress, and illness. In the course of treating patients they observed that it was often the case that a range of major life events seemed to precede physical illness. These changes were both positive and negative events that had one thing in common – they involved change. Change requires psychic energy to be expended i.e. it is stressful. Holmes and Rahe, suggested that this affected health.

DeLongis *et al.* (1982) suggested that the ongoing (chronic) strains of daily living – hassles – would provide a better measure of stress than looking at acute events.

Many scales have been criticised because they ignore ongoing stressors such as noise, don't include any assessment of perceived importance nor do they assess how much support an individual is receiving. All of these factors would affect the amount of stress actually experienced.

An observation: stress behaviour
an alternative for activity 18

1. Decide on a situation that will create mild stress. This could involve:

   • a student delivering a short talk to the class

   • observing behaviour while doing the Stroop test – compare behaviour while reading colour conflicting lists and non-conflicting lists.

2. Conduct a pilot study observing one or more individuals and noting any behaviours that indicate stress.

3. Draw up a coding system (see pages 65 and 68).

4. Decide on a sampling procedure (see page 65).

5. Use your coding system to record observations.

To analyse your data, possibilities might be:

• If more than one observer records the same individual, you can calculate inter-observer reliability by counting the number of agreements. Divide the total number of agreements by the total number of observations to produce inter-observer reliability (see page 67).

• Compare males and females. What can you conclude about stress-related behaviour?

Note: see
http://www.atkinson.yorku.ca/~psyctest/ *for access to questionnaires that could be used for performing correlational analyses e.g. body image scale.*

Survey of Recent Life Experiences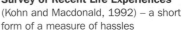
(Kohn and Macdonald, 1992) – a short form of a measure of hassles

Below is a list of experiences that many people have at some time or other. Please indicate for each experience how much it has been a part of your life **over the past month**.

Intensity of experience over the past month:

1 = not at all part of my life
2 = only slightly part of my life
3 = distinctly part of my life
4 = very much part of my life

1. Disliking your daily activities
2. Disliking your work
3. Ethnic or racial conflict
4. Conflicts with in-laws or boyfriend's/ girlfriend's family
5. Being let down or disappointed by friends
6. Conflicts with supervisor(s) at work
7. Social rejection
8. Too many things to do at once
9. Being taken for granted
10. Financial conflicts with family members
11. Having your trust betrayed by a friend
12. Having your contributions overlooked
13. Struggling to meet your own standards of performance and accomplishment
14. Being taken advantage of
15. Not enough leisure time
16. Cash flow difficulties
17. A lot of responsibilities
18. Dissatisfaction with work
19. Decisions about intimate relationship(s)
20. Not enough time to meet your obligations
21. Financial burdens
22. Lower evaluation of your work than you think you deserve
23. Experiencing high levels of noise
24. Lower evaluation of your work than you hoped for
25. Conflicts with family member(s)
26. Finding your work too demanding
27. Conflicts with friend(s)
28. Trying to secure loans
29. Getting "ripped off" or cheated in the purchase of goods
30. Unwanted interruptions of your work
31. Social isolation
32. Being ignored
33. Dissatisfaction with your physical appearance
34. Unsatisfactory housing conditions
35. Finding work uninteresting
36. Failing to get money you expected
37. Gossip about someone you care about
38. Dissatisfaction with your physical fitness
39. Gossip about yourself
40. Difficulty dealing with modern technology (e.g. computers)
41. Hard work to look after and maintain home

Appendix IV Websites

General psychology sites for AQA A that include research methods

Both sites are full of information, quizzes and links to elsewhere:
psYonline http://psyonline.edgehill.ac.uk/
s-cool http://www.s-cool.co.uk/default.asp

An OCR site but has useful material and good links:
http://www.holah.karoo.net/links.htm

Another vast collection of psychology material, including research methods:
http://psychology.about.com/

Gerry Kegan's site for Scottish Higher Psychology, again full of useful materials:
http://www.gerardkeegan.co.uk/

Research methods

An interactive site for learning about research methods:
http://www.mcli.dist.maricopa.edu/proj/res_meth/index.html

syNAPse, the A level psychology website developed by Northampton & District A-Level Psychology Teachers Group (NAP). The site is packed full of resources and activities to help A level students learn about psychology and in particular psychological research methods.
http://nap.northampton.ac.uk/

Discovery Psychology (hosted by Philip Zimbardo) – a series of half hour films that can be viewed on the Internet. One is on research methods:
http://www.learncr.org/resources/series138.html

Psychological research on the net

Site full of links to a vast array of psychology experiments to take part in:
http://psych.hanover.edu/Research/exponnet.html

Yahoo list of online tests and experiments:
http://dir.yahoo.com/Social_Science/Psychology/Research/Tests_and_Experiments/

Ethical guidelines

APA code http://www.apa.org/ethics/code.html

BPS code www.bps.org.uk/documents/Code.pdf

Descriptive statistics

A nicely presented introduction to descriptive statistics:
http://www.mste.uiuc.edu/hill/dstat/dstat.html

Sites where you can try out correlation simulations (and other statistics)

http://www.stattucino.com/berrie/dsl/regression/regression.html
http://davidmlane.com/hyperstat/prediction.html
http://www.ruf.rice.edu/~lane/rvls.html
http://www.statsoft.com/textbook/stathome.html

Observation coding systems and checklists

Checklists, observations forms etc:
http://www.umchs.org/umchsresources/administration/forms/umchsforms.html#education

Coding Rules for the Hall/Van de Castle System of Quantitative Dream Content Analysis:
http://psych.ucsc.edu/dreams/Coding/index.html

Questionnaires

Claims to be the world's largest testing centre, tests and questionnaires on everything:
http://www.queendom.com/

Various health surveys and other scales:
http://www.rand.org/health/surveys.html

Site providing access to copyrighted psychological tests that can be downloaded and used by student researchers, including dieting beliefs scale and self-esteem scales:
http://www.atkinson.yorku.ca/~psyctest/

AQA site

Section called 'guidance' contains the Teacher Support Document. Also contains specification, past papers and mark schemes, report on each exam (check comments on research methods), and details of support meetings:
http://www.aqa.org.uk/qual/gceasa/psyA.html

Glossary

Words in CAPITALS are AQA KEY WORDS. Words in *italics* are explained elsewhere in the glossary.

An edited version of this glossary can be found in AQA supplementary materials on the Nelson Thornes website, www.nelsonthornes.com/researchmethods, so that you can make the definitions into a game – paste the descriptions onto cards and then ask students to identify what terms are being defined.

ABBA A form of *counterbalancing* to deal with *order effects* in which participants do condition A, then B, then B and finally A.

aims A statement of what the researcher(s) intend to find out in a research study, (pp. 1, 16).

ALTERNATIVE HYPOTHESIS A testable statement about the relationship between two variables. Sometimes called the 'experimental hypothesis'. See *hypothesis* and *research prediction*, (p. 7).

attrition The loss of participants from a study over time. Those participants who are less interested or who have done less well may not be available for re-assessment in a *longitudinal study* or in the second condition of a *repeated measures design*, which means that the remaining sample is biased in favour of those who are more interested/motivated/doing well.

Availability sampling See *opportunity sample*.

BAR CHART A graph used to represent the frequency of data; the categories on the *x*-axis have no fixed order, and there is no true zero. See *histogram*, (p. 15).

behaviour checklist A list of the behaviours to be recorded during an observational study. Similar to a *coding system*, (pp. 65, 69).

bias A systematic distortion. It is a problem in research studies (e.g. *experimenter bias, interviewer bias, observer bias, sample bias, social desirability bias, volunteer bias*), (p. 44).

boredom effect A kind of *order effect*. In a repeated measures design, participants may do less well on one condition rather than another because they have not completed it first and become 'bored', (p. 19).

case study A research investigation that involves a detailed study of a single individual, institution or event. Case studies provide a rich record of human experience but are hard to generalise from, (p. 72).

clinical method (clinical interview) A form of semi-structured or *unstructured interview* similar to the kind of interview used by a GP, (p. 46).

closed questions In a questionnaire, questions that have a range of answers from which respondents select one. Produces *quantitative data*. Answers are easier to analyse than those for *open questions*, (p. 44).

coding system A systematic method for recording observations in which individual behaviours are given a code for ease of recording. Similar to a *behaviour checklist*, (pp. 65, 69).

conclusions The implications drawn from the findings of a study; what the findings tell us about people in general rather than about the particular participants in a study, (pp. 14, 16).

concurrent validity A form of *external validity* related to questionnaires and interviews. It aims to demonstrate the extent to which performance on a test correlates positively with other tests of the same thing. If a test is a good one, we would expect a high *positive correlation*, (p. 51).

confederate An individual in an experiment who is not a real participant and has been instructed how to behave by the investigator/experimenter. May act as the *independent variable*, (p. 13).

confidentiality An *ethical issue* concerned with a participant's right to have personal information protected, (pp. 33, 35, 47, 67).

confounding variable A variable that is not the independent variable under study but may be found to have an effect on the dependent variable, thus confounding the findings of the study. See *extraneous variable*, (pp. 12, 26, 31).

content analysis A kind of *observational study* in which behaviour is observed indirectly in written or verbal material. A detailed analysis is made of, for example, books, diaries or TV programmes. It is possible to count the frequency of particular behaviours using categories, (p. 69).

continuous observation Every instance of a behaviour is recorded in as much detail as possible. This is useful if the behaviours you are interested in do not occur very often, (p. 65).

CONTROL refers to the extent to which any variable is held constant or regulated by a researcher, (pp. 12, 25).

control condition In an experiment, the condition that provides a baseline measure of behaviour without the experimental treatment, so that the effect of the experimental treatment may be assessed. See *experimental condition*, (p. 36).

control group In an experiment, a group of participants who receive no treatment. Their behaviour acts as a baseline against which the effect of the independent variable may be measured. See *experimental group*, (p. 36).

controlled observation A form of investigation in which behaviour is observed but under controlled conditions, in contrast with a *naturalistic observation*, (pp. 64, 66).

CORRELATION (CORRELATIONAL ANALYSIS) Determining the extent of a relationship between two variables; *co-variables* may not be linked at all (*zero correlation*), they may both increase together (*positive correlation*), or as one co-variable increases, the other decreases (*negative correlation*). Usually a *linear correlation* is predicted, but the relationship can be *curvilinear*, (pp. 48, 49, 52).

CORRELATION COEFFICIENT A number between −1 and +1 that tells us how closely the *co-variables* in a correlational analysis are related, (pp. 48, 49).

counterbalancing An experimental technique designed to overcome *order effects*. Counterbalancing ensures that each condition is tested first or second in equal amounts, (p. 9).

co-variables When one conducts a correlational analysis there is no *independent variable* or *dependent variable* – the two measured variables are called co-variables, (p. 48).

covert observations See *undisclosed observations*.

cross-cultural study A kind of *natural experiment* in which the IV is different cultural practices and the DV is a behaviour such as attachment. This enables researchers to investigate the effects of culture/socialisation, (p. 72).

cross-sectional design One group of participants of a young age are compared with another, older group of participants, with a view to finding out the influence of age on the behaviour in question, (p. 72).

curvilinear correlation A non-linear relationship between *co-variables*. For example, arousal and performance do not have a *linear* (straight line) relationship. Performance on many tasks is depressed when arousal is too high or too low; it is best when arousal is moderate, (p. 52).

debriefing A post-research interview designed to inform participants of the true nature of the study and to restore them to the same state they were in at the start of the experiment. It may also be used to gain useful feedback about the procedures in the study. Debriefing is <u>not</u> an *ethical issue*; it is a means of dealing with ethical issues, (pp. 13, 34, 35).

deception An *ethical issue*, most usually where a participant is not told the true aims of a study (e.g. what participation will involve) and thus cannot give truly *informed consent*, (pp. 32, 35, 47, 67).

DEMAND CHARACTERISTICS Features of an experiment that a participant unconsciously responds to when searching for clues about how to behave. These may act as a *confounding variable*, (pp. 26, 45).

DEPENDENT VARIABLE (DV) A measurable outcome of the action of the *independent variable* in an experiment, (p. 4).

difference studies Studies in which two groups of participants are compared in terms of a *DV* (such as males versus females, or extraverts versus introverts). This is not a true *experiment* because the apparent *IV* (gender or personality) has not been manipulated, (p. 31).

DIRECTIONAL HYPOTHESIS Predicts the kind of difference (e.g. more or less) or relationship (positive or negative) between two groups of participants or between different conditions. See *non-directional hypothesis*, (p. 7).

disclosed observations See *undisclosed observations*.

double blind A research design in which neither the participant nor the *experimenter* is aware of the condition that an individual participant is receiving, (pp. 12, 26).

DV see *dependent variable*.

ecological validity A form of *external validity*, concerning the ability to generalise a research effect beyond the particular setting in which it is demonstrated to other settings. Ecological validity is established by *representativeness* (mundane realism) and *generalisability* (to other settings), (pp. 28, 29, 31, 36, 69).

ethical committee A group of people within a research institution that must approve a study before it begins, (pp. 34, 35, 67).

ethical guidelines Concrete, quasi-legal documents that help to guide conduct within psychology by establishing principles for standard practice and competence, (pp. 34, 35, 67).

ETHICAL ISSUES An ethical issue arises in research where there are conflicts between the research goals and the participant's rights, (pp. 13, 32, 33, 34, 35, 47, 67).

event sampling An observational technique in which a count is kept of the number of times a certain behaviour (event) occurs. See *time sampling*, (p. 65).

EXPERIMENT A *research method* that involves the direct manipulation of an *independent variable* in order to test its possible causal relationship with a *dependent variable*. See *laboratory experiment, field experiment, natural experiment*, (pp. 4, 49).

experimental condition In a repeated measures design, the condition containing the *independent variable*. See *control condition*, (p. 36).

experimental control The use of techniques designed to eliminate the effects of *extraneous variables* in an experiment. See *control*.

EXPERIMENTAL DESIGN A set of procedures used to control the influence of participant variables in an experiment (*repeated measures design, independent groups design or matched participants design: RIM*), (p. 8).

experimental group In an independent groups design, a group of participants who receive the experimental treatment (the *independent variable*). See *control group*, (p. 36).

EXPERIMENTAL HYPOTHESIS The *alternative hypothesis* in an experiment, (p. 7).

experimental realism The extent to which participants take an experiment seriously. If the simulated task environment is sufficiently engaging, the participants pay attention to the task and not to the fact that they are being observed, thus reducing *participant reactivity*, (p. 26).

experimental validity Concerns the legitimacy of an *experiment* – the way in which it is carried out, the conclusion(s) drawn and its implications for understanding related aspects of real life. Includes both *internal* and *external validity*, (p. 28).

experimenter The person who directly interacts with participants when an experiment is carried out. The study may be designed by someone else, called the *investigator*, (p. 4, 27).

experimenter bias The effect that the experimenter's expectations have on the participants and thus on the results of the experiment. See *investigator effect*, (p. 27).

external reliability A calculation of the extent to which a measure varies from another measure of the same thing over time. This can be assessed using the *test-retest* method. See also *reliability*, (p. 50).

EXTERNAL VALIDITY The degree to which an experimental effect can be generalised, for example, to other settings (*ecological validity*), other people (*population validity*) and over time (*historical validity*), (pp. 28, 31, 51, 67).

EXTRANEOUS VARIABLE In an experiment, any variable other than the *independent variable* that might potentially affect the *dependent variable* and thereby confound the results. If this happens, an extraneous variable becomes a *confounding variable*, (p. 12).

face validity A form of *external validity* related to questionnaires and interviews. The extent to which the items look like what the test claims to measure, (p. 51).

fatigue effect A kind of *order effect*. In a repeated measures design, participants may do less well on one condition rather than another because they have become tired or bored, (p. 9).

FIELD EXPERIMENT This is a controlled experiment that is conducted outside a laboratory. The key features are that the *independent variable* is still manipulated by the experimenter, and therefore causal relationships can be demonstrated; it is conducted in a more natural setting than a laboratory experiment and may therefore have greater *ecological validity*; and participants are usually unaware that they are participating in an experiment, thus reducing *participant reactivity*, (p. 24, 25, 28, 29, 31, 49).

field study Any study that takes place away from the laboratory and within the context in which the behaviour normally occurs, (p. 24, 28, 29).

findings The factual data produced in a study, *quantitative* or *qualitative* data. *Conclusions* may be drawn from findings *if* the study was *valid* and *reliable*, (p. 16).

forced choice question The participant must choose one item or alternative from (usually) the two offered, (p. 44).

generalisability The degree to which the findings of a particular study can be applied to the *target population*, (pp. 28, 29).

give voice A technique used when analysing *qualitative data*. The report of the findings uses selective quotations from participants to illustrate points made.

graph A pictorial representation of the relationship between variables, (pp. 15, 16, 48).

Greenspoon effect The tendency for an interviewee's responses to be affected by the interviewer's reaction (e.g. saying 'mm-hmm' or 'uh-huh'), an example of operant conditioning.

grounded theory A technique used when analysing *qualitative data*. It is an emergent research process in which theoretical explanations 'emerge' during the course of the investigation.

Hawthorne effect The tendency for participants to alter their behaviour merely as a result of knowing that they are being observed. It acts as a *confounding variable*, (pp. 25, 26).

HISTOGRAM A type of frequency distribution in which the number of scores in each category of continuous data are represented by vertical columns. In contrast to a bar chart, the data in a histogram have a true zero and a logical sequence, there are no spaces between the bars, (p. 15).

historical validity A form of *external validity*, concerning the ability to generalise a research effect beyond the particular time period of the study, (p. 28).

homage to formal terms (Coolican, 2004b).The problem that technical terms create an illusion that things are 'black and white'. They aren't. You should focus on the 'general drift' and not be fazed when you find that there are slightly different meanings as your understanding increases, (p. 27).

HYPOTHESIS A precise and testable statement about the world, specifically of the relationship between data to be measured. It is a statement about *populations* and not *samples*. Usually derived from a theoretical explanation, (p. 7).

independent groups design An *experimental design* in which participants are allocated to two (or more) groups representing different conditions. Allocation is usually done using *random techniques*. Contrast with *repeated measures design and matched participants design* (RIM), (pp. 8, 9, 72).

independent variable (IV) Some event that is directly manipulated by an experimenter in order to test its effect on another variable (the *dependent variable*), (p. 4).

informed consent An *ethical issue* and an *ethical guideline* in psychological research whereby participants must be given comprehensive information concerning the nature and purpose of a research study and their role in it, in order that they can make an informed decision about whether to participate, (pp. 32, 35, 67).

inter-interviewer reliability The extent to which two interviewers produce the same outcome from an *interview*, (p. 47).

internal reliability A measure of the extent to which something is consistent within itself. For a psychological test to have high internal reliability, all test items should be measuring the same thing. This can be assessed using the *split-half method*. See also *reliability*, (p. 50).

INTERNAL VALIDITY An experiment is internally valid if the observed effect can be attributed to the experimental manipulation rather than some other factor. A questionnaire or observation is internally valid if it is measuring what it was intended to measure (rather than some other behaviour), (pp. 26, 31, 51, 67).

inter-observer reliability The extent to which there is agreement between two or more observers involved in observations of a behaviour. This is measured by correlating the observations of two or more observers. A general rule is that if (total number of agreements) / (total number of observations) > 0.80, the data have inter-observer reliability, (pp. 50, 67, 69).

inter-rater reliability See *inter-observer reliability*.

interval data Data is measured using units of equal intervals, such as when counting correct answers or using any 'public' unit of measurement. Many psychological studies use *plastic interval scales* in which the intervals are arbitrarily determined so we cannot actually know for certain that there are equal intervals between the numbers. However, for the purposes of analysis, such data may be accepted as interval. Remember NOIR, (pp. 15, 95).

Intervening variable A *variable* that comes between two other variables that is used to explain the relationship between two variables. For example, if a positive correlation is found between ice cream sales and violence, this may be explained by an intervening variable – heat – which causes the increase in violence.

INTERVIEW A *research method* that involves a face-to-face, 'real-time' interaction with another individual and results in the collection of data. See *structured interview* and *unstructured interview*, (pp. 46, 47, 50, 51).

interviewer bias The effect of an interviewer's expectations, communicated unconsciously, on a respondent's behaviour, (p. 47).

investigator The person who designs a research study and *may* conduct it. In some cases someone else (sometimes referred to as the *experimenter*) is the one who directly interacts with participants. See *investigator effects*, (p. 27).

investigator bias The effect that the investigator's expectations have on the participants and thus on the results of the experiment. See *experimenter bias*.

INVESTIGATOR EFFECT Anything that the investigator/experimenter does which has an effect on a participant's performance in a study other than what was intended. This includes direct effects (as a consequence of the investigator interacting with the participant) and indirect effects (as a consequence of the investigator designing the study). Some people only include direct effects in their definition of an investigator effect – the unconscious cues from the investigator/experimenter. Investigator effects may act as a *confounding variable*. Investigator effects are not the same as *participant effects*.

IV see *independent variable*, (pp. 12, 26, 27, 31).

John Henry effect A *control group* might try extra hard to show that the old way is just as good or better than a new approach. This is a form of *participant effect* and a threat to *internal validity*, (p. 36).

laboratory Any setting (room or other environment) specially fitted out for conducting research. The laboratory is not the only place where scientific experiments can be conducted. It is, however, the ideal place for experiments because it permits maximum control. Laboratories are not used exclusively for experimental research; e.g. *controlled observations* are also conducted in laboratories, (p. 24).

LABORATORY EXPERIMENT An experiment carried out in the controlled and specially designed setting of a *laboratory* and that enables the experimenter to draw conclusions about the causal relationship between the *independent* and *dependent variable*. Not all laboratory experiments have low *ecological validity,* although there is usually a balance to be struck between *control* and *generalisability*, (pp. 24, 25, 28, 29, 31, 49).

leading question A question that is phrased in such a way (e.g. 'Don't you agree that…?') that it makes one response more likely than another. The form or content of the question suggests what answer is desired, (pp. 44, 47).

Likert scale A means of providing an answer to a question where respondents can indicate the extent to which they agree or disagree with a statement. There are usually five levels ranging from 'strongly agree' through 'neutral' to 'strongly disagree', (p. 44).

linear correlation A systematic relationship between *co-variables* that is defined by a straight line. See *curvilinear correlation*, (p. 52).

longitudinal design A form of *repeated measures design* in which participants are assessed on two or more occasions as they get older. The *IV* is age. See *longitudinal study*, (p. 72).

longitudinal study A study conducted over a long period of time usually to compare the same individual(s) at different ages.

matched participants design An *experimental design* in which pairs of participants are matched in terms of key variables such as age and IQ. One member of each pair is placed in the *experimental group* and the other member in the *control group*, so that *participant variables* are better controlled than is usually the case in an *independent groups design* experiment, (p. 9).

MEAN A *measure of central tendency*. The arithmetic average of a group of scores, calculated by dividing the sum of the scores by the number of scores. Takes the values of all the data into account (whereas the *mode* and *median* just take all the data into account – but not the values), (p. 15).

MEASURES OF CENTRAL TENDENCY A descriptive statistic that provides information about a 'typical' response for a set of scores. See *mean, median, mode*, (p. 15).

MEASURES OF DISPERSION A descriptive statistic that provides information about how spread out a set of scores are. See *range, standard deviation*, (p. 15).

MEDIAN A *measure of central tendency*. The middle value in a set of scores when they are placed in rank order, (p. 15).

MODE A *measure of central tendency*. The most frequently occurring score in a set of data, (p. 15).

mundane realism Refers to how an experiment mirrors the real word. The simulated task environment is realistic to the degree to which experiences encountered in the environment will occur in the real world, (pp. 25, 29, 31).

NATURAL EXPERIMENT A *research method* in which the experimenter cannot manipulate the *independent variable* directly, but where it varies naturally and the effect can be observed on a *dependent*

variable. Strictly speaking, an experiment involves the deliberate manipulation of an IV by the experimenter, so causal conclusions cannot be drawn from a natural experiment. In addition, participants are not *randomly allocated* to conditions in a natural experiment, which may reduce *external validity*. See also *quasi-experiment*, (pp. 30, 69, 72).

NATURALISTIC OBSERVATION A *research method* carried out in a naturalistic setting, in which the investigator does not interfere in any way but merely observes the behaviours in question, (pp. 64, 65, 66, 67, 68, 69).

NEGATIVE CORRELATION A relationship between two *co-variables* such that as the value of one co-variable increases, that of the other decreases, (p. 48).

NOIR An acronym to help remember the four levels of measurement of data: *nominal*, *ordinal*, *interval* and *ratio*.

nominal data The data are in separate categories, such as grouping people according to their favourite football team (e.g. Liverpool, Inverness Caledonian Thistle, etc.), remember NOIR (pp. 15, 95).

NON-DIRECTIONAL HYPOTHESIS A form of hypothesis that proposes a difference, correlation or association between two variables but does not specify the direction (e.g. more or less, positive or negative) of such a relationship, (p. 7).

non-participant observations Observations made by someone who is not participating in the activity being observed, (p. 66).

normal distribution A symmetrical bell-shaped frequency distribution. This distribution occurs when certain variables are measured, such as IQ or the life of a light bulb. Such 'events' are distributed in such a way that most of the scores are clustered close to the mean.

null hypothesis An assumption that there is no relationship (difference, association, etc.) in the population from which a sample is taken with respect to the variables being studied, (p. 7).

observational study Participants are observed engaging in whatever behaviour is being studied. The observations are recorded. There are *naturalistic observations* and *controlled observations*. Observational methods may also be used in an experiment – in which case observation is a *research technique* instead of a *research method*.

observation techniques The application of systematic methods of observation in an *observational study, experiment* or other study, (p. 65).

observational systems Systematic methods for recording observations such as a *coding system* or *behaviour checklist*, (p. 65).

observer bias In observational studies, there is the danger that observers might 'see' what they expect to see. This reduces the *external validity* of the observations, (pp. 67, 69).

one-tailed hypothesis See *non-directional hypothesis*.

open questions In an interview or questionnaire, questions that invite the respondents to provide their own answers rather than select one of those provided. Tend to produce *qualitative* data. Answers are more difficult to analyse than those for *closed questions*, (p. 44).

OPERATIONALISATION Ensuring that variables are in a form that can be easily tested. A concept such as 'educational attainment' or 'social development' needs to be specified more clearly if we are going to investigate it in an experiment or observational study. The researcher lists various behaviours that can be measured, for example, 'social development' can be broken down into the following operations: the tendency to seek the company of others, to show enjoyment when with others, to have a number of friends, to display social skills such as negotiating with friends, etc, (pp. 11, 25, 44, 65).

OPPORTUNITY SAMPLE A *sample* of participants produced by selecting people who are most easily available at the time of the study. Sometimes called an availability sample, (p. 10).

order effect In a repeated measures design, a *confounding variable* arising from the order in which conditions are presented, e.g. a *practice effect* or *fatigue effect*. Counteracted by using *counterbalancing*, (p. 9).

ordinal data Data are ordered in some way, e.g. asking people to put a list of football teams in order of liking. Liverpool might be first, followed by Inverness, etc. The 'difference' between each item is not the same; i.e. the individual may like the first item a lot more than the second, but there might only be a small difference between the items ranked second and third. Remember NOIR, (pp. 15, 95).

participant effects A general term used to acknowledge the fact that participants react to cues in an experimental situation and that this may affect the validity of any conclusions drawn from the investigation, for example, *demand characteristics*. Participant effects are not the same as *investigator effects*, (p. 26).

participant observations Observations made by someone who is also participating in the activity being observed, which may affect their objectivity, (p. 66).

participant reactivity The bias in responses that occurs because a participant knows they are being studied. See *participant effects*, (pp. 26, 31).

participant variables Characteristics of individual participants (such as age, intelligence, etc.) that might influence the outcome of a study, (pp. 9, 72).

PILOT STUDY A small-scale trial of a study run to test any aspects of the design, with a view to making improvements, (p. 6).

placebo A condition that should have no effect on the behaviour being studied so can be used to separate out the effects of the *IV* from any effects caused merely by receiving *any* treatment, (p. 71).

plastic interval scale See *interval data.*

population All the people in the world. In any study, the sample of participants is drawn from a *target population*, (p. 10).

population validity A form of *external validity,* concerning the extent to which the findings of a study can be *generalised* to other groups of people besides those who took part in the study, (p. 28).

positive correlation A relationship between two *co-variables* such that as the value of one co-variable increases, this is accompanied by a corresponding increase in the other co-variable, (p. 48).

practice effect A kind of *order effect*. In a repeated measures design, participants may do better on one condition rather than another because they have completed it first and are therefore more 'practiced'.

presumptive consent A method of dealing with lack of *informed consent* or *deception*, by asking a group of people who are similar to the participants whether they would agree to take part in a study. If this group of people consent to the procedures in the proposed study, it is presumed that the real participants would agree as well, (pp. 34, 35).

privacy An *ethical issue* that refers to a zone of inaccessibility of mind or body and the trust that this will not be 'invaded'. Contrast with *confidentiality*, (pp. 33, 35, 47, 67).

procedures Includes design decisions as well as all the steps taken when a research study is conducted. See *standardised procedures*, (p. 16).

protection from psychological harm An *ethical issue*. During a research study, participants should not experience negative psychological effects, such as lowered self-esteem or emabarrassment, (pp. 32, 35).

qualitative analysis Any form of analysis that focuses more on words (i.e. what participants say) than on other forms of numerical data. Qualitative analyses interpret the *meaning* of an experience to the individual(s) concerned. See *give voice, grounded theory* and *thematic analysis*, (p. 46).

QUALITATIVE DATA Data that express a complete account of what people think or feel. Qualitative data cannot be counted or quantified. Qualitative data can be turned into *quantitative data* by placing them in categories, (pp. 44, 46, 66).

quantitative analysis Any form of analysis (e.g. descriptive statistics) that uses numerical data as the basis for investigation and interpretation, (p. 46).

QUANTITATIVE DATA Data that represent how much or how long, or how many, etc. there are of something; i.e. a behaviour is measured in numbers or quantities, (pp. 44, 46, 66).

quasi-experiment Experiments that are not true experiments, either because the *IV* is not directly manipulated and/or because participants are not *randomly allocated* to conditions. Therefore, we cannot claim to investigate cause and effect relationships.

QUESTIONNAIRE A *research method* in which data is collected through the use of written questions, which may be *open* or *closed questions*. Also called a survey, (pp. 44, 45).

questionnaire fallacy The erroneous belief that a questionnaire actually produces a true picture of what people do and think.

quota sample See *stratified sample*.

random allocation Allocating participants to experimental groups or conditions using random techniques, (pp. 9, 10, 31).

RANDOM SAMPLE A *sample* of participants produced by using a *random technique* such that every member of the *target population* being tested has an equal chance of being selected, (p. 10).

random technique Any technique in which there is no systematic attempt to influence the selection or distribution of the items or participants that form part of the investigation, (p. 10).

RANGE A *measure of dispersion* that measures the difference between the highest and lowest score in a set of data, (p. 15).

ratio data There is a true zero point, as in most measures of physical quantities. Remember NOIR. (pp. 15, 95).

RELIABILITY A measure of consistency both within a set of scores or items (*internal reliability*) and also over time such that it is possible to obtain the same results on

subsequent occasions when the measure is used (*external reliability*). The reliability of an experiment can be determined through *replication*, (pp. 50, 67).

repeated measures design A type of *experimental design* in which each participant takes part in every condition under test. Contrast with *independent groups design* and *matched participants design* (RIM), (pp. 8, 9, 72).

replication The opportunity to repeat an investigation under the same conditions in order to test the *reliability* of its findings, (pp. 28, 29, 50).

representative sample A *sample* selected so that it accurately stands for or represents the *population* being studied, (p. 10).

representativeness The extent to which an experiment mirrors the real world. This is *mundane realism*, (pp. 28, 29).

research The process of gaining knowledge through the systematic examination of data derived empirically or theoretically.

RESEARCH DESIGN The overall plan of action to maximise meaningful results and minimise ambiguity using systematic research techniques, (p. 1).

research method A way of conducting research (such as an *experiment* or a *questionnaire*) as distinct from the *research design* of the investigation, (pp. 1, 45, 64).

research prediction A prediction about the outcome of a study based on the *hypothesis*. The research prediction is about *samples*, whereas the hypothesis is about *populations*, (p. 11).

research technique The specific techniques used in a variety of research methods, such as *control* of variables, *sampling* methods and *coding systems*, (pp. 45, 64).

response set A tendency for interviewees to respond in the same way to all questions, regardless of context. This would *bias* their answers, (p. 51).

right to withdraw An *ethical issue* that participants should be able to stop participating in an experiment if they are uncomfortable with the study, (pp. 33, 35).

RIM An acronym to help remember the three experimental designs (*repeated measures, independant groups* and *matched participants*).

role play A controlled observation in which participants are asked to imagine how they would behave in certain situations, and act out the part. This method has the advantage of permitting one to study certain behaviours that might be unethical or difficult to find in the real world, (p. 72).

sample A selection of participants taken from the *target population* being studied and intended to be *representative* of that population, (p. 10).

sample bias A particular problem with questionnaire studies as certain types of people are more likely to complete and return the questionnaire.

sampling The process of taking a sample, (p. 10).

sampling technique/procedure The method used to *sample* participants, such as *random, opportunity* and *volunteer sampling*, or to sample behaviours in an observation such as event or *time sampling*, (p. 10, 65).

SCATTERGRAPH A graphical representation of the relationship (i.e. the *correlation*) between two sets of scores, (p. 48).

screw you effect A participant who knows the aims of an experiment deliberately behaves in a way to spoil an experiment. This is a form of *participant effect* and a threat to *internal validity*, (p. 26).

semantic differential technique A method of assessing attitudes by measuring the affective component using bipolar adjectives. This means that an attitude can be evaluated on a number of different dimensions, whereas the *Likert scale* only represents one dimension of an attitude (agreement or disagreement), (p. 44).

significance A statistical term indicating that the research findings are sufficiently strong to enable us to reject the *null hypothesis* and accept the research hypothesis under test, (p. 49).

single blind A type of *research design* in which the participant is not aware of the research aims or of which condition of the experiment they are receiving, (pp. 9, 26).

social desirability bias A tendency for respondents to answer questions in such a way that presents themselves in a better light, (pp. 26, 44, 47).

split-half method A method of determining the *internal reliability* of a test. Test items are split into two halves and the scores on both halves compared. Scores should be similar if the test is reliable, (p. 50).

STANDARD DEVIATION A *measure of dispersion* that shows the amount of variation in a set of scores. It assesses the spread of data around the mean, (p. 15).

standardised instructions A set of instructions that are the same for all participants so as to avoid *investigator effects*

caused by different instructions, (p. 12).

standardised procedures A set of *procedures* that are the same for all participants so as to enable *replication* of the study to take place, (p. 12).

stratified sample A *sampling technique* in which groups of participants are selected in proportion to their frequency in the population in order to obtain a *representative sample*. The aim is to identify sections of the population, or strata, that need to be represented in the study. Individuals from those strata are then selected using a *random technique* for the study. If the sample is not randomly selected from the stratum, it is then a *quota sample*, (p. 10).

structured interview Any *interview* in which the questions are decided in advance, (p. 46).

structured observations The researcher uses various 'systems' to organise observations, such as a *sampling technique* and an *observational system*, (p. 65).

STUDIES USING A CORRELATIONAL ANALYSIS See *correlation*.

survey See *questionnaire*.

systematic sample A method of obtaining a representative sample by selecting every 5th or 10th person. This can be random if the first person is selected using a random method; then you select every 10th person after this, (p. 10).

target population The group of people that the researcher is interested in. The group of people from whom a *sample* is drawn. The group of people about whom *generalisations* can be made, (p. 10).

test-retest method A method used to check *reliability*. The same test or interview is given to the same participants on two occasions to see if the same results are obtained, (p. 50).

thematic analysis A technique used when analysng *qualitative* data. Themes or concepts are identified before starting a piece of research; then responses from an *interview* or *questionnaire* are organised according to these themes.

time sampling An *observational technique* in which the observer records behaviours in a given time frame, e.g. noting what a target individual is doing every 30 seconds. You may select one or more categories from a checklist. See *event sampling*, (p. 65).

two tailed hypothesis See *directional hypothesis*.

undisclosed observations Observing people without their knowledge, e.g. using one-way mirrors. Knowing that your

behaviour is being observed is likely to alter your behaviour, (p. 66).

unstructured interview The interview starts out with some general aims and possibly some questions, and lets the interviewee's answers guide subsequent questions, (p. 46).

unstructured observation An observer records all relevant behaviour but has no system. The behaviour to be studied may be largely unpredictable, (p. 65).

VALIDITY Refers to the legitimacy of a study, the extent to which the findings can be applied beyond the research setting as a consequence of the study's *internal* and/or *external validity*, (pp. 26, 28, 29, 31, 36, 51, 67).

variables Anything of relevance in a study that can vary or change. See *independent variable* and *dependent variable*, *extraneous* and *confounding variable*.

volunteer An individual who, acting on their own volition, applies to take part in an investigation, (p. 10).

volunteer bias A form of *sampling bias* because *volunteer* participants are usually more highly motivated than randomly selected participants, (p. 10).

VOLUNTEER SAMPLE A *sample* of participants produced by a *sampling technique* that relies solely on volunteers to make up the sample, (p. 10).

x-axis The horizontal axis on a graph, going across the page. Usually the *IV*.

y-axis The vertical axis on a graph, going up the side of the page. Usually the *DV* or 'frequency'.

zero correlation No relationship (*correlation*) between *co-variables*, (p. 48).

References

Baddeley, A. D. and Longman, D. J. A. (1978) The influence of length and frequency on training sessions on the rate of learning type. *Ergonomics*, 21, 627–635, (p. 29).

Bandura, A., Ross, D. and Ross, S.A. (1961) Transmission of aggression through imitation of aggressive models. *Journal of Abnormal and Social Psychology*, 63, 575–582, (pp. 25, 64, 68).

BEO (2004) Behavioural observation, University of Bern http://www.psy.unibe.ch/beob/proj_ex.htm and http://www.psy.unibe.ch/beob/home_e.htm (accessed September 2004), (p. 67).

Bickman, L. (1974) Clothes make the person. *Psychology Today*, 8(4), 48–51, (p. 24).

Brugger, P., Landis, T. and Regard, M. (1990) A 'sheep–goat effect' in repetition avoidance: extra sensory perception as an effect of subjective probability. *British Journal of Psychology*, 81, 455–468, (p. 52).

Charlton, T., Gunter, B. and Hannan, A. (eds) (2000) *Broadcast television effects in a remote community*. Hillsdale, NJ: Lawrence Erlbaum, (p. 30).

Coolican, H. (1996) *Introduction to research methods and statistics in psychology*. London: Hodder & Stoughton, (p. iv).

Coolican, H. (2004a) Personal communication, (p. 30).

Coolican, H. (2004b) *Research methods and statistics in psychology* (3rd edition). London: Hodder & Stoughton, (p. iv).

Crabb, P.B. and Bielawski, D. (1994) The social representation of material culture and gender in children's books. *Sex Roles*, 10(1/2), 65–75, (p. 68).

Craik, F.I.M. and Lockhart, R.S. (1972) Levels of processing: a framework for memory research. *Journal of Verbal Learning and Verbal Behavior*, 11, 671–684, (p. 130).

Craik, F.I.M. and Tulving, E. (1975) Depth of processing and the retention of words in episodic memory. *Journal of Experimental Psychology*, 104, 268–294, (p. 130).

Dicks, H. V. (1972) *Licensed mass murder: a socio-psychological study of some S.S. killers*. New York: Basic Books, (p. 36).

Ekman, P. and Friesen, W. V. (1978) *Manual for the facial action coding system*. Palo Alto, CA: Consulting Psychology Press, (p. 68).

Festinger, L., Riecken, H. W. and Schachter, S. (1956) *When prophecy fails*. Minneapolis: University of Minnesota Press, (p. 68).

Fick, K. (1993). The influence of an animal on social interactions of nursing home residents in a group setting. *American Journal of Occupational Therapy*, 47, 529–534, (p. 65).

Gilligan, C. and Attanucci, J. (1988) Two moral orientations: dender differences and similarities. *Merrill-Palmer Quarterly*, 34, 223–237, (p. 46).

Harms, T., Clifford, R. M. and Cryer, D. (1998) *Early childhood environment rating scale*, (revised edn), New York, NY: Teachers College Press (p. 68).

Hofling, K. C., Brontzman, E., Dalrymple, S., Graves, N. and Pierce, C. M. (1966) An experimental study in the nurse–physician relationship. *Journal of Mental and Nervous Disorders*, 43, 171–178, (pp. 29, 36).

Holmes, T. H. and Rahe, R. H. (1967) The social readjustment rating scale. *Journal of Psychosomatic Research*, 11, 213–218, (p. 132).

Jenness, A. (1932) The role of discussion in changing opinion regarding matter of fact. *Journal of Abnormal and Social Psychology*, 27, 279–296, (p. 131).

Jones, W. H., Russell, D. W., and Nickel T. W. (1977) Belief in the Paranormal Scale: an instrument to measure beliefs in magical phenomena and causes. *JSAS Catalogue of Selected Documents in Psychology*, 7:100 (Ms. no. 1577), (p. 60).

Jost, A. (1897). Die assoziationsfestigkeit in iher abhängigheit von der verteilung der wiederholungen. *Zeitschrift für Psychologie*, 14, 436–472, (p. 29).

Kendrick K. M., da Costa, A. P., Leigh A. E., Hinton, M. R. and Pierce, J. W. (2001) Sheep don't forget a face. *Nature*, 414, 165–166.

Kohlberg, L. (1978) Revisions in the theory and practice of moral development. *Directions for Child Development*, 2, 83–88, (p. 46).

Kohn, P. and Macdonald, J. E. (1992). The Survey of Life Experiences: a decontaminated hassles scale for adults. *Journal of Behavioral Medicine*, 15, 221–236, (p. 132).

Lamb, M. E. and Roopnarine, J. L. (1979) Peer influences on sex-role development in preschoolers. *Child Development*, 50, 1219–1222, (p. 64).

Lewis, M. K. and Hill, A. J. (1998). Food advertising on British children's television: a content analysis and experimental study with nine year olds. *International Journal of Obesity*, 22, 206–214, (p. 69).

Mandel, D. R. (1998) The obedience alibi: Milgram's account of the Holocaust reconsidered. *Analyse und Krtik: Zeitschrift für Sozialwissenschaften*, 20, 74–94, (p. 36).

Middlemist, D. R., Knowles, E. S. and Matter, C. F. (1976) Personal space invasions in the lavatory: suggestive evidence for arousal. *Journal of Personality and Social Psychology*, 33, 541–546, (p. 31).

Milgram, S. (1963) Behavioural study of obedience. *Journal of Abnormal and Social Psychology*, 67, 371–378, (p. 29, 36).

Peterson , L. R. and Peterson, M.J. (1959) Short-term retention of individual verbal items. *Journal of Experimental Psychology*, 58, 193–198, (p. 25).

Piliavin, I. M., Rodin, J. and Piliavin, J. A. (1969) Good Samaritanism: an underground phenomenon. *Journal of Personality and Social Psychology*, 13, 1200–1213, (p. 25).

Rank, S. G. and Jacobsen, C. K. (1977) Hospital nurses' compliance with medication overdose orders: a failure to replicate. *Journal of Health and Social Behaviour*, 18, 188–193, (p. 29).

Roethlisberger, F. J., and Dickson, W. J. (1939) *Management and the worker: an account of a research program conducted by the Western Electric Company, Chicago*. Cambridge, MA: Harvard University Press, (p. 25).

Rosenthal, R. and Fode, K. L. (1963) The effect of experimenter bias on the performance of the albino rat. *Behavioural Science*, 8(3), 183–189, (p. 19).

Ryback, R. S. (1969) The use of the goldfish as a model for alcohol amnesia in man. *Quarterly Journal of Studies on Alcohol*, 30, 877–882, (p. 4).

Schellenberg, E.G. (2004). Music lessons enhance IQ. *Psychological Science*, 15, 511–514, (p. 30).

Schultheiss, O.C., Wirth, M. M. and Stanton, S. (2004) Effects of affiliation and power motivation arousal on salivary progesterone and testosterone. *Hormones and Behavior*, 46(5), 592–599.

Schunk, D. H. (1983) Reward contingencies and the development of children's skills and self-efficacy. *Journal of Educational Psychology*, 75, 511–518, (p. 25).

Stroop, J. R. (1935) Studies of interference in serial verbal reactions. *Journal of Experimental Psychology*, 18, 643–662, (p. 6).

Veitch, R. and Griffitt, W. (1976) Good news, bad news: affective and interpersonal effects. *Journal of Applied Social Psychology*, 6, 69–75, (p. 25).

Waynforth, D. and Dunbar, R. I. M. 1995. Conditional mate choice strategies in humans – evidence from lonely-hearts advertisements. *Behaviour*, 132, 755–779, (p. 69).

Weick, K. E., Gilfillian, D. P. and Keith, T. A. (1973) The effect of composer credibility on orchestra performance. *Sociometry*, 36, 435–462, (p. 4).

White, G. L., Fishbein, S. and Rutstein, J. (1981) Passionate love and the misattribution of arousal. *Journal of Personality and Social Psychology*, 41, 56–62, (p. 14).

Widdowson, E. M. (1951) Mental contentment and physical growth. *Lancet*, 1, 1316–1318, (p. 30).

Williams, T. M. (1985) Implications of a natural experiment in the developed world for research on television in the developing world. *Journal of Cross Cultural Psychology*, 16(3) Special issue, 263–287, (p. 30).

Zimbardo, P. G., Banks, P. G., Haney, C. and Jaffe, D. (1973) Pirandellian prison: the mind is a formidable jailor. *New York Times Magazine*, 8 April, 38–60, (p. 72).

Zuckerman, M. (1994) *Behavioral expressions and biosocial bases of sensation seeking*. New York: Cambridge University Press, (p. 51).